The Persistent Prison?
Rethinking Decarceration and Penal Reform

The prison system is widely believed to be an immutable element of contemporary society. Many criminologists and sociologists of deviance believe that decarceration movements have failed to yield progressive reform, and that feasible alternatives to the prison system do not exist.

Maeve McMahon challenges these views. Reconstructing the emergence of critical perspectives on decarceration, she examines analytical and empirical problems in the research. She also points out how indicators of community programs and other penalties serving as alternatives to prison have typically been overshadowed through a critical focus on their effects in 'widening the net' of control.

McMahon presents a detailed analysis of decreasing imprisonment, and of the part played by alternatives in this, during the postwar period in Ontario. Drawing from extensive documentary research, and from interviews with former correctional officials, she charts the changing climates of opinion, and socio-economic factors, which facilitated decarceration.

By situating her analysis in the context of theoretical and political arguments about the possibility of decarceration, McMahon provides in her work a stimulus to the development of progressive penal politics not just in Canada, but in all western countries.

MAEVE W. MCMAHON is a Canada Research Fellow in the Centre of Criminology, University of Toronto. She is co-author, with Richard V. Ericson, of *Policing Reform: A Study of the Reform Process and Police Institution in Toronto*.

The Persistent Prison?
Rethinking Decarceration
and Penal Reform

MAEVE W. McMAHON

UNIVERSITY OF TORONTO PRESS
Toronto Buffalo London

© University of Toronto Press Incorporated 1992
Toronto Buffalo London
Printed in Canada

ISBN 0-8020-2817-9 (cloth)
ISBN 0-8020-7689-0 (paper)

∞

Printed on acid-free paper

Canadian Cataloguing in Publication Data

McMahon, Maeve W. (Maeve Winifred), 1957–
  The persistent prison?

  Includes bibliographical references and index.
  ISBN 0-8020-2817-9 (bound)   ISBN 0-8020-7689-0 (pbk.)

  1. Imprisonment – Ontario.   2. Correctional law – Ontario.
  3. Criminal justice, Administration of – Ontario.   I. Title

HV9509.05M25 1992   365'.9713   C92-094068-4

For the joyful
memory of Margaret Browne
who was my friend and mentor
in the arts of living, loving, and reflection

Contents

Figures and Tables

Figures

Tables

Foreword

The punishment of criminal offenders is a barometer of culture. As it represses undesirable conduct, punishment simultaneously expresses civility. Punishment signifies a society's values, morality, sensibilities, and reasoning.

Dr Maeve McMahon offers a reading of our culture through an examination of criminal punishment in Ontario over the past forty years. She considers how the scale of punishment and forms of penal practice articulate with the reasoning of social scientists and penal administrators in the context of wider cultural, social, political, and economic forces. She pursues her inquiry through the difficult work of fine-grained empirical analyses, providing a refreshing contrast to the overabundance of literary and metaphorical depictions that characterize recent research in this field. The result is a superb book that challenges most aspects of conventional wisdom about punishment in Canadian culture.

The most significant and unique contribution of this book is the challenge it presents to the conventions and wisdom that prevail in academic culture. Dr McMahon treats the prevailing academic orthodoxy as a core analytical problem.

The orthodoxy has it that there is no such thing as a liberative penal system. All criminal punishment is negative and repressive. Whenever anything new is tried, it ends up making things worse. Prison regimes designed to rehabilitate prisoners end up being more punitive than if rehabilitation had not been a consideration. Community programs established as alternatives to imprisonment do not reduce the use of imprisonment, bring more people within the ambit of the penal system, and intensify and prolong sanctioning. Everything is read in the negative logic of social control, and nothing works.

This discourse of critical criminology has advanced by debunking other forms of scientific reasoning and showing how that reasoning has led to conservative and repressive penal practice. For example, the knowledge of forensic psychiatry, psychology, social work, and clinical criminology has been picked apart by critical criminologists. These fields have been found lacking in terms of scientific merit. What they claim they are offering in the interest of rehabilitating the offender actually punishes the offender more, but serves the professional interests and administrative convenience of penal operatives.

Dr McMahon's approach is to similarly pick apart the reasoning of critical criminologists. She lays bare the flaws in their scientific reasoning. She shows how their discourse, presented as an oppositional stance, also ends up as part of the penal complex and serves some of its more negative features.

In their rush to politicize the field, critical criminologists have overlooked some important scientific tenets. They often fail to exhibit balanced reasoning through hypothesis testing. A critical posture is taken as a point of departure, rather than as a conclusion that might or might not be reached. Critical criminologists are not out to test their own conventional wisdom. Failing to use a more sensitive aperture that would permit other ways of seeing, they miss a lot. The result is ideology as a procedure not to know.

Dr McMahon shows that many things are missing in the analyses of critical criminologists. In addition to serious flaws in their methodology – for example, misreading their own data, juxtaposing incompatible forms of data, and basing their conclusions on insufficient evidence – critical criminologists have become self-enclosed on whole fields of inquiry. Self-enclosure largely results from the fact that their primary value is 'against power,' and the resultant vision is to see every thing in terms of more social control. The one-dimensional conception of power leads to an obsession with failure. This obsession in turn means that critical criminologists miss instances of success, such as cases where new penal policies have actually reduced the use of imprisonment. It has led them to prefer simple condemnation of new community alternatives to imprisonment over the hard work of exploring scientifically the origins and development of these alternatives. Perhaps most surprisingly, the focus on demystifying the benign face of community-corrections initiatives has meant that, in many studies, empirical examination of imprisonment itself has been largely overlooked. Critical criminologists have fostered an analytical displacement of imprisonment. They typically take for granted that the maintenance and growth of imprisonment are inexorable. A paradox results: imprisonment is central to the arguments critical criminologists make about penal expansion and repression, yet is peripheral as a focus of their empirical inquiries. Meanwhile critical criminologists have entirely overlooked other forms of criminal punishment – in particular, the fine – that have a significant influence on rates of imprisonment.

Dr McMahon also makes it clear that critical criminology is not a unique form of scientific reasoning that can somehow escape being entwined with penal practice. In keeping with all other forms of scientific reasoning, critical criminology offers a discourse that both forms and is formed by practice. Facing the implications of their eternally recurrent argument that reform is of no benefit in light of a recalcitrant penal system, critical criminologists retreat into nihilism and an abstentionist political stance. Meanwhile, as Dr McMahon documents, their key terms have been taken on by policy officials and used rhetorically to serve the administrative convenience of the penal system. Ironically, while the stance of critical criminologists urges sensitivity to co-optation by the penal system, they themselves have had their work co-opted. Ironically, while they aspire to a progressive penal politics, critical criminologists systematically undermine their own aspirations.

It is her painstaking empirical analyses that allow Dr McMahon to make such a convincing case against the orthodoxy of critical criminology. She provides rich data regarding a number of important issues and themes that are sure to have a significant influence on all future research in this field.

The research shows that, from the 1950s to the early 1970s, the rehabilitative ethos prevailed in Ontario and had many positive consequences for prisoners. The impact of the rehabilitative ethos was not direct or necessarily seen in the measured effectiveness of experimental programs. Rather, the ethos provided more sensitive and benevolent penal officials with a legitimating rationale to ameliorate some degrading aspects of prison life. While the gains were small and typically limited to mundane matters, they did make a difference to those experiencing the pains of imprisonment.

Dr McMahon has produced important data indicating that the growth of probation – the fundamental community-based sanction in Ontario – was not associated with an overall expansion in the penal system. As probation grew in the 1970s and early 1980s, the overall population under penal jurisdiction in Ontario remained stable, and even decreased slightly. This situation is attributable to several factors, including the likelihood that judges were using probation as an alternative to imprisonment, the fact that probation terms were shortened, and the fact that breach-of-probation charges resulting in imprisonment were rare.

While probation was not associated with bringing more people under control, it did intensify sanctioning of those serving their sentences in non-custodial settings. Intensification occurred because new community-based penal programs in Ontario, such as community-service and victim–offender reconciliation programs, were initiated as conditions of probation orders. Hence probationers, who had previously been subject to no more than occasional reporting to a police station or probation officer, were now often compelled to meet substantial additional obligations, such as forced unpaid labour and restitution to people they had victimized.

The research documents that decarceration did occur in Ontario. After charting a substantial decrease in rates of imprisonment in the 1960s and early 1970s, Dr McMahon pursues multiple lines of inquiry to explain her findings.

The first line of inquiry is consideration of the fine as a penal sanction. The fine is a neglected topic in criminological research. It is the criminal sanction that is used most, but thought about least. The empirical investigation shows that decarceration occurred largely as a result of a decrease in the rate of fine-default admissions to Ontario prisons. In the early 1950s one-half of all committals to Ontario prisons resulted from an inability to pay fines following conviction for intoxication in a public place and for other liquor-related offences! Changing practices in relation to such cases over the following two decades shut the prison door to many who previously had it opened for them on a regular basis.

The second line of inquiry is an investigation of what led to the use of alternatives to imprisonment for those found intoxicated in public places. Dr McMahon reports that a series of interrelated changes occurred throughout the criminal-justice system. Police modified their charging practices; pre-trial detention was used less so that many failed to appear and were never subsequently captured; and magistrates gave lighter sentences, including lesser fines and suspended sentences instead of fines. The law relating to public intoxication was eventually modified in support of de-escalation. At the same time social scientists documented the futility of using imprisonment for these offenders, and joined policy officials in advocating non-penal alternatives, such as detoxification centres.

Dr McMahon emphasizes that trends differ for different types of offenders, a point typically overlooked. Public intoxication offenders in Ontario were subject to moderation in penal control in the 1960s, while probationers were subject to intensification in the 1970s and 1980s. She also documents that, even with respect to a particular type of offender, there is considerable variation by place. For example, while public intoxication and related liquor offences became all but ignored in Toronto, they remained central to the definition of order in towns such as Kenora, where the police continued to imprison Native persons at an astounding rate for liquor-related infractions.

The third line of inquiry focuses on police contributions to rates of imprisonment. In Ontario, a high proportion of admissions to prison, albeit for very short terms, continue to be for infractions of a regulatory nature. Chief among these are liquor and traffic infractions, and default on payment of fines regarding those infractions. Indeed, the police routinely bypass the prosecution, adjudication, and sentencing phases of the criminal process by picking up fine defaulters on committal warrants and sending them directly to jail. Further substantial decarceration could be effected by simply eliminating imprisonment as an alternative for persons in default of payment of fines for minor regulatory offences.

The finding that decarceration occurred up to the early 1970s, but not subsequently, presents a puzzle. The advent of the official reform discourse of decarceration also occurred in the early 1970s, precisely at the point when the actual decline in rates of imprisonment halted. Why is it that decarceration reform discourse became prominent in public political culture only after the practice it advocated had taken place? Did the reform discourse arise from the practice, serving as an after-the-fact rationalization of what had already occurred? If the answer to this question is yes, then the reform discourse was clearly out of synchronization with present and emerging trends, and there was a sharp disjuncture between policy and practice.

Dr McMahon addresses the above questions through interviews with key policy officials in Ontario corrections and the use of secondary sources. She discovered that the decarceration reform discourse that emerged in the 1970s marked a discursive shift by Ministry of Corrections officials, and was aimed at dealing with problems of organizational maintenance, legitimacy, and fiscal restraint. Faced with prison overcrowding, a loss of jurisdiction over sentenced juveniles to the Ontario Ministry of Community and Social Services, fiscal restraint affecting all areas of provincial government spending, and a tarnished image resulting from sporadic negative publicity, corrections officials searched for sources of innovation and, in effect, new markets.

In a classic case of an idea borne out of necessity, officials began to organize things under the umbrella of 'alternatives' and to deploy the associated knowledge-base of the emerging critical-criminology literature on alternatives. Officials admitted in interview that what they did in the name of alternatives was not intended to have a substantial impact on the scale of imprisonment. As one official expressed it: 'Programs we already had became alternatives. They weren't alternatives before ... [It was] in the restraint period that they became alternatives.' In particular, within the Ministry of Corrections, where the prison branch had always dominated, community-corrections alternatives were supported to the extent that they contributed to the administrative convenience of the prison system. While conventional wisdom views community corrections as a means of reducing the state's size, budget, and involvement in public life, the opposite consequences ensued in the case of Ontario. Community corrections, and later the privatization of corrections, became an entrepreneurial strategy for the expansion of the ministry's activities in face of state fiscal restraints, legitimacy problems, and prison-population management problems. At least from the viewpoint of Ministry of Corrections officials, community corrections was a major success.

Given her challenge to academic orthodoxy, Dr McMahon is sensibly reflexive about her own contributions to knowledge. She is careful to pinpoint the limitations of the data she uses, especially those culled from official sources, which are subject to the vagaries of administrative classification and record-keeping. Canada ranks almost as poorly in the world league of statistics on punishment as it does in practices of punishment. Dr McMahon is also sensitive to the fact that she has produced local knowledge, a study of one place as a particular time, that begs comparative research. She is especially reflexive in the concluding chapter, in which she articulates preferred values and visions that might solve the paradox of a liberative punishment on the side of more liberation. She points to the successes of the Dutch penal system. She favours abolitionist criminology, fostered by academics and reformers in the Netherlands and other parts of Western Europe, as a means of replacing the negative logic of orthodox critical criminology.

The final chapter completes the task of turning the field on its head. One hopes that, once critical criminologists have recovered from their dizziness, they will take up the challenge and pursue the myriad questions for research and practice posed by this work.

I have only touched upon some of the more significant contributions of the research reported in the pages that follow. This book is the embodiment of criminology as a multidisciplinary and multifaceted field. It presents a history of punishment in Ontario in the late twentieth century. It contributes to the social-scientific study of social policy and reform. It addresses the core interest of political scientists in the role of the state in social reform and change. It offers lessons in social-science research methodology, especially by using critiques of methodology in existing research to demonstrate the relation between preferred techniques and preferred ideologies. It is a contribution to the sociologies of science and knowledge, showing the ways in which scientific knowledge about punishment is entwined with penal policy, practice, and reform. Scholars in all of the above-mentioned fields, and everyone involved in and concerned about penal practice and reform, will find this work of enormous value. This book is a landmark in criminology, and marks Dr McMahon as an important scholar in the field.

RICHARD V. ERICSON

Acknowledgments

Writing a book can be an isolating process. There were times when the social highlight of the workday consisted of my distractedly looking up from mounds of paper in the library to respond to the animated knocking and waving of a friendly window cleaner who was suspended outside, thirteen floors up.

Happily, however, even this primarily documentary and statistically based work has brought me into contact with numerous people. Through visits to state and community agencies and interviews with criminal-justice officials and reformers; through making presentations at academic gatherings (including in Canada, Scandinavia, Britain, Germany, and Spain), and receiving feedback on various parts of the manuscript from colleagues; and through those 'title-partyers' kind enough to bring their suggestions, preparing this book has also had intensely sociable, and pleasurable, aspects. Let me first, then, generically acknowledge all of those people who have responded to my requests, and who have debated and commiserated with me on issues of penal reform.

More specifically, for assistance during the period of data collection, I thank Tom Anderson, Leonard Crispino, Michael Crowley, Cheri Davis, Relva Khan, Patrick Madden, Diana Sepejak, Mark van Steen, and Paul Whillans, at the Ontario Ministry of Correctional Services; Roger Boe, Gail Cole, Orest Fedorowycz, Lothar Goetz, Brian Grainger, Helen Lacey, Dave Lester, Paul McPhie, Margaret Parlor, and Bert Soubliere, at the Canadian Centre for Justice Statistics; Lise Champagne at Statistics Canada; and Dorothy Gonsalves-Singh and Robert Harris at the Ontario Ministry of the Attorney General.

Many of these people not only assisted with gathering data, but provided useful comments and advice. I am particularly grateful to the official at the Canadian Centre for Justice Statistics who, in responding to my request for Ontario sentencing data through the 1970s and into the 1980s, straightforwardly laughed in my face, and suggested that I go hunting 'in boxes in rat-infested attics.' His frank acknowledgment that the data did not exist in any coherent form was helpful in terminating what had been becoming a lengthy tour of Ontario criminal-justice bureaucracies where more polite officials had courteously been referring me on to the next.

My extended conversations with those who consented to be interviewed for this study were both helpful and enjoyable. All of the interviews took place between October 1987 and February 1988. I warmly thank Don Sinclair, Glenn Thompson, Andrew Birkenmayer, and Art Daniels, all of whom, at the time of interview, were formerly of the Ontario Ministry of Correctional Services; Dennis Conly, then with the Canadian Centre for Justice Statistics; Stan Jolly, of the Ontario Ministry of the Attorney General; and Ruth Morris, activist and abolitionist. I especially thank Don Evans, also formerly of the Ministry of Correctional Services at the time of interview, not just for consenting to several lengthy interviews, but also for being instrumental in getting this research going, and for numerous insightful discussions on the perils of penal reform. The accumulated wisdom of these interviewees deserves far more elaboration than has been possible here.

For comments on this work during its various incarnations, I thank Keith Bottomley, Nils Christie, Stanley Cohen, David Downes, David Garland, Willem de Haan, Roger Hood, Lorna Marsden, Roger Matthews, Bob Menzies, Hans Mohr, Andrew Scull, Diana Sepejak, Dorothy Smith, Graham Stewart, Rene van Swaaningen, Tony Ward, and Peter Young. I also thank my anonymous reviewers.

This book has been initiated, developed, and completed through the support of the Centre of Criminology at the University of Toronto. In particular, I thank Richard Ericson for educating, challenging, supporting, and tolerating me. No expression of my appreciation could be sufficient. I also thank Janet Chan (now with the University of New South Wales, Australia), who, along with Richard, made my involvement in this project possible, and provided helpful commentaries.

Also at the Centre, I thank Anthony Doob who, during his period as director, could not have been more responsive in facilitating my work. His successor, John Beattie, has likewise been very helpful. Clifford Shearing, Philip Stenning, and Susan Addario provided multifaceted assistance and encouragement. Kevin Haggerty has been a superb research assistant. Larry White was also a great help in the final stages. At the Centre's library, Jane Gladstone has been a fount of information, and extremely patient in responding to my endless requests. I am also grateful to Catherine Matthews, Tom Finlay, and Renana Almagor for expediting my use of library materials. For looking after me administratively not only within, but well beyond the call of duty, I especially thank Rita Donelan and Bea Caulfield. Thanks also go to Marie Pearce, Gloria Cernivivo, and Monica Bristol. Overall, the intellectually stimulating and supportive collegiality I have experienced at the Centre has greatly enhanced my enjoyment of this work.

Financially, my travails have been supported by the University of Toronto, through a Canada Research fellowship, Open Fellowships, and fellowships from the Centre of Criminology; by the Ontario government, through a grant to the Centre of Criminology from the Ministry of Correctional Services, an Ontario Graduate Scholarship, and a Queen Elizabeth II Ontario Scholarship; by the Council of Europe, through a Criminological Research Fellowship (supported by the Universities of Oslo, Edinburgh, and Cambridge, and the Centre de Recherches Sociologiques sur le Droit et les Institutions Pénales, Paris); and by the Government of Canada, through a Canada Research Fellowship, and a Social Sciences and Humanities Research Council postdoctoral fellowship. I have been indirectly facilitated by the Ministry of the Solicitor General of Canada, through the contributions program to the Centre of Criminology. I also thank my money-lending friends.

The day after this manuscript was submitted to the University of Toronto Press, I took up a political staff position as policy adviser to the Minister of Correctional Services in Ontario (who concurrently served as Solicitor General). During the editorial period of this book's production, therefore, I was in daily contact with correctional policy makers and officials. I would like to thank these civil servants for tolerating my vehement, and not always diplomatic, expressions of opinion that the prison is a futile institution which reproduces wider structures of oppression, and that alternatives are a viable proposition. I warmly thank the minister – Mike Farnan, MPP – for hiring and listening to me, and for organizing the time of contract in a way that facilitated the book's production. It was only when I later became executive assistant to the subsequent minister (involving additional responsibilities in relation to policing and public safety) that I fully realized just how difficult it is to pay attention to corrections: in the wider and hectic world of criminal-justice politics and policy, driven by media and other pressures, issues of policing and the courts always seem to take precedence.

Curious readers might wonder whether my experience as an 'insider' at the political and bureaucratic apex of corrections made me want to change anything in the analysis I had already written, which is presented here. The short answer is no. A longer answer would elaborate on how I became more acutely aware of various issues, including the pains of imprisonment, especially for inmates, but also for staff; the general lack of public information about what is going on in relation to prisons; the significance of correctional officers' unions as a political force that needs to be taken account of, and worked with, in any proposals for progressive change; the ongoing dominance of institutions within the correctional sphere, despite the ever-more-polished rhetoric of alternatives; the continuing subsuming of the expression of values and feelings about punishment in favour of the amoral language and dehumanizing practices of management; and, last but not least, the difficulties involved in doing anything to change all of this experienced by the many people working in the system who do care, including those supposedly in positions of power. But a full elaboration of this would take another book.

For an excellent job in editing and producing this book, I thank Virgil Duff, Managing Editor, and his colleagues – especially Beverley Beetham Endersby for her copy editing – at the University of Toronto Press. Thanks also go to Laura Houle for producing the index. This book has been published with the help of a grant from the Social Science Federation of Canada, using funds provided by the Social Sciences and Humanities Research Council of Canada. With respect to chapters 3 and 4, I thank the editors of *The British Journal of Criminology* for allowing me to draw on material that was first published there.

Despite these numerous debts of gratitude, responsibility for any errors or omissions in what follows must be considered solely my own.

Finally, it is a pleasure to thank Jan Anderson, Zaheer Baber, Mary Condon, Ron Cavalucci, Dany Lacombe, John Stix, Wendell Block, and b.h. Yael, who are foremost among the friends, and loves, who have borne with me through the various stages of this work. Along with my parents, any pleasure in its publication belongs to them too.

THE PERSISTENT PRISON?
RETHINKING DECARCERATION
AND PENAL REFORM

1

Imprisonment, Alternatives, and Penality

Imprisonment and Alternatives

As we approach the end of the twentieth century, issues of imprisonment are topical. Overcrowding, riots, prisoner suicides, staff discontent, and abysmal conditions are regularly reported. Answers to the question of what should be done about the prison system are regularly disputed by politicians, penal policy makers, academics, reform groups, the mass media, and the public, as well as by prisoners themselves.

Criticisms of prisons and proposals for reform of the penal system are not recent phenomena. Since the inception of imprisonment as a major form of punishment about two hundred years ago, criticism of it has been 'endemic to its history' (Ignatieff 1978: 19). Yet, despite how consistently imprisonment has remained an issue, neither its nature nor that of the broader power to punish has remained static over the past two centuries. Just as the practices of punishment have undergone a series of transformations, so have strategies and discourses of penal reform.

In this book, I explore trends in imprisonment and penal reform since the Second World War, with the purpose of illuminating some postwar transformations of the power to punish. I also seek to shed light on changing criminological and sociological perspectives on penal reform. As is often the case in social-scientific analyses, my interest in my subject – imprisonment and penal reform – is not only scholarly. It is my hope that, by better understanding the situation as it exists, we may enhance our ability to challenge and change conditions that smother, rather than foster, human liberty and potential.

What major trends in imprisonment and penal reform have developed during the contemporary period? The answers that might be given to this question vary according to the perspective from which it is viewed. Lawyers might point to increasing pressure for, and accomplishment of, legal intervention in the matters of prison conditions and prisoners' rights. Philosophers might point to how, in discussions of punishment, the expression of liberal and humanitarian values has been superseded by that of more pragmatic ones. Economists might point to huge increases in the costs of crime, and of responses to it.

Such legal, philosophical, and economic observations are pertinent to this inquiry. But, from the sociological and criminological perspective adopted here, the most striking feature of postwar penal trends has been a dramatic increase in alternatives to imprisonment, both in discussion and in implementation. My primary concern in this book is with related developments – often encapsulated in the notion of 'decarceration' (e.g., Scull 1977, 1984, 1991; Chan and Ericson 1981; Cohen 1979a, 1985).

The postwar watershed in this movement towards alternatives occurred in the early 1970s. At that time – as I document in more detail later – the prison as an institution, and its programs, came under attack from political and reformist sources. One of the distinctive features of what was, after all, but another in a long series of critiques of imprisonment was its rigour. Supported by numerous social-scientific studies documenting the various failures of imprisonment, the attack was also distinguished by its emphasis on non-institutional alternatives as a solution to the problems of prisons: given that imprisonment as a penal strategy appeared to be beyond meaningful reform, reformers began looking for other ways of dealing with offenders.

Prior to this watershed in penal reform, punitive practices other than imprisonment already existed for dealing with offenders, and, in fact, some predated its use. Moreover, in many Western countries, an expansion of correctional alternatives to imprisonment had already been occurring during the 1950s and 1960s. But this tendency towards adopting alternatives received a major boost from the penal-reform debates of the early 1970s. Viewed as appealing by reformers and administrators for humanitarian, fiscal, and utilitarian reasons, existing programs, such as probation, temporary release, and halfway houses, gained a more prominent public profile and underwent an accelerated rate of expansion. A sometimes bewildering range of new community programs were also developed, including, for example, community service orders, victim–offender reconciliation schemes, and bail supervision. In sum, the postwar period – most obviously after the early 1970s

– has been an era in which penal policy makers and reformers have sought to bring the issues and practices of corrections beyond the prison and into the community.

That imprisonment continues to be criticized is an indication of the perceived limitations of this reformist endeavour. Issues of prison over-crowding, of disturbances within prisons, and of staff and prisoner grievances are often seen as manifestations of the overriding problem of the large size of prison populations. Many observers believe that the promises made about alternatives have not been realized. They argue that, despite the introduction of alternatives, prison populations have remained stable, and, in some places, have even increased. Alternatives, therefore, are believed to have had little or no effect in constraining and reducing the use of imprisonment. The prison, it is said, has displayed a remarkable immunity, not only to historical attempts at reform within its walls, but also to contemporary efforts at bringing inmates outside them. David Downes's (1988: 4) summary of perceptions of the situation in England and Wales resonates in many Western countries: 'Reforms are tried and found wanting – parole, suspended sentences, community service orders – in the pursuit of a reduced prison population. Its continuing rise is then declared something akin to a natural law, beyond the realms of political choice or informed decision-making.'

In relation to the common perception that, especially in conditions of rising crime rates, reducing prison population is 'hardly to be expect-ed or induced,' Downes raises the question: 'Does it have to be so?' (1988: 4). In responding, he turns to an analysis of incarceration in The Netherlands compared with that in England and Wales. For, viewed from an expansionist British perspective, postwar penal trends in The Netherlands have been anomalous: even during a period of increasing crime rates, the Dutch accomplished a substantial reduction in impris-onment from 1950 to 1975, with the subsequent prison population remaining relatively low. Dutch prison conditions are also compara-tively more liberal and humane than those in England and Wales. Downes charts those aspects of Dutch social and penal policy that facil-itated this decarceration and amelioration of the pains of imprisonment. His findings present a challenge to the many observers who see prison populations as constant and conditions as beyond reform.

In this book, my major concerns – similar to those of Downes – are with the possibilities and practicalities, as well as the explanations of penal reform. But, rather than looking elsewhere – to the proverbial other side of the hill where the grass so often appears greener – I present a re-examination of the situation in some jurisdictions where it has been claimed that the use of imprisonment has expanded, along with the use of alternatives. At issue are the questions: Has the growth of imprisonment been inexorable in these jurisdictions as commentaries suggest? Has the use of alternatives during the postwar period been as ineffective in influencing constraint and reduction in the use of imprisonment as many experts would have us believe? Is the increasingly popular picture of penal reform as merely accomplishing the 'further consolidation of carceral power' (Ignatieff 1978: 220) impeding our ability to recognize any accomplishment of progressive ideals that may have occurred?

In re-examining postwar penal trends, my major focus is on the Canadian province of Ontario. This province is known far beyond its borders for the strength of its commitment to community programs (Dodge 1979). By the mid-1980s, the Ontario Ministry of Correctional Services, which is responsible for the administration of provincial prisons and community correctional programs, could report that 'institutional custody or "imprisonment" makes up just a fraction of the ministry's scope of activity. On any given day, more than 85 per cent of offenders under the ministry's care are serving their sentences under community supervision by ministry probation and parole personnel' (*Annual Report* 1986: 5).

In more critical circles, however, the province of Ontario has been known not only for the scale of its adoption of alternatives, but also for its failure in constraining the use of imprisonment. As Chan and Ericson (1981: 9) have expressed it, in Ontario, and in Canada as a whole, 'not only are more people coming under the system, more are being sent to prison as well.' Reference to their study as indicating that the movement to decarceration has been marked by failure has been made by criminologists from many countries, including Britain, the United States, Israel, Norway, and Australia (e.g., Austin and Krisberg 1981; Bottoms 1983; Chan and Zdenkowski 1986; Cohen 1985; Mathiesen 1983, 1986, 1990; Scull 1984, 1987, 1991).

Given that penal trends in Ontario have been seen as paradigmatic of the tendency for imprisonment to increase in the face of penal reform, the province provides a good case for re-examination of trends in, and issues of, decarceration. In contrast to previous analysis, I argue that a substantial reduction in imprisonment *did* occur in Ontario during the postwar period, and that penal reform played an important part in this reduction. I further argue that my different conclusions about decarceration are not merely a matter of more, better, or different data.

Rather, the conclusions I draw signal fundamental issues about the social organization and construction of knowledge in critical criminology. In raising these issues of knowledge, I am both drawing from, and responding to, some theoretical developments in critical criminology itself, as well as in the sociologies of deviance, punishment, and control.

Criminological Knowledge and Penality

While knowledge has traditionally been seen as the aim or *object* of criminological study, in recent years it has increasingly been made a constituent part of the *subject* of the inquiry. This shift in emphasis is related to broader developments in social-scientific and literary criticism (Cohen 1988a). But, for students of the power to punish, Michel Foucault's work – particularly *Discipline and Punish: The Birth of the Prison* (1977) – has precipitated recognition of the importance of discourse in the penal realm.

According to Foucault, 'the exercise of power itself creates and causes to emerge new objects of knowledge and accumulates new bodies of information' (1980: 51). The birth of the prison represented an important example of this power–knowledge symbiosis. As those incarcerated were subject to forms of observation conducive to the formation of clinical knowledge, the prison yielded a basis for the emergence of the social-scientific field of criminology. Although Foucault's focus in *Discipline and Punish* is primarily on the prison, he also reveals the significance of the 'carceral network' more generally in making the human sciences historically possible. For the last few centuries, the penal exercise of power and the generation of social-scientific knowledge have intersected with, and reinforced, each other.

A similar concern with issues of knowledge and power is reflected in many recent sociological studies of deviance and control. The concept of 'penality,' for example, has been advanced by David Garland and Peter Young (1983). 'Penality' refers to the whole of the 'penal complex, including its sanctions, discourses and representations' (Garland 1985b: 10). Much literature on contemporary developments in criminal justice can be read as analyses of penality: the concern is with the penal realm, but goes far beyond that of studies that limit their attention to 'prisons,' 'the courts,' 'the police,' and other components of the criminal-justice system.

In social analyses of penality, attention is given to discursive as well as more tangible aspects of criminal justice, punishment, and control.

At issue is not only empirical identification of what is going on in prisons, courts, and elsewhere, but also the perceptions and depictions of what is, and should be, occurring, by officials, reformers, and others active in the area of criminal justice. Through this approach, critical analysts have identified disjunctures between penal rhetoric and practices, and between intentions and effects. Their attention to discursive aspects of the exercise of power has provided insights on the partial nature of knowledge, and on the ideological elements of social-scientific and other discourses on justice. In turn, these insights have furthered understanding of the dialectical constitution and reproduction of dominant penal and social orders: penality is not just produced by, but is productive of, the wider social environment (e.g., Burton and Carlen 1979; Chan and Ericson 1981; Cohen 1983, 1985, 1988b; Ericson 1983; Ericson and Baranek 1982; Edelman 1977; Garland 1986, 1990; Garland and Young 1983; Gusfield 1981; de Haan 1990; McBarnet 1981; Melossi 1987; Menzies 1989; Smith 1983, 1984).

This book is also informed by, and seeks to inform, the understanding of penality. In addition to re-examining trends in the use of imprisonment and alternatives, I analyse the assumptions and understandings that have permeated this field of penal reform. There is one important respect, however, in which this study differs from many others concerned with penality. Social analysts of penality have typically taken a critical-outsider stance, have deconstructed reformist rhetoric, and have proceeded to elaborate on what is 'really' going on within the system (with these revelations usually being even sadder stories than those officials and reformers tend to tell). By taking this approach, analysts of penality have presented themselves as ideologically, politically, and intellectually separate from the penal complex. But, what critical analysts have insufficiently considered is that critical discourse itself – although typically in oppositional stance – can also be considered as part of the penal complex.

The point is that attention to issues of penality requires more than exploring the dialectical relationships of conservative discourse to the exercise of power. The situation of more critical discourse in relation to the exercise of power must also be examined. What has critical criminology's position been in the wider network of power–knowledge relationships? Is it enough to deconstruct the hidden agenda and consequences of official, correctionalist, managerial, and reformist discourses? Should critical criminologists not be more reflexive about the nature of their own assumptions, concepts, and interpretations? In what ways might critical analyses be vulnerable to usurpation by those with more repressive or conservative interests, and influence, in the power to punish? Can the usurpation of critical analysis be avoided? Are there conceptual or analytical strategies that might be conducive to the attainment of what Garland and Young (1983: 33) aptly describe as 'the paradox of a liberative penality'?

My approach to the study of imprisonment and alternatives has been shaped by these concerns about critical criminology's situation in relation to the power to punish. For, as I elaborate, critical analyses of alternatives to imprisonment are amenable to, and have been used in, correctional officials' attempts to extend, rather than diminish, the power to punish.

Where this study differs from others, therefore, is in that, rather than taking previous critical studies of the failures of decarceration as a knowledge base on which to build, it considers such studies as a core analytical problem to be addressed. What have been the logic, insights, and limitations of critical analyses of imprisonment and alternatives? Are critical analyses of decarceration satisfactory in light of a re-examination of postwar penal trends? To what extent have critical analysts of decarceration succeeded in divorcing themselves from the more conservative correctionalist stances they opposed?

Towards addressing these issues, I first provide a historical retrospective on changing social-scientific perspectives on imprisonment and corrections, and on how they facilitated the emergence of alternatives to prison as a dominant reform strategy (chapter 2). I then analyse opposition to correctionalist criminology, the development of critical perspectives on issues of decarceration, and problematic aspects of this literature (chapters 3 and 4). I further address the insights and limitations of critical perspectives on decarceration through an analysis of postwar penal trends in Ontario: substantial decarceration actually occurred (chapter 5); the development of community corrections played some – but not a major – part in this decarceration (chapter 6); changes in the administration of fines, particularly in the case of intoxication offenders who defaulted, were of greater significance in the accomplishment of decarceration (chapters 7 and 8); I then analyse the significance of Ontario community corrections (chapter 9) and wider penal trends (chapter 10). And, in the final chapter, I return to fundamental issues of knowledge, power, and praxis in critical theory and the desire of such theory to ameliorate the power to punish.

2

The Prison, Criminology, and Rehabilitation

The Prison, Criminology, and the Ascendancy of Rehabilitation

As Foucault's (1977) work suggests, and as Garland (1985b) has elaborated, the exercise of penal power through the prison, and the genesis of criminological ideas, have historically been interwoven. The emergence of a distinctively critical criminology in the late 1960s represented a concerted attempt to break with this correctionalist stance. Critical criminologists sought to move away from technicist concerns with criminals, the causes of crime, and the effectiveness of penal programs; what they considered to be at issue were deeper, more political questions about the significance of deviance, its definition, and its control, in the reproduction of an oppressive social order. This sociopolitical focus of critical criminologists brought them far beyond the walls of the prison and into the wider penal realm.

Yet, in some respects, critical criminologists' analytical movement away from the prison reflected a tendency that was also becoming evident in mainstream criminology itself. One way of recapitulating the history of criminological ideas, therefore, is to examine criminology's initial preoccupation with, and gradual movement away from, the institution of imprisonment.

The rapid spread of imprisonment as a major social institution during the nineteenth century provided a basis for criminology as a field of inquiry. Originally, what was considered to be at issue in the formation of knowledge was not the nature of imprisonment itself, but rather that of those who were incarcerated. By virtue of their confinement within the prison, prisoners were spatially, socially, legally, and administratively segregated from society at large. They became amenable to social-scientific inquiry. The prison thereby provided the 'institutional surface for the emergence of the concerns, techniques and data of the new discipline,' and early criminology can safely be described as its 'offspring' (Garland 1985: 80, 82). Generated from within the institution, criminological knowledge – in its biological, psychological, and sociological forms – was synonymous with that of prisoners. As Garland (ibid: 82) has expressed it:

> The prison provided a kind of experimental laboratory, a controlled enclosure in which the new knowledge could develop. It provided the possibility for the long-term observation of criminals who could be examined, measured, photographed and catalogued in an organised manner. It produced statistical data on conviction rates, recidivism patterns and criminal careers which were invaluable criminological materials unavailable elsewhere. It even allowed a degree of experimentation in so far as various regimes of labour, diet, discipline and so on could be compared with one another to assess the effects of each upon the prison population and the causes of crime.

Pioneering criminologists took a positivist approach in studying prisoners: their scientific objective was to identify the individual and social characteristics of offenders, and so to discover the factors underlying criminal behaviour. From the late nineteenth century, attempts were made to establish relationships between physical appearance and criminality, for example, by Lombroso (1876) in Italy, Goring (1913) in England, Kretschmer (1921) in Germany, and Hooton (1939) and Sheldon (1936, 1940, 1942, 1949, 1954) in the United States. With the growth of criminology as a field of inquiry, and a broadening of disciplinary approaches, further hypotheses were developed about the significance of mental deficiency, of hereditary and biological defects, and of psychiatric abnormalities in contributing to criminality (Vold 1979). Sociologists also studied life within the prison, attempting to determine, for example, if criminal behaviour was learned through association with other criminals (ibid; Lynd and Lynd 1929; Hayner and Ash 1939; Taft 1942; Haynes 1948; Sykes 1958). Such sociological studies often followed the occurrence of prison disturbances and 'riots,' with efforts at explaining them furthering prison administrative, as well as social-scientific, interests.

From the outset, positivist inquiries in the prison setting were not solely scientific endeavours. They fused with utilitarian and reformist efforts to discover the causes of, and thereby suitable treatment for, criminal behaviour. The social-scientific genesis of criminology paralleled and reinforced the emergent policy-reform discourse of rehabilitation. As the rehabilitative ethos gathered support among social scientists, and correctional reformers and practitioners, the orientation of punishment changed: the earlier emphasis on the offence, and on legal and classical principles of justice, was moderated by growing attention to the offender and the utility of strategies of classification, differentiation, and individualization in the provision of treatment (Cullen and Gilbert 1982). Over time, penal practices increasingly incorporated rehabilitative strategies. The use of indeterminate sentences grew. The political, legal, and administrative groundwork was laid for the development of treatment-oriented programs such as probation, parole, and halfway houses.

Of course, the pace of the advancement of criminological knowledge, and of the rise of rehabilitation, varied greatly from place to place. Nevertheless, by the time criminology was being institutionalized in university and other settings during the 1950s and 1960s, commitment to, and practices based upon, the ideas of treatment and rehabilitation were reaching a peak. While there was no lack of debate about specific causal factors and preferable reform strategies, the early postwar period was the one in which rehabilitation 'received its fullest and widest support' (Young 1983: 98). Until the late 1960s, rehabilitation 'remained unchallenged as the dominant correctional ideology' (Cullen and Gilbert 1982: 82).

Ironically, while studies from the prison had facilitated the rise of criminology and of rehabilitation, this approach also carried the seeds of its own demise: later studies centring on imprisonment, and the effects of rehabilitation programs, provided an important basis for challenges to positivist criminology and the programs with which it was associated. These challenges were to be most forcefully expressed during the watershed in penal reform in the early 1970s.

Negative Findings about Rehabilitation

Until Robert Martinson published his 1975 'Nothing Works' article in a liberal magazine, not many people noticed the many sociological research studies and essays purporting to show that prisons do not rehabilitate. For example, Walter Bailey's 1966 review of reports on the effectiveness of 100 treatment programs concluded that correctional programs rarely correct, but few people paid any attention to the review. No one yelled, 'Nothing Works!' (Cressey 1982: xix)

Until the mid-twentieth century, the prison provided a basis for the formation of criminological knowledge emphasizing the desirability of rehabilitation. But, after the Second World War, literature embodying negative findings about the 'effectiveness' of rehabilitative programs proliferated rapidly. The changing interpretation and reception of these findings in the academic, policy, and public cultures represents a substantial transformation in the social organization of correctional knowledge: where studies with negative findings were initially used to advance rehabilitation, in the 1970s they facilitated the speedy demise of the rehabilitative ideal. A brief sketch of relevant discourses indicates the changing perspectives on imprisonment and corrections with which the effectiveness literature was associated.

As with the genesis of criminological inquiry more generally, the development of research on the effectiveness of rehabilitation programs was stimulated by a combination of utilitarian, reformist, and positivist scientific interests. With the development and expansion of vocational, education, medical, counselling, and other therapeutic programs, various constituencies sought knowledge of their effects: state officials, with budgetary and other responsibilities in the exercise of penal control, sought assurance that correctional programs were not only having their intended effects, but were doing so in a cost-efficient manner; reformers, both in state and in civil society, sought support for their humanitarian objectives, and for their claims about the benefits of rehabilitation as a penal strategy; and social scientists sought to further their knowledge of the causes of criminal behaviour through examination of the results of treatment. Given these utilitarian, reformist, and scientific interests, the issues of costs, of humaneness, and especially of effectiveness, were consistently in the forefront in the criminological literature on rehabilitation.

From mid-century on, the advancement of criminology as a social-scientific field, and the availability of funding, further facilitated effectiveness studies. In North America, benevolent organizations such as the Russell Sage and Ford foundations provided resources to encourage the involvement of social scientists in carrying out relevant research (McKelvey 1977: 345–8; Ohlin 1956; Laub 1983). Issues of rehabilitation and the successful treatment of offenders also figured prominently in the establishment of government- and university-based criminology institutes, such as the British Home Office Research Unit (established in 1957), the Institute of Criminology at Cambridge University (established in 1959), the Institute of Criminology and Criminal Law at the University of Oslo (established in 1954), and the Centre of Criminology at the University of Toronto (established in 1963) (Edwards 1960, 1964, 1984; Olaussen and Sørensen 1977; Radzinowicz 1988; Rock 1988). While the extent of liaison among private, government, and university-based agencies varied greatly in different contexts, similar correctionalist concerns underlay their stated objectives.

In assessing treatment and correctional programs, and in evaluating whether they 'worked,' rates of recidivism emerged as the crucial criterion. The phenomenon of recidivism, or the tendency of an offender to relapse into crime, had long been a concern of correctional authorities (Garland 1985b: 61–2; Mannheim, 1960; Ohlin 1956: 41ff; Third International Congress of Criminology 1955). Attempts to counter this tendency were an important rationale of treatment programs informed by positivist principles. Evaluators compared the subsequent criminal careers of prisoners subjected to treatment programs with those of control groups who were not. They measured the probability of reoffending on release after short-term incarceration against that following longer periods of incarceration. Evaluators also compared the results of the imposition of probation, fines, and other non-incarcerative dispositions with those of imprisonment. This 'continuing quest for correctional goals' by academics and administrators received further impetus with improvements in research techniques (McKelvey 1977: 367).

Without elaborating the details of this extensive literature on effectiveness (for reviews, see Bailey 1966; Martinson 1974), the conclusions that were to become best known can be summarized concisely: treatment programs apparently had little effect on recidivism. Moreover, it appeared that imprisonment was no more effective than non-incarcerative dispositions in reducing recidivism. As Radzinowicz, for example, remarked (1961: 169): 'the similarity of success and failure rates, as measured by the after-conduct of offenders, irrespective of whether they were put on probation, fined, [or] sentenced to short-term imprisonment, or to longer corrective detention, is indeed striking.'

What is most pertinent here is not the repeated finding that treatment and correctional programs apparently had little effect on recidivism, but the manner in which this result was initially construed so as to reaffirm positivist and rehabilitative ideals. Thus, for example, George Vold – in response to the repeated finding of continuing recidivism in face of a wide variety of treatment programs – did not question the basic tenets or underlying principles of such programs, but instead highlighted the recursive relationship between theory, research, and practice. According to him (1958: 302): 'more adequate theory on which to base a more adequate treatment program may only be expected with more fruitful research into, and a more complete understanding of, crime causation.' In sum, the recurrently negative findings of the effectiveness literature were not initially used in diminishing commitment to rehabilitation, but rather served to justify more of the same: the issue was not whether the idea of rehabilitation itself was conceptually flawed, but how the goals of rehabilitation could be better accomplished. Efforts at classifying criminals so as to identify 'good risks,' and the development and refinement of rehabilitation programs, therefore proceeded apace.

Although the early negative findings of the effectiveness literature did little to change the substance of rehabilitation programs, they did provide support for changes in their context: growing documentation of the limited effectiveness of rehabilitation, and of the similarity of success and failure rates in institutional and community correctional settings, helped to fuel the expansion of non-incarcerative programs for offenders. Specifically, given that community correctional programs had outcomes similar to those of institutional ones, and that they also had the apparent virtues of being less costly and more humane than imprisonment, support for community corrections grew in the social-scientific, policy, and public cultures. Community correctional advocates argued that rehabilitation could be accomplished in the community as well as, or better than, in the institutional context. During the postwar period, commitment to progressive penal policies increasingly included reference to the promise of community corrections. In the United States, the publication of the report of the Corrections Task Force of the President's Commission on Law Enforcement and the Administration of Justice in 1967 constituted the official 'blessing' of community-based correctional programs (Conrad 1973). In Canada, the report of the Ouimet committee (1969) played a similar role. Ironically, growing documentation about the limits of rehabilitation within the prisons facilitated its expansion in the form of community corrections.

In the early 1970s, although the empirical content of the effectiveness literature remained similar to that of earlier studies, a dramatic turn-about occurred in its interpretation. This interpretive transformation was linked to other emergent attacks on the wider sociopolitical underpinnings of rehabilitation. Within criminology, however, Robert Martinson's (1974) article, entitled 'What Works? Questions and Answers about Prison Reform,' had a pivotal role in shifting perspectives on rehabilitation.

Martinson and his colleagues had originally been employed by the New York State Governor's Special Committee on Criminal Offenders. The state correctional system had been moving towards rehabilitation, and sought knowledge of the most effective approaches. The researchers systematically surveyed 231 studies carried out between 1945 and 1967 that were considered to have been methodologically satisfactory. This analysis led researchers to the gloomy conclusion that, rather than affirming rehabilitation, '*with few and isolated exceptions, the rehabilitative efforts that have been reported so far have had no appreciable effect on recidivism*' (1974: 25; emphasis in original).

Viewed retrospectively, this conclusion appears merely to replicate previous ones. However, Martinson's project stood out not only because of the scope and apparent rigour of the analysis, but also because of the critical inferences he drew. Specifically, where previous analysts had tended to use such conclusions in bolstering arguments about the need for expanding and trying new forms of rehabilitation, Martinson raised questions about the viability of rehabilitation itself. Having queried whether the lack of effectiveness might reflect only the need for 'a more full-hearted commitment to the strategy of treatment,' Martinson (1974: 49) stated: 'It may be, on the other hand, that there is a more radical flaw in our present strategies – that education at its best, cannot overcome, or even appreciably reduce, the powerful tendency for offenders to continue in criminal behaviour. Our present treatment programs are based on a theory of crime as a "disease" – that is to say as something foreign and abnormal in the individual which can presumably be cured. This theory may well be flawed.'

Martinson's conclusions about the effects of rehabilitation programs rapidly became encapsulated in the buzz phrase 'nothing works.' As Cullen and Gilbert (1982: 112) have documented, the response to Martinson's study differed greatly from that to previous ones in that, rather than serving as 'the starting point for yet another liberal campaign to save the criminal and the delinquent,' the dictum '"nothing works" became a code word for the more sobering belief that rehabilitation *cannot work*' (emphasis in original). This contention soon became entrenched in correctional analyses. As Cressey (1982: xix) ruefully observed: 'Now, dozens of people are handed salaries of up to $50,000 a year just for standing up in an occasional meeting on prison policy, and shouting "Nothing works!" Others are receiving gold stars, pay raises and royalties for writing essays whose only message is a negative one: "Nothing works."'

Significantly, although Martinson's article, along with related developments in the social-scientific, political, and public cultures, fundamentally undermined the ideals of rehabilitation, the movement towards community corrections was not weakened, but received added impetus from the critique. As already indicated, while the initial orientation towards community correctional programs was largely stimulated by the rehabilitative ethos, it had also gathered support from recognition of the limitations of rehabilitation programs in the institutional context. The combined advancement of community corrections, along with the declining faith in the potential for accomplishing rehabilitation within prisons, is, therefore, not as contradictory as it might at first appear.

The rationales underlying the growing force of the community-corrections movement were evident in Martinson's own article. The studies reviewed by him also included community correctional programs, notably probation and parole. Here, in contrast to his otherwise pessimistic conclusions, Martinson identified 'one encouraging set of findings.' Observing that such programs had cost advantages, and that offenders in them did not do any worse than those in institutional contexts, Martinson contended that 'the implication is clear: *if we can't do more for (and to) offenders, at least we can safely do less*' (1974: 48; emphasis in original).

In sum, the negative findings of the effectiveness literature, initially by implication, and later more explicitly, contributed to the demise of discourse on rehabilitation and the ascendancy of that on community corrections. In their growing critique of prison programs, and preference for community ones, these analyses mirrored the direction of developments in other social-scientific and political arenas.

Intellectual and Political Movements Away from the Prison

PERSPECTIVES ON DEVIANCE AS A PRODUCT OF CONTROL

Martinson's endorsement of 'doing less' echoed similar exhortations across the liberal intellectual and political spectrum. But, where Martinson's adoption of this position stemmed primarily from his identification of the ineffectiveness of rehabilitation programs, for many other liberal critics growing recognition of the repressive aspects of these penal practices influenced calls for their diminution in favour of deinstitutionalization, decarceration, and other such movements.

In the 1960s, and just as rehabilitation was reaching its zenith in the official and public cultures, an influential literature on deviance and social reaction emerged in the social sciences. In particular, sociological analyses from the phenomenological, ethnomethodological, and symbolic-interactionist traditions challenged the explanatory circumscriptions of positivist approaches to criminality. These publications provided more sympathetic views of the context of deviant behaviour, and pointed to the stigmatizing, scapegoating, and often unjust social reactions to which deviants were subject (Garfinkel 1956; Kitsuse 1962; Becker 1963, 1970; Matza 1964; Wilkins 1964; Downes 1966; Erikson 1966; Douglas 1967; Cicourel 1968; Cohen 1971; Schur 1971).

Through these inquiries, particular aspects of penal and social control were brought more clearly into view: deviance and criminality were now largely posited as 'a product of agencies of social control' (Cicourel 1968: 22), with the activities of these agencies effectively 'amplifying deviant behaviour' (Vold 1979: 264; see Lemert 1951, 1967, 1971). Contentions about the socially constructed nature of deviance, and the effects of control, were supported through studies of the management of deviance and criminality by the police (Skolnick 1966; Bittner 1967, 1970; Reiss 1971; Manning 1972, 1977), the courts (Sudnow 1965; Emerson 1969) and other criminal-justice agencies and institutions (Scheff 1966; Cicourel 1968; Ericson 1975b).

Where imprisonment was concerned, studies from the labelling and social-reaction perspectives pointed to the contingent nature of decisions to incarcerate, given the discretionary nature of police and judicial decision making. The arbitrariness involved in classification procedures, in the administration of indeterminate sentences, and in the granting of parole was similarly highlighted. With recognition of the socially defined nature of deviance, and the normality and prevalence of much behaviour subject to such definition, positivist assumptions about the sick and different character of criminals were challenged. Sociologists also drew on critiques of psychiatric procedures and practices in pointing out the coercive and repressive aspects of rehabilitation programs. They argued that 'treatment' was often better understood as punishment; they revealed how those subject to rehabilitation were rarely afforded the protections of due process. In short, many social scientists now ascribed pathology to the correctional system itself, rather than to those being processed by it (e.g., Goffman 1961; Greenberg 1970, 1972, 1977; AFSC 1971; Kittrie 1971; Frankel 1972; Conrad 1973; Mitford 1973; Rosenhan 1973; Gaylin 1974).

Although analysts of labelling and social reaction were more or less explicitly critical of positivism, their policy conclusions were quite similar. Drawing on the effectiveness literature indicating the limited impact of treatment programs on recidivism, as well as pointing to the 'humane and economical' benefits of non-institutional programs, analysts agreed that 'there is a strong argument for turning efforts to the search for alternatives outside the prison system' (Ericson 1975b: 135). As did their positivist colleagues, labelling analysts supported the view that, 'by doing as little as possible, we may be doing as little harm as possible' (Wilkins 1969, quoted in Ericson 1975: 135). By advocating a search for alternatives 'outside the prison system altogether,' and a policy of radical non-intervention (Schur 1971), labelling and social-reaction analysts provided support for broader movements away from the prison, and towards the rise of community alternatives.

LIBERAL SCEPTICISM ABOUT STATE BENEVOLENCE

The conclusions of positivist criminologists, and of sociologists of deviance and control, resonated with those in the liberal political culture more generally. The social, cultural, and political events of the 1960s and early 1970s had already generated much scepticism about the state's role in 'doing good' through criminal-justice and other institutions. As Cullen and Gilbert have expressed it, the 'turmoil' of the 1960s, and the emergence of the civil rights movement, 'marked the beginning of a period in which the legitimacy of state authority was subjected to continued and widespread debate among liberal forces.' For those of liberal and leftist orientations, 'optimism about the possibilities for genuine reform within the confines of existing institutional arrangements would be replaced by a deep sense of pessimism' (1982: 104–5).

Authorities' responses to civil rights movements on both sides of the Atlantic; the continuing u.s. involvement in Vietnam; the Canadian implementation of the War Measures Act; the multifaceted revelation of the coercive, unethical, repressive, and inequitable aspects of Western states – all contributed to the shaking of complacent liberal sentiments. In the correctional context, however, it was prison disturbances and riots, such as those at Attica, New York, and Kingston, Ontario, in 1971, that hastened the already waning credibility of penal practices (Badillo and Haynes 1972; Caron 1985; McKelvey 1977; Oswald 1972; Swackhamer 1972; Wicker 1978). As Cullen and Gilbert have explained, with reference to Attica and the United States (1982: 108):

Traditionally, reformers had championed the infusion of the rehabilitative ideal into the criminal justice system and the expansion of discretionary powers that would allow for the individualized treatment of offenders. While the difficulties surrounding correctional programs were not ignored in the past, many liberals nevertheless had held tenaciously to the belief that the state could ultimately be induced to exercise these powers in a benevolent manner. But the bloody suppression of the uprising at Attica compelled even the most adamant supporters of enforced therapy to re-examine this assumption. In focusing attention on the plight of society's captives, Attica revealed how badly the liberals' faith in the state had been misplaced. It was now clear that the state used its discretion not to better inmates but to brutalize them, not to effect individualized treatment but to incarcerate only the poor and non-white.

Liberal discontent with penal practices was frequently articulated in terms of the 'crime of treatment,' and the 'limits' and 'prisoners' of benevolence (AFSC 1971: 83; Gaylin et al 1978; Glaser 1978). Rehabilitation was described as a myth that fostered the victimization of prisoners themselves (Cullen and Gilbert 1982: 125). In the reform culture of progressive officials and civil-libertarian and other reformers, the theme of doing 'less harm,' rather than 'more good,' also became common. Towards the end of minimizing harm, both outsider and insider reformers called for 'deinstitutionalization,' 'diversion,' 'decriminalization,' and other destructuring policies.

In sum, a crisis in penal reform was precipitated in the early 1970s. At that time, the political, academic, and public cultures converged in seeking to release deviants and offenders from the purview of the state, its professional experts, and its institutions. In the case of imprisonment, a movement towards community corrections was posited as a strategy conducive to the accomplishment of the lesser of two evils.

Discursive and Strategic Movements Away from the Prison

As documented here, although the prison was central in the early formation of criminological knowledge, the evolution of the field can be described in terms of a movement away from the prison. In particular, the outcome of studies of rehabilitation programs, coupled with the insights of the sociology of deviance and control, had important repercussions: attention was shifted from the nature of prisoners to that of the penal practices to which they were subjected. As the limitations of therapeutic programs in the prison context became apparent, correctional analysts and reformers increasingly sought to further their utilitarian, humanitarian, and scientific interests through alternative correctional programs.

The incipient movement away from the prison was most dramatically and coherently expressed during the penal-reform watershed of the early 1970s. In conjunction with vociferous criticism of prisons and their programs, a range of 'destructuring' strategies was advocated (Cohen 1988a: 11–12). Drawing from legal critiques (e.g., Packer 1968) of existing arrangements, many reformers primarily turned their attention to legal issues. They sought reduction in the exercise of discretion by state agents and agencies through adoption of the 'justice' model. Under this model 'just deserts' would be a key principle of sentencing, sentences would be legislatively fixed and determinate, and any participation by prisoners in rehabilitation programs would be on a voluntary basis (Cullen and Gilbert 1982: 125–31). For more legally oriented reformers, therefore, due process and the rule of law were seen as the means of reducing the arbitrary exercise and excesses of state power. Additional recommendations, such as decriminalization, delegalization, and diversion, sought to remove particular categories of deviants and offenders from the legalistic criminal-justice system altogether.

In the field of corrections, the destructuring movement was most usually expressed in terms of calls for deinstitutionalization and the use of community-correctional alternatives to imprisonment. Enjoying the support of both insider and outsider reformers, this movement had an effect. The already increasing use of programs such a probation and halfway houses accelerated. Many new community-correctional programs – for example, community service orders – were initiated and highly publicized.

As talk about, and practices of, community corrections and alternatives to prison became more common during the 1970s and 1980s, attention was again turned to the consequences of programs. In their assessment, much of this criminological literature has evidenced more sophisticated conceptualizations of 'success' than those found in the earlier literature on the effectiveness of rehabilitation. In particular, critical criminologists – seeking to transcend the correctionalist stance of their mainstream predecessors – have examined the rhetorical and ideological, as well as the substantive, aspects of community corrections.

Rather than restricting their attention to technicist matters of the effectiveness of penal measures, critical criminologists have raised more fundamental issues of power, control, and penality.

In the following chapters, my re-examination of the critical literature on community corrections reveals some of the insights provided by critical criminologists about the complexities of community-correctional rhetoric as against practice, and intentions as against effects. However, by shaping this re-examination of the literature in light of the recognition that critical discourse itself is also a part of the phenomenon of 'penality,' unwarranted assumptions and associated limitations of the decarceration literature are brought into focus. Ironically, these problematic aspects of the critical literature on community corrections derive, in part, from critical criminologists following their mainstream predecessors' tendency of moving away from the prison. The problematic aspects of the critical literature on community corrections also derive from critical criminologists' unwitting retention of empiricist logic in evaluating the effects of penal reform.

3

The Evolution and Assumptions of Critical Literature on Community Corrections

The Genesis of Critical Analysis of Correctional Issues

> Mainstream criminology has compromised itself too far and too much because of its close connexions with the institutions and ideology of the correctional system. It has complacently thought that there are no problems of competing values and interests. At worst, this has led to an unquestioning acceptance of official goals and policies; at best it has led to sustained and well informed criticism of these policies if not the goals. (Cohen 1974: 35)

Why did a purposefully critical literature on community corrections and penal control begin to emerge after the mid-1970s? What have been the major arguments and characteristics of this literature? What was its relationship to the wider emergence of distinctively critical criminology? In this chapter, I trace the genesis of the critical community-corrections literature, and examine its key assumptions about interrelationships between imprisonment and community programs. Primarily at issue here is *what*, or the typical social organization of critical views on the interrelationships of imprisonment and alternatives. In the next chapter, I analyse the *how*, or the discursive and analytical tactics that were used in reinforcing key assumptions and assertions about decarceration.

One of the characteristics of the decarceration literature is that – unlike the approach taken in many previous studies in the correctional field – a critical stance is taken as a point of departure rather than as a conclusion that might or might not be reached. This perspective contrasts, for example, with that of the earlier effectiveness literature on rehabilitation, where analysts usually concurred with the correctional goals of state officials. Although they repeatedly identified the limited effectiveness of rehabilitation programs, their correctionalist perspective – emphasizing the desirability of rehabilitation – rendered their findings negative rather than critical.

Growing opposition to the correctionalist orientation of mainstream criminology was one important source of the critical approach often taken in the later analysis of community corrections. This anti-correctionalism was influential in the institutionalization of distinctively critical and 'new' (Taylor, Walton, and Young 1973) criminologies from the late 1960s. While the new criminologies incorporated a variety of perspectives, including, for example, 'conflict,' 'radical,' 'idealist,' 'Marxist,' and 'abolitionist,' they all sought to be critical, both in their analysis of previous approaches and in their proposals for a future agenda.[1] Critical criminologists – cognizant of broader theoretical debates in sociology – voiced their dissatisfaction with the conservatism of functionalist and positivist approaches in criminology (Cohen 1974, 1981, 1988a; de Haan 1990; Hall and Scraton 1981; Sim, Scraton, and Gordon 1987). They also drew on the commentaries of C. Wright Mills (1959) and others (e.g., Blackburn 1969; Nicolaus 1973; Gouldner 1970; Becker and Horowitz 1972; Poulantzas 1973) in calling attention to the utilitarian nature of social research, and its service in the interests of the state and other powerful institutions. They repudiated mainstream criminology's links with state agencies, and denigrated the empiricist manner in which positivists had 'probed and prodded the heads and bodies' of the 'captive population' of prisoners (Sim, Scraton, and Gordon 1987: 11). A major objective of critical criminology was to avert and supersede correctionalist constraints.

Where imprisonment has been concerned, critical criminology's attempt to break with more conservative approaches involved several different, and sometimes contradictory, tendencies: politically, and especially during the early stages of critical criminology, there was involvement with prison issues, but, conceptually, the major tendency has been a distancing from inquiries into imprisonment, as critical criminologists have tended to focus on broader aspects of penal and social control.

The political identification of many critical criminologists with prison issues reflected one strategy for separating themselves from mainstream criminology. Where more traditional criminologists were seen as tending, *de facto*, if not by intent, to be aligned with the interests of correctional authorities, critical criminologists actively associated themselves with the interests of those subject to incarceration. This identification also reflected critical criminologists' more general politicization of the situation of deviants, and commitment to an interventionist politics (Sim, Scraton, and Gordon 1987). In efforts to support the interests of inmates, critical criminologists made contact with prisoners and ex-prisoners, and participated in the prisoner movements of the late 1960s and 1970s. Informed by this involvement, they published accounts of current prison conditions, and highlighted the need for change, in radical, popular, and reformist, as well as in academic, publications (e.g., Greenberg 1970, 1972; Cohen and Taylor 1972; Mitford 1973; Wright 1973; Stratton 1973; Mathiesen 1974; Ericson 1974; Bianchi, Simondi, and Taylor 1975; Taylor, Walton, and Young 1975; PREAP 1976; MacDonald and Sim 1978; Cohen 1979b; Fitzgerald and Sim 1982; MacBride 1980; Platt and Tagaki 1982; Carlen 1983; Tomlinson and Rolston 1986; Bianchi and van Swaaningen 1986; Scraton and Chadwick 1987; Sim 1986; Platt 1988; Scraton, Sim, and Skidmore 1988. For accounts of decreasing participation in radical penal groups, and of related changes in political conditions and consciousness from the late 1970s, see Leander 1990; Mathiesen 1990; Ryan and Ward 1990; van Swaaningen 1990).

While this literature has usually focused on penal conditions and politics in specific contexts, views expressed during the 1980s about overall tendencies in the institution of imprisonment accorded with those of the critical literature on decarceration and penal control. Prison systems have been said to have 'expanded' (Mathiesen 1986: 84), and it has been considered 'clear' that 'the structure of power in prisons and in the state remains intact with the institutional centres of power consolidating their strength' (Sim, Scraton, and Gordon 1987: 18).

Paradoxically, the political identification with imprisonment that occurred was accompanied by a conceptual distancing from it. This movement away from the prison accorded with that which was occurring in criminology more generally. But it was further reinforced by the premises of critical criminology. Seeking to transcend positivist 'obsession' with causation (ibid: 5) and the factors likely to lead individuals into – and away from – crime, critical criminologists resolutely brought sociopolitical aspects of the definition and control of crime to the centre of the analytical agenda. The scope of the field was broadened, with attention being given to issues of power, conflict, class, and ideology as played out on the criminal-justice terrain. More traditional understandings of criminality were deconstructed, demystified, and reformulated. Cohen has nicely summarized key demystifying themes of critical criminology (1988a: 31):

'Crime' is not real, but the product of faulty categorization, moral
enterprise, or class-based attribution in the interest of the powerful;
'criminals' were not what they appeared to be, but were elevated into
rebels or demoted into ordinary people just like everyone else, while the
'real' criminals were invisible; the 'crime problem' was the product of
manipulation by the media and the powerful; 'prostitution,' 'blackmail,'
and 'theft' were just labels attached to transactions and social arrangements endemic to this society; 'rape' was just an extension of normal
male sexuality; the designation of some drugs rather than others as illicit
was irrational, arbitrary, and prejudiced; 'mental illness' was not really
an illness, but a myth, a metaphor, a label attached to certain people
under certain circumstances; 'benevolence' and 'reform' were really
hidden forms of coercion; psychiatry, social work, and treatment were
all forms of social control; and so on.

These alternative definitions of the situation of deviance and control, along with critical criminologists' emphasis on structural conditions, resulted in a relative displacement of attention to crime and
criminals, traditionally defined. It has been argued that this critical
approach resulted in the 'loss of a criminology' (J. Young 1986: 12).
Agreement with this contention depends on how one defines the field of
criminology itself. Nevertheless, there is little doubt that the analytical
orientation generated by critical criminology resulted in issues of
imprisonment – along with those of crime and criminals – being shifted
to the periphery of studies of penal control.

No doubt, the difficulties of research access to prisons and prisoners encountered by critical criminologists (see Cohen and Taylor 1977)
contributed to the lack of research on imprisonment. But the inclina-
tions of critical criminologists to inquire into hitherto neglected topics,
and to document the subtle and complex aspects of social control, were
also important factors. For those of a critical orientation, the repressive
aspects of imprisonment were already clear. By contrast, repressive
aspects of the police (with their rhetoric of 'citizens in uniform'), and of
the courts (with their discourse of 'due process'), were in greater need of
documentation. Critical consciousness of the pervasiveness and subtlety of penal control also brought other institutions, such as the media,
social welfare, and education, to critical-criminological attention.

Rather than focusing on the institution of imprisonment per se,
critical criminologists sought to theoretically situate it in relation to

broader trends in penal and social control. Moreover, as revisionist historians were rapidly accomplishing this objective with respect to segregative institutions and the penal exercise of power in the past (Rothman 1971, 1980; Foucault 1977; Ignatieff 1978; Scull 1979, 1981), the analytical gap with respect to contemporary developments became more apparent. The publication of Michel Foucault's *Discipline and Punish* (1977) was particularly influential as it facilitated the move 'to a sociology of control.' The work of analysts of agencies of control acquired 'a theoretical refinement and a political importance which it had not had before' (Garland 1987: 2). Informed by Foucauldian conceptions (ibid), the growth of revisionist historical literature was followed by contemporary 'revisionist' literature seeking to demystify correctional discourses and practices, and to locate them in the context of currently evolving control systems.

One of the accomplishments of Foucault's *Discipline and Punish* is that, although his analysis centres on the institution of imprisonment, with its explicit punitive functions, he skilfully argues that disciplinary mechanisms pervade the 'carceral continuum' more generally, with leniency itself being an important technique of control. This argument clearly resonated with the critique of treatment and rehabilitation, which had already been developed. Critical analysts drew upon it as they embarked upon examination of community corrections, which were rapidly superseding rehabilitation in constituting the benign face of corrections.

Unlike Foucault, however, critical criminologists did not make observations about the carceral continuum from the vantage of the prison. On the contrary, they took community corrections as their major focus, and, from this basis, made assertions about the prison. The social organization of critical arguments about decarceration acquired a distinctive structure: although community correctional alternatives were the immediate object of inquiry, much of the powerful critique that ensued still came to rest on assumptions about trends in prison populations themselves. In short, although the prison was empirically shifted to the periphery of inquiry, contentions about prison populations remained central in critical theorizing of contemporary trends in penal control. A re-examination of early analysis of decarceration, and of the subsequent conventional wisdom of the critical literature on community corrections, reveals the emergence of key assumptions about trends in imprisonment.

Changing Understanding of Decarceration and Community Corrections

> Until the 1970s, literature on various community correctional pro-
> grammes was largely descriptive, theoretical or exhoratory and without
> meaningful empirical interest. (Blomberg 1987: 218)

> Why should community corrections itself, not be subjected to suspicion
> about benevolent reform? A large dose of such skepticism, together with
> a much firmer location of the new movement in overall structural and
> political changes, is needed for a full scale critique of community
> corrections. (Cohen 1979a: 343)

Until the mid-1970s, studies dealing with community corrections were
usually presented in the traditional correctionalist vein abhorred by critical criminologists: their relative advantages over imprisonment in
terms of costs, effectiveness, and humaneness were repeatedly emphasized, and the movement was lauded across the political spectrum
(Greenberg 1975: 1). While some critical criminologists were sceptical of
these claims, and were conscious that community-correctional programs had been allowed to proliferate 'largely free from critical scrutiny' (ibid: 2), early critical inquiries tended to be speculative, and lacked
empirical specification of overall correctional trends. For example
Cohen (1977: 217) predicted 'the decline of the asylum as such and its
supplementation by new forms of social control.' At the same time, he
acknowledged that 'our information is imprecise and open to multiple
interpretations.'

Nevertheless, these initial critiques identified important issues that
would recur in the literature on community corrections. For example,
the benign notion of 'community' was questioned, with Greenberg raising the question as to 'why, if the community is so therapeutic, the
offender got into trouble there in the first place?' (1975: 4–5). Claims of
'humaneness' and 'effectiveness' were similarly questioned. Compla-
cency about community corrections was challenged. Questions were
raised about the potential implications of community corrections for
social control.

With the publication of Andrew Scull's (1977) *Decarceration: Community Treatment and the Deviant – A Radical View*, critical study of
contemporary trends in corrections was moved to a more systematic,
and structural, level of analysis. In dialectical fashion, the debate of
other critical analysts with Scull yielded a conventional wisdom about
community corrections and their interrelationship with imprisonment.

Imprisonment was no longer seen as 'declining' (Cohen 1977: 227), but came to be understood to be a thriving and even expanding institution; Scull's *Decarceration* was the precipitating factor in the shift in understanding.

As used by Scull (1977, 1983, 1984) and others, the term 'decarceration' encapsulates processes associated with deinstitutionalization, diversion, and the general movement towards non-institutional responses to crime and deviance during the postwar period. In the corrections context, the concept of decarceration is used in analysing the interrelationships of prisons with alternatives such as probation, parole, community service orders, diversion schemes, temporary absence, and other community programs. Given that penal measures other than imprisonment have existed since the inception of the prison (not to mention prior to it), 'decarceration' has been conceptually aligned with ideologies seen as characterizing the recent historical juncture. Processes related to decarceration are presented as somehow new, as well as continuous with what was already going on (Cohen 1977: Chan and Ericson 1981: 4). For example, according to Scull (1977: 45): 'the rise of "community corrections" has meant not so much the introduction of radically novel approaches, but rather the transformation of traditional mechanisms so as to promote the return to the outside world of many who would previously have been incarcerated, and to develop special incentives designed to speed up the process.'

Scull theorized that a fiscal crisis of the state had prompted the shift towards community corrections. He identified the period from the mid-1950s until the early 1970s in the United States as being characterized by 'a marked decline in the rate of imprisonment,' with the same period experiencing 'increasing emphasis on noninstitutional controls' (1977: 47). He also pointed to British indications of an 'increasing reliance on noncustodial dispositions.' One example he cites of such indications is the fact that, in 1958, of every 1,000 adult men convicted of indictable offences, 396 were imprisoned, but, by 1972, the number imprisoned had dropped to 197 (ibid: 57). Pointing to the growth of welfare states during the postwar period, and to the threat of fiscal crisis this entailed, Scull interpreted the apparent decline in the use of segregative methods of control as a means of curtailing expenditure. Rather than being a paradox, the concurrent growth of expenditure on wider welfare services and reduction of that on 'problem populations,' reinforced each other: 'it is precisely the expansion of one which made possible and desirable the contraction of the other' (ibid: 135).

Given that fiscal interests were the primary factor underlying the decarceration movement, Scull argued that liberal rhetoric on the issue of community corrections was a useful 'ideological camouflage' that allowed 'economy to masquerade as benevolence and neglect as tolerance' (1977: 152). This interpretation was supported by his report of the situation in Massachusetts where, following the sudden closure of juvenile reform schools in the state, 'not even token efforts had been made to develop an infrastructure capable of providing community supervision or control over those released' (ibid: 142). Further support was provided by his highlighting the low percentage of total corrections budgets allocated to community corrections in the United States and the high volume of case-loads assigned to probation officers (ibid: 142–3). According to Scull, the neglect ensuing from economy was resulting in unsupervised ex-inmates and other deviants roaming the 'new emerging "deviant ghettoes,"' and 'sewers of human misery' in the cities. The former institutional population had been shifted to the streets, to Salvation Army and other hostels, as well as to the burgeoning range of 'community care' programs (ibid: 150–2).

In short, Scull's thesis about penal populations had three major elements: 1 / threatened fiscal crisis of the state had prompted the shift towards decarceration and community corrections; 2 / deinstitutionalization was actually occurring; and 3 / community-correctional programs were being used in lieu of imprisonment.

Subsequently, each of these claims about penal populations was disputed.[2] Other critical criminologists castigated Scull for his economism and functionalism, as well as for his underestimation of the importance of ideology in reform processes. Most notably, they also charged that Scull had posited community programs as *alternatives* to prisons, when they should more accurately be seen as *complements* to the institutions (Chan and Ericson 1981: 9; Matthews 1979: 101, 109).

Swayed by such critiques, Scull, in his later writing on decarceration, highlighted the 'striking increases in prison populations,' the 'widening of the net' phenomenon, and the 'expansionist direction' in criminal justice generally (1984: 178, 177). In making these observations, Scull modified his story of decarceration, so that, where alternatives were earlier seen by him as representing the neglect of deviants, they were later posited as involving more control of offenders; and, where prison populations were seen as decreasing, they were later presented as subject to increases. In face of a forceful critique of his arguments by analysts from various countries, Scull adapted his interpretation to the extent that it later fully accorded with the conventional wisdom of the critical literature on community corrections.

The Conventional Wisdom of the Decarceration Literature

'Widening the net' describes the nightmare of the benevolent state gone haywire. This horror has already been vividly portrayed in Orwell's *1984*, Solzhenitsyn's *Cancer Ward*, Kesey's *One Flew Over the Cuckoo's Nest*, and Burgess's *Clockwork Orange*. Social scientists and criminologists have just caught up with the humanists. (Austin and Krisberg 1981: 188–9)

Although there is now a voluminous critical literature concerned with decarceration in Western countries, the major tenets of studies can be summarized quite briefly, since the major features of correctional trends are largely taken for granted. Where issues arise, and where the literature becomes more complex, is in explanations of trends. Drawing heavily on the work of revisionist historians (Ignatieff 1978; Foucault 1977; Scull 1979; Rothman 1980; Cohen and Scull 1983), critical debates centre around issues such as whether organizational or political economic theories, functionalist or instrumentalist interpretations, or ideological contradictions or professional interests should predominate in analysing the interrelationship between prison and alternatives, and particularly the perceived disjunctures between stated intentions and actual consequences in the criminal-justice field.

This critical consensus about empirical trends in imprisonment and alternatives was clearly evident by the mid-1980s. The core elements of the conventional wisdom are apparent, for example, in Cohen's (1985: 44) state-of-the-art summary of what is really going on 'inside the system':

Let us start with the (apparently) simple question of whether the decarceration strategy has worked in reducing the rates of juvenile and adult offenders sent to custodial institutions. The obvious index of success is not simply the proliferation of new programmes, but whether custodial institutions are being replaced, phased out or at least are beginning to receive fewer offenders overall. The statistical evidence here is by no means easy to decipher and there are complicated methodological problems in picking out even the crudest of changes. But all the

evidence here indicates failure – that in Britain, Canada and the USA
rates of incarceration are not at all declining and in some spheres are
even increasing. Community control has supplemented rather than
replaced traditional methods.

Similar messages about the limited effects of community corrections
have repeatedly appeared in the critical literature. For example, Canadian authors Lowman, Menzies, and Palys (1987: 211) confidently state
that, 'designed originally to provide a community *alternative* to incarceration ... these programmes have become a *supplement* to them.
Instead of *fewer* individuals going to prison, there are now more than
ever. And instead of directing individuals out of the criminal justice system, the new programmes have directed more people *into* it ... The bot-
tom line, therefore, is that more and more individuals are becoming
subject to the scrutiny and surveillance of criminal justice personnel.'

One notable characteristic of the critical literature on decarceration
has been the tendency to express the empirical basis of arguments as
much through metaphors and analogies as through specific statistical
statements about identifiable penal populations. In the course of this
analytical strategy, the language and theme of net-widening have
become prominent in depicting the scenario whereby alternatives
become add-ons to pre-existing prison populations. Probation, parole,
and other community programs have been said to have reduced liberty,
and to have introduced many new people into the 'control net'
(Matthews 1979: 115). As the process of 'widening the net' is said to
have been accompanied by that of 'thinning the mesh,' the predominant
image is that of a system in perpetual expansion: deviants are continu-
ally subjected to new, more intense and pervasive forms of control that
are woven into, and beyond, traditional institutional networks of penal
control (Austin and Krisberg 1981; Blomberg 1980; Chan and Ericson
1981; Cohen 1979a, 1983, 1985; Lowman, Menzies, and Palys 1987;
Muncie and Coventry 1989; Scull 1984; Van Dusen 1981).

As the notions of 'widening' and 'thinning' suggest, the development
of alternatives is seen by critics as not only yielding an expansion in the
numbers of people subject to penal control, but also giving rise to an
intensification of the substance of control. When these changes are
depicted, the concept of 'net-widening' is typically allied with – and often
presented as incorporating – those of 'stronger' and 'different' nets.
Again, Cohen (1985: 44) has provided an adroit specification of these
key images. According to him, with the development of alternatives

(1) there is an increase in the total number of deviants getting into the system in the first place and many of these are new deviants who would not have been processed previously (wider nets);

(2) there is an increase in the overall intensity of intervention, with old and new deviants being subject to levels of intervention (including traditional institutionalization) which they might not have previously received (denser nets);

(3) new agencies and services are supplementing rather than replacing the original set of control mechanisms (different nets).

In turn, the overarching concept of 'net-widening' is linked to other evocative images. The prison, for example, is described as the 'hard end' of the system, with the boundaries between it and other control institutions becoming increasingly 'blurred.' Community and private institutions – such as the family, school, neighbourhood, and workplace – are seen as subject to 'penetration' and 'absorption' by formal modes of social control. As the 'hard end' gets harder, and as the 'soft end' gets wider, 'bifurcation' is said to be occurring. Meanwhile, the processing of deviants 'accelerates.' In light of these developments, the 'holy trinity' of reform rhetoric about the virtues of alternatives in terms of costs, effectiveness, and humaneness, is revealed as mythical. The 'dreams' of progressive reformers are said to be better understood as 'nightmares.'

Analysts of decarceration portray the net effect of these trends as involving a 'dispersal of discipline': the prison retains its institutional strength, and is interwoven with, and dependent on, a 'carceral continuum' that powerfully pervades social life in ever more subtle, complex, and effective ways (Blomberg 1977; Bohnstedt 1978; Chan and Ericson 1981; Cohen 1979a, 1983; Ericson and Baranek 1982: ch. 7; Garland and Young 1983; Greenberg 1975; Hylton 1981a, 1982; Lerman 1975; Mathiesen 1983; Matthews 1979; Scull 1983, 1984; Warren 1981). These key empirical points of the conventional wisdom can be expressed more mundanely: prison populations are maintained and increased, while community alternatives proliferate. The predominant penal trend is that of an expansion of penal control.

Perceptions of the Maintenance and Increase of Imprisonment

While claims about net-widening are most clearly expressed in the literature on decarceration, wider debates about penal control also tend to reinforce perceptions about prison and penal expansion. For example, in an important article, 'Neglected Features of Contemporary Penal Systems,' Anthony Bottoms (1983) calls attention to developments that have been overlooked by analysts of decarceration, and points to the need for an empirically based research agenda. Yet, at the same time, he accepts that increasing numbers of people in different countries are being subjected to imprisonment.

Bottoms's analytical objective is a critique of the 'extension of discipline' thesis, particularly as advanced by Cohen (1979a) and Mathiesen (1983). In developing his points, Bottoms identifies the *proportionate* decline in the use of imprisonment for indictable offences in England and Wales when figures for 1938, 1959, and 1980 are compared. On the basis of sentencing data for these years, Bottoms goes on to make a convincing argument that the gap has been filled, not, as one might expect, by a proportionate increase in the use of probation or discharge, but rather by the imposition of fines: as the use of imprisonment proportionately decreased, that of fines increased.

Bottoms does not use these data to dispute the net-widening thesis. More at issue for him is the question of whether these trends accord with wider perceptions of the 'dispersal of discipline.' Decarceration analysts have emphasized the growth of 'disciplinary' penalties, such as probation. But, according to Bottoms, the fine is a non-disciplinary penalty, the area in which the most dramatic increases have taken place. For Bottoms, therefore, analytical issues about the disciplinary or non-disciplinary nature of penal dispositions are very important.

Questions about whether specific penal practices should or should not be classified as 'disciplinary' are interesting and difficult to answer. Related debates derive largely from the translation of Foucault's *Surveillir et punir* as *Discipline and Punish*. Had *surveillir* been translated as 'supervision,' 'inspection,' or 'observation,' rather than 'discipline' (see Sheridan 1979), issues of the 'disciplinary society' would hardly have come to such prominence. The ambiguity of the notion of 'discipline,' as exacerbated by the idiosyncracies of Foucault's literary approach and its translation, has given rise to stimulating disputes about the character of contemporary penal control and preferred concepts in elucidating it (Mathiesen 1983; Nelken 1989; O'Neill 1986; Santos 1985). At this point, however, I am more concerned with the empirical than with the theoretical aspects of the debate. Of particular interest is Bottoms's acceptance of observations about the maintenance and growth of imprisonment.

Pointing to Bottoms's agreement about the growth of imprisonment may initially appear puzzling in light of his emphasis on the proportionate decline in the imposition of imprisonment compared to other dispositions. But, stability or growth in imprisonment, coupled with a proportionate decline in its use in sentencing, is possible when there is a growth in the numbers of those convicted in the first place. Such a trend indeed occurred in England and Wales. Therefore, in conjunction with his observations about the proportionate decline in imprisonment, Bottoms makes the 'very important' observation: 'many more people are being sent to prison per annum now than before the Second World War.' One example he cites is that the 'number of adults given prison sentences in England and Wales rose from less than 13,000 in 1938 to 36,000 in 1980' (1983: 183–4). According to Bottoms, this represents the 'same kind of result' as that represented by Hylton's (1981) data for the Canadian province of Saskatchewan, which demonstrate an increasing imprisonment rate both in absolute numbers and in rates per 100,000 population. He also points to Chan and Ericson's (1981) study of Canadian data as showing such an increase. Bottoms further notes that these studies demonstrate concurrent and rapid increases in community supervision, with those put on probation growing in rates per head of population as well as in absolute numbers.

Where Bottoms takes issue with Hylton, and Chan and Ericson, is with respect to their omission of broader sentencing data. This omission, he says, leads them to overlook the possibility of increasing numbers of people being convicted, and a declining proportion being sentenced to imprisonment. Such data could lead to different inferences about developments in the nature of power exercised by the state. By contrast – and despite Bottoms's focus on the methodologies of Hylton's and Chan and Ericson's studies – he does not take issue with what they include. Bottoms thereby accepts their propositions that both prison and probation populations are growing in Canada. In sum, whether or not one considers that the 'features' Bottoms has identified fit with the 'dispersal of discipline' thesis, they certainly do accord with the conventional wisdom of the decarceration literature: an international trend of growth in those subject to imprisonment – and to criminal-justice processing more generally – is clearly identified.

Similarly, those who have taken up Bottoms's challenge to the 'dispersal of discipline' thesis do not question the empirical basis of fundamental statements about prison populations. For example, while agreeing with Bottoms that the current dispersal of social control in corrections does not necessarily represent an extension of disciplinary punishment per se, Shearing and Stenning (1984) contend that, contrary to

Bottoms's assertions, current developments in private policing and security do represent an extension of discipline. In their article, Shearing and Stenning focus on the notion of 'discipline' as originally advanced by Foucault, and its analytical relevance for the transformations in privatized control they have documented (1981, 1983b, 1987).

The absence of any reference to correctional populations by Shearing and Stenning implies an acceptance of the usual assumptions of growth in that realm. As such, a similar reading can be made of their, and of Bottoms's, articles. The perception of growth in correctional populations remains intact, and – however one might conceptually or theoretically express it – the conventional wisdom of increasing control at all levels of the system is supported. Thus, Shearing and Stenning's observations are not that public police are in substantial decline numerically, but that, while that system of policing continues, another private system is developing. For them, public policing is of secondary importance, as the growth of private policing has become far more rapid and analytically significant.

What Bottoms and Shearing and Stenning have in common is a focus on what is usually ignored (i.e., fines and private policing), rather than an attempt to dispute the substance of what is usually included. To use the terms of the conventional wisdom, one could say that they are bringing 'alternative' systems of control to our attention, but ones that are clearly 'add-ons' rather than substitutes. They suggest that the implications of these systems may be more crucial to understanding current trends in penal control than are the mechanisms – such as public police, prisons, and probation – that are most frequently studied.

In the afterword to the second edition of *Decarceration*, Scull's response to Bottoms's observations is instructive. While, in the first edition, Scull (1977: 57) had used precisely the point of a decreasing proportionate use of imprisonment in England and Wales to bolster his original argument that a shift away from imprisonment was occurring, he now (1984: 176) relegates Bottoms's critique to a footnote:

> We need to bear in mind, of course, that long continued secular increases in crime rates have generated a much larger population eligible for the attentions of the criminal justice system. To an extent, therefore, one might reasonably argue that diversionary programs have enabled the authorities to avoid some of the expenditures for prison accommodation they would otherwise have incurred [reference to Bottoms (1983)]. But obviously one can push this argument only so far, and in the United

States in particular, the sheer size of the increase in prison populations, which has occurred alongside and despite a dramatic rise in the use of probation and other non-institutional forms of punishment, suggests the need for a fundamental reassessment of the significance of recent 'reforms.'

Here, even while alluding to the proportionate decline in judicial use of imprisonment, for Scull, it is the sheer volume of perceived growth in both prisons and community programs that should be emphasized. The decreasing importance ascribed to the proportionate decline in the use of imprisonment by Scull in the first and second editions of *Decarceration* is symbolic of his changing emphasis, from highlighting evidence of decarceration itself, to accepting the conventional wisdom, and contributing to it, by emphasizing the continuance of penal institutions coupled with the proliferation of alternatives. Thus, in the first edition, Scull advanced the opinion that the 'decline is real, rather than being simply a statistical artifact' (1977: 57). Later, citing studies by other community-corrections critics, Scull's observations centre on growth, net-widening, and the general expansion of social control. The reader is left with the impression that growth, within and without the prison, has been documented, and the primary task, already being addressed but still to be completed, is to examine the issue of why these trends have occurred (Scull 1984: 177).

Other critical analysts either downplay or ignore the potential importance of Bottoms's observations about the relevance of proportionate declines in the use of imprisonment in sentencing. Cohen (1985: 84, 295), for example, makes only passing reference to the phenomenon, and cites Bottoms in a note. In the main narrative, he goes on to say: 'beyond all the complex empirical problems, historical comparisons and implied value judgements, there is the over-riding fact of proliferation, elaboration and diversification.' Again, while the analytical significance of events may be disputable, the factuality of penal expansion is not. Meanwhile, Bottoms (1987) himself has pointed to the proportionate decrease in the use of fines that occurred in the 1980s, at least partly in favour of the use of imprisonment. These more recent trends may render it even more unlikely that Bottoms's historical observations will disturb conventional-wisdom analyses.

Adherence to the conventional wisdom has, on occasion, been associated with extremely deterministic views about penal reform. According to Roger Matthews (1979: 115), for example: 'the introduction of parole, probation, indeterminate sentences, diversion programmes, and the whole array of recent control strategies have served, *invariably*, to ... increase lengths of incarceration, loss of liberty, or surveillance ... and to introduce many, particularly the young, into the control net for "offences" that prior to the setting up of such programmes would have gone unnoticed or seem to be inconsequential' (emphasis added). While Matthews (1987, 1989) has now modified his view, many critical criminologists have continued to assume that the development of alternatives yields an expansion of the prison and penal system.

An article by Muncie and Coventry (1989) is a prototype of this kind of thinking. Muncie and Coventry's subject is the non-custodial sanction of the Youth Attendance Order (involving community work and activities), introduced in the Australian province of Victoria in 1988. While making customary reference to the possibility of different experiences in different places, and having acknowledged that no evaluative research on the new community program is available to them, the authors grant themselves 'poetic licence' in using the findings of decarceration research elsewhere to make predictions about the consequences of the program.

Through this approach, and in the absence of data on the Youth Attendance Order in Victoria, Muncie and Coventry confidently state that, several years hence, it will have been seen that the community order program 'acts as a funnel towards custody rather than a route out of it'; that the order 'is not treated as a true alternative to custody'; that the order 'is used as an *addition* rather than an *alternative* to existing sentencing options'; that it is 'net-widening,' and is but one in the series of reform innovations that have 'established a system which appears to be forever expanding' (1989: 185–6; emphasis in original). For Muncie and Coventry, conventional-wisdom knowledge provides a basis for social-scientific premonition.

In sum, the critical literature on alternatives sees them as not simply different, but more intense, and more ominous, than earlier forms of control. The portrait is of an oppressive situation that appears to be becoming worse. In making this argument, statements about the persistence and growth of imprisonment are central: evidence for the worsening nature of the situation largely derives from the observation that alternatives are merely 'add-ons' to imprisonment. If alternatives 'really' were alternatives, and prison population was declining, arguments about the expansion of penal control would lose much of their analytical force.

Yet, while statements about imprisonment are fundamental to arguments about net-widening and penal expansion, empirical examination of imprisonment has often been secondary. For many critical criminologists, the maintenance and growth of imprisonment have become assumptions. The primary research objective of critical criminology has been to demystify the benign face of alternatives, and to make new discoveries about penal control beyond the prison. The ensuing paradox is that trends in imprisonment have simultaneously been central to arguments about net-widening and penal expansion, and peripheral as a focus of empirical inquiry.

Given that statements about the continuance and growth of imprisonment, along with the occurrence of net-widening, often underlie, and always reinforce, critical analysis of the increasingly sinister nature of penal control, this lack of attention to imprisonment needs to be redressed. In the next chapter, I develop the argument that some of the most important statements in the literature about prison populations and net-widening have been methodologically problematic. First, however, it is necessary to briefly examine the political context of analyses of net-widening, since methodological problems in the decarceration literature arguably reflect and reinforce problems of praxis in critical criminology more generally.

Political Rationales for Challenging Net-widening

Why – particularly from within a critical criminological perspective – should one be cautious in accepting contentions about net-widening? In contrast, for example, to critical ambiguity about the role of unemployment in affecting imprisonment rates (e.g., Box 1987; de Haan 1990; W. Young 1986), there has been much agreement about the role of alternatives in expanding penal control. Moreover, given that populations involved with alternatives are better understood as 'add-ons' to pre-existing prison populations, official and reformist discourse about the virtues of community corrections in terms of costs, effectiveness, and humaneness can be incisively deconstructed. The argument of 'net-widening' also has theoretical appeal, as analyses of contemporary penal development reaffirm many of the penetrating observations of influential revisionist historians (Foucault 1977; Ignatieff 1978; Rothman 1980; Scull 1979).

The net-widening argument is politically problematic. The prospects it yields for praxis are pessimistic and conservative. Although critical analysts have sought to reject the empiricism, correctionalism, and positivism of mainstream criminologists, the logic of their analyses is often very similar to that of those they have criticized. While critical criminologists sought to avert and supersede the concern with issues of 'success' and 'failure' characteristic of the positivist literature on the effectiveness of rehabilitation, their own critique of penal trends has arguably merely broadened, rather than changed, the parameters of criminological debate. They have adopted and generalized the conclusion attributed to Martinson (1974) that 'nothing works': where the 'nothing works' argument was initially applied by positivists observing that correctional programs had a limited impact in rehabilitating offenders, critical criminologists have subsequently argued that penal reform in general can have little impact on the predominantly repressive tendencies of the criminal-justice system itself. In effect, critical criminologists have substituted the recalcitrant criminal-justice system for the recalcitrant offender of the positivist criminology they sought to criticize. With this shared conservatism about the prospects for penal reform, critical perspectives have remained conventional.

For mainstream criminologists and penal policy makers, the belief that 'nothing works' – particularly concerning rehabilitation – has contributed to the development of primarily administrative and regulatory approaches to dealing with crime and criminals (Melossi 1979; Bottoms 1983; Peters 1986; J. Young 1986). Community alternatives, and related processes of privatization, played an increasing part in the evolution of this managerial approach to criminal justice. By contrast, for more critical criminologists, the perception that 'nothing works' – particularly in reform of the criminal-justice system – has contributed to the emergence of a political and policy-making void. Critical criminology – in dealing with issues of penal reform – appears restricted to developing ever-more-penetrating critiques of contemporary developments. Participation in reform activity seems counter-productive. Rather, the findings of their analyses often involve critical criminologists in the depressing task of advising and informing well-meaning reformers that they are doing 'no good' (see Cohen 1985).

The politically problematic status of 'net-widening' also derives from the use of related arguments by penal authorities. For example, in Ontario in 1984, government officials advanced a proposal to terminate a bail program that sought to divert accused persons awaiting trial from custodial to non-custodial supervision. In doing so, the correctional minister was able to 'emphasize our concern that the program may be expanding the net of social control' (*Hansard*, 7 June 1984: J-166). In actuality, the major reason for attempting to terminate the bail program was to release funding for the rapidly expanding (and more politically popular) community-service-order program in the province. Moreover, while internal ministry evaluations were uncertain about whether the bail program was 'net-widening' or not, at the outset of the community-service-order program the minister of corrections had already acknowledged that 'we have nothing under our act to deal with the Community Service Order in lieu of incarceration' (*Hansard*, 30 May 1978, 2999). In short, in this case, the 'net-widening' argument was used by officials to effect the diminution of a program whose 'net-widening' effects were questionable, in favour of a program where such effects were clear.

The service of the 'net-widening' literature in the interests of correctional officials, and predominantly more conservative ones, was confirmed in interview with Donald Evans, former executive director of the Community Programmes Division of Ontario corrections. Evans especially identified Stanley Cohen's writings as providing a language amenable to being 'captured' by correctional officials. As he explained: 'I always kept up on the literature – I began to discover all the people using nice phrases [e.g., 'decarceration']. Cohen, of course, turned out to be great from a management point of view because he's a great categorizer ... You'd do things in chart form, and stuff that you could easily translate and use and make [into] management presentations if you wanted to. They looked good on overhead transparencies!'

According to the former director, the critical literature was 'read in a political sense, in a managerial sense' whereby the ideas and analyses 'were decontexted [*sic*] from their theoretical bases' and 'rhetoric was easily entered into ministry speeches.' Further, while the literature was originally used by those such as himself who, although sensitive to potential pitfalls, fostered the development of community programs in the hope that they could be alternatives, it was later most forcefully used by those in the ministry who sought a renewed emphasis on imprisonment. As the former director explained:

> And then what happened was institutional people [within the ministry] would discover the articles in the journals I had circulated, photocopy them, and use them for their own arguments internally ... community corrections programmes were not solving their overcrowding problem, so they should stop getting money.
> Police also became aware of this claim. You would go to your

conferences with local police, and they would stand up and say – 'you guys, you're not doing anything, all you're doing is churning out people and your programs don't work ... It would be better if these people were at least incapacitated, they wouldn't commit any crimes.'

Over time, according to Evans, officials' uses of critical arguments about community corrections, coupled with a growing emphasis on 'risk management,' resulted in a situation whereby 'community corrections caseload profiles [have] become an argument for prison building.' Clearly, the 'net-widening' argument is amenable to use by correctional authorities whose interests and objectives can be at odds with those of critical criminologists who developed the argument in the first place.

So far, such usurpations of the 'net-widening' argument have been little discussed in the critical literature. But there are signs of a growing sensitivity to questions of the relationship of critical analyses of alternatives to strategies for a more progressive penal politics. The inherent pessimism, and related conservatism, of the perspective have now been acknowledged by some authors. For example, Roger Matthews has highlighted what he describes as the 'impossibilism' of much of the decarceration literature. In doing so, he focuses on Scull's gloomy remarks in the 'Afterword' to the second edition of *Decarceration*. Here, Scull accorded with the conventional wisdom in his statement that (1984: 165, quoted in Matthews 1987: 351) 'only a confirmed Pangloss can view the realities of a traditional penal system with equanimity, but what I have learned about the community corrections movement simply reinforces my conviction that tinkering around with the criminal justice system in a radically unjust society is unlikely to advance us very far toward justice, equity or (come to that) efficacy. Perhaps the best I can do is to persuade others to share my sense of discomfort.'

For Matthews (1987: 351–2), 'This is the impossibilist stance in a nutshell. Prisons are a disaster, community corrections are invariably worse, realistic reform cannot be achieved without a fundamental transformation of the social structure, which is unlikely to occur in the foreseeable future, so there is nothing that can be done.'

While Matthews's summary critique may be considered unduly harsh by some (particularly in light of his [1979: 115] own earlier identification of alternatives as 'invariably' being associated with a greater loss of liberty and 'net-widening'), the proposals he advances towards countering impossibilism merit serious consideration. In addition to identifying the need for political routes out of this policy impasse, Matthews addresses problematic aspects of the *analytical* perspective embodied in studies of community corrections and 'net-widening.' He argues that impossibilism reinforces, and is reinforced by, the 'globalism' and 'empiricism' of the literature. Globalism involves the tendency to over-generalize from the particular, especially when the instance lends support to the broader argument. Empiricism involves the juxtaposition of trends in different areas, and the use of one to explain the other, rather than attempting 'to decipher underlying relations' (Matthews 1987: 347).

For Matthews, the impossibilism of Scull and others stems from 'commitment to a functionalist metaphysic' (1987: 352). In its place, he recommends that analysts pay greater attention to the role of progressive reforms, and particularly to the contradictory aspects of capitalist social relations and of the state: 'any comprehensive theory of social control must take these tensions and contradictions as its point of departure' (ibid: 354).

Stanley Cohen has also pointed to the 'analytical despair' and 'adversarial nihilism' of much of the literature (1985: 241). He has further observed that 'the results of the destructuring movements were indeed complicated, ambiguous, contradictory – and dialectical. But it was only the dark side of the dialectic that was exposed' (1987: 364). Cohen has also been more frank than others in acknowledging the shifting critical perspectives and affiliations involved in the entrenchment of the conventional wisdom (ibid: 366; emphasis in original):

> the proponents of the original destructuring/abolitionist ideas were not always 'them'; that is, the people who the theories were criticizing: the managers, bureaucrats, technicist criminologists, the powerful. They were us. *We* were the ones who wanted to abolish prisons, to weaken professional monopolies, to find forms of justice and conflict resolution outside the official system, to undermine the power of the centralized state, to create possibilities for real community and social justice. Critical scholarship has very well exposed the problems of this critical agenda – but the very effectiveness of this demystification job is a little embarrassing. You have to distance yourself from those original ideas and reforms, dismiss your enthusiastic support for them as matters of false consciousness or perhaps a product of over-enthusiastic youthful exuberance. Life seems more complicated as you get older; about that early love you say 'well, yes, I wasn't really in love at the time, I only thought I was.'

In seeking a way out of the ensuing pessimistic position, Cohen suggests a reaffirmation – albeit cautious – of the original destructuring values. Adopting a position of 'moral pragmatism,' he suggests that programs and developments should be assessed politically in terms of their potential for realizing preferred values (Cohen 1985).

Where analysis of penal trends is concerned, Cohen has also made some important suggestions: there should be a *'slightly different reading of the literature on social control,'* and one that would include 'first, a sensitivity to success (however ambivalent), and second, an experimental and inductive attitude' (1987: 368, 369; emphasis added).

It is precisely the endeavor of a slightly different reading of the critical literature on alternatives that is being undertaken here. Rather than taking statements about 'net-widening' and the expansion of penal control at face value, I consider the social organization of this knowledge a core problematic to be explored. Preliminary review of the literature has revealed that, in critical analyses of decarceration, examination of incarceration itself has paradoxically been shifted to the periphery of inquiry. Moreover, the argumentative emphasis on prison and penal expansion has restricted recognition of any accomplishments in the constriction of imprisonment and penal control that may have occurred. A more detailed re-examination of the critical literature, and particularly of its statements about imprisonment, illuminates the discursive and analytical tactics that have reinforced pessimism about the prospects for penal reform.

4

Problematic Aspects of the Decarceration Literature

Characteristics of Analyses of Net-widening

> When we examine the problem-setting stories told by the analysts and practitioners of social policy, it becomes apparent that the framing of problems often depends upon metaphors [u]nderlying the stories which generate problem setting and set the directions of problem solving ... we can spell out the metaphor, elaborate the assumptions which flow from it, and examine their appropriateness in the present situation. (Schön 1979: 255)

The conventional wisdom that the development of alternatives typically leads to net-widening and penal expansion is politically problematic. It hinders recognition of any progressive accomplishments of penal reform. It undermines the prospects for developing progressive penal politics. These political problems intersect with theoretical and methodological ones: the conventional wisdom is analytically problematic. It denies the importance of human agency in the making of history. The intentions and efforts of penal reformers are seen as repeatedly thwarted by more structural factors, which are the prime movers of history. Sometimes, these moving forces are identified as economic or bureaucratic. More often than not, they are unspecified, and are articulated through the discourse of 'unintended consequences.' The problem with this way of thinking is that unintended consequences have become synonymous with ominous or repressive ones. But surely unintended consequences can also, at least occasionally, be desirable ones. The critical literature has failed to identify aspects of penal reform that have been beneficial to its subjects, even when they have occurred only by accident.

Through critical criminologists' metaphorical adoption of the discourse of net-widening, some important aspects of penal reform and its consequences have escaped their attention. One way of identifying these omissions is to take a closer look at the social organizations of knowledge characteristic of critical analysis of decarceration. Questions underlying this re-examination include: What has been the structure of critical analyses of the failure of decarceration? Upon what evidence have statements about net-widening been based? Has the evidence been adequate? What methodological and analytical tactics have reinforced pessimism about alternatives and penal reform? Are there other ways of looking at correctional data and experience that might be more conducive to the development of a progressive penal politics?

Preliminary re-examination of the decarceration literature has identified some of its key characteristics. Much attention has been devoted to revealing, and developing explanations for, the net-widening effects of alternatives. But little corresponding attention has been paid to counter-indications of net-widening and penal expansion. Abstract theoretical issues have been debated, but some basic empirical trends have remained undocumented. Most notably, the emphasis on matters of discipline and the quest for new discoveries in penal control have usurped the attention paid to imprisonment.

This analytical displacement of imprisonment is understandable in light of the wider theoretical and political concerns of critical criminology. However, in the context of arguments about alternatives and net-widening, it must be considered serious. For, in the net-widening argument, assertions about the maintenance and increase of imprisonment are fundamental to the broader association of alternatives with penal expansion. One way, then, of further re-examining critical analyses of decarceration is to keep issues of trends in imprisonment as a central focus. While reviewing relevant statistical data appears mundane compared to engaging in literary and metaphorical depictions of transformations in penal control, the necessity of undertaking such prosaic tasks must be considered crucial for adequately analysing and understanding penal trends.

The following re-examination specifies limitations in conventional-wisdom arguments about decarceration. Documentation of trends in imprisonment has been partial. Insufficient evidence has been provided to support contentions about the maintenance and increase of imprisonment. Incompatible forms of data on imprisonment and probation have been juxtaposed. The conclusions that have been drawn from research appear to be far stronger than the data on which they are based should have allowed. Such methodological problems of individual studies have been exacerbated with their assimilation into international literature. As has happened in other social-scientific areas, 'ambiguities and qualifications are expressed, but then ignored as conclusions are drawn, and forgotten as they reach other arenas and transmitters. A fact is not a near-fact, maybe-fact or convenient fact. It becomes reality' (Gusfield 1981: 59).

In short, arguments about net-widening have often had a questionable empirical basis. Metaphorical depictions of net-widening have sometimes obscured as much as they have revealed. These observations can be illuminated, in the first instance, through a re-examination of widely cited Canadian studies of decarceration.

Canadian Analysis of Decarceration and Net-widening

It's a bit amazing that in Canada you can tell how much margarine people are consuming and the brand as compared to butter, and you can't tell how many people are put in jail. (Yvon Dandurand, director of research and statistics, federal justice department; quoted in Strauss 1985: 15)

Hylton's data on one province in Canada are a microcosm of the trend to expand in systems committed to community control (Cohen 1985: 49).

In the international literature on imprisonment and alternatives, the Canadian experience has been posited as paradigmatic. Specifically, research by Hylton (1981a) and by Chan and Ericson (1981) has frequently been drawn on in studies associating growing populations in community programs with the maintenance and increase of prison populations. Reference to Canadian data as confirming the tendency of community programs to 'widen the net' rather than to decrease prison populations has been made by authors from many countries, including the United States, Britain, Australia, Israel, and Norway (e.g., Austin and Krisberg 1982; Bottoms 1983; Chan and Zdenkowski 1986a; Cohen 1985; Mathiesen 1986; Scull 1984).

That the work of Hylton, and Chan and Ericson, is frequently cited in the literature is not surprising in light of their critical approaches and unequivocal conclusions. Hylton sets his analytical framework by referring to 'the publication of extensive literature on the net-widening effects of community corrections programs,' and presents a case-study of the province of Saskatchewan from 1962 to 1979, when a 'number of so-called alternative programs were developed and implemented on a broad scale in order to reduce reliance on correctional institutions.' He states that 'throughout the period steady increases in the number and rate of admissions to prison and in the number and rate of persons incarcerated on any given day were observed' (1982: 367, 345). In his analysis, there is no doubt that the penal control apparatus expanded in conjunction with the province's commitment to community alternatives.

Chan and Ericson are similarly unambiguous. They follow other critics in positing community programs as *complements* to, rather than *substitutes* for, institutions. Using quantitative data for the province of Ontario, and for Canada as a whole, they argue that the population of community programs, as well as that of prisons, is increasing: 'not only are more people coming under the system, more are being sent to prison as well.' Having provided provincial and national empirical support for these assertions, Chan and Ericson state that their study confirms Rothman's (1980: 8) revisionist historical observation that 'innovations that appeared to be substitutes for incarceration became supplements to incarceration.' They also state that their study confirms Cohen's (1979a) about the effects of alternatives in '"thinning the mesh and widening the net"' (1981: 9, 59, 45).

Clearly, these Canadian studies accord with the critical conventional wisdom. A central theme of their accounts is that no decrease in imprisonment occurred with the development of alternatives. But, although these arguments have been influential, a re-examination of the work of Hylton, and Chan and Ericson, reveals serious flaws in their methods, data, and analytical frameworks. Their documentation of trends in imprisonment has been especially problematic. Their conclusions overgeneralize from the data and are conducive to misinterpretation by others. That misinterpretation of the basis and scope of their findings has occurred in practice is evident, for example, in the use of their work by Cohen (1985) in his state-of-the-art analysis of contemporary penal trends.

A RE-EXAMINATION OF HYLTON'S RESEARCH

According to Cohen (1985: 49), Hylton's data for Saskatchewan are microcosmic of the tendency towards expansion in jurisdictions committed to community alternatives. He also considers Hylton's research as 'exemplary' in involving 'a detailed follow-through of the overall dispositional patterns of one correctional system over time.' Summing up

Hylton's findings, Cohen states that 'institutions now process more offenders than at any time in the province's history and all trends indicate that this expansion is increasing' (ibid: 47, 49).

One of the reasons for the frequent use of Hylton's research in the critical literature on alternatives is that the quantitative inquiry it provides is far superior to that of most other studies. Indeed, as Austin and Krisberg (1982: 377) observe following their careful review of the literature on alternatives to incarceration and net-widening, 'while the research on alternatives offers important information on policy, the quality of the research is, in general, poor. We reviewed scores of studies, but found only a few employing rigorous methods.' Addressing the specific question of whether community programs have reduced imprisonment, they report that 'only one study was found that attempted to evaluate the effects of community correctional programs on the institutional population' (ibid: 386). Naming Hylton, they go on to summarize his conclusions about the relationship between the expansion of community correctional and institutional populations in Saskatchewan.

Given the continuing dearth of rigorous quantitative studies, it is all the more important to realize that there are important omissions in Hylton's analysis. In particular, Hylton has identified only partial trends in the prison population, and his conclusions about overall expansion in the correctional system must be treated with caution.

Hylton's (1981a) analysis includes both count and admissions data for the province's correctional system. Count data refer to the number of people in the system on a given day. Admissions data refer to the total number of committals to the system in a year. In estimating the count of people in Saskatchewan's correctional system, Hylton provides statistics on the 'average daily count in the institutions, the year-end probation caseload, and the year-end count in the CTR's [Community-Training Residences, which are halfway houses] for each year from 1962 to 1979' (ibid: 203). In estimating the number of admissions to the Saskatchewan correctional system, he provides statistics on sentence admissions to institutions, probation intakes, and fine-option completions.

Specific to the prison population, Hylton states that 'the average daily count per 100,000 in Saskatchewan institutions increased from 55.23 in 1962 to 84.87 in 1979 – an increase of some 54 percent in 18 years.' Meanwhile, the 'number of admissions per 100,000 population increased from 434.85 in 1962 to 688.72 in 1979 – an increase of some 58 percent' (1981a: 196, 197). From these figures there appears to be no doubt that the prison population has grown considerably. But, although

Hylton has shown that certain components of the prison population in Saskatchewan have increased, he has by no means demonstrated that the prison population as a whole has increased.

In Canada, prison population is administratively divided into two major sections. One section comes under the jurisdiction of the federal (i.e., national) government. The other section comes under the jurisdiction of the provincial governments. Specifically, prisoners with longer sentences, of two years and over, are the responsibility of the federal government and its correctional agency; prisoners with shorter sentences, of less than two years, and remand prisoners are the responsibility of provincial governments and their correctional agencies. Documenting the whole of the prison population in any given province, therefore, requires examining both federal and provincial prisons in the province.

One of the crucial omissions of Hylton's research is that he does not include the two categories of federal and provincial prisoners. Rather, he excludes 'Saskatchewan offenders under supervision of the federal correction authority, that is, those sentenced to a period of incarceration for two years or more.' His focus is restricted to 'correctional programs administered by the provincial correctional authority,' that is, persons sentenced to periods of less than two years. According to Hylton, the omission of offenders incarcerated in federal institutions is 'not difficult to justify,' since these offenders 'made up only a small fraction of the total offender population in Saskatchewan.' Hylton goes on to explain in a footnote that 'admissions to the sole federal penitentiary in Saskatchewan represent less than one percent of the total admissions to the provincial correctional system in Saskatchewan' (1981a: 202, 214).

Hylton's omission of federal prisoners, on the basis of their constituting a small proportion with respect to prison admissions, overlooks the very different distribution that can prevail with respect to counts. To take the case of Ontario, for example, while admissions to federal penitentiaries in 1962 constituted less than 3 per cent of total sentenced admissions to prison, they accounted for 30 per cent of prisoner counts. In 1984, while they represented 4 per cent of total sentenced admissions to institutions, they accounted for 34 per cent of prisoner counts. Meanwhile, as regards Canada as a whole, Chan and Ericson's (1981: 77) data for 1955–77 show that the federal portion usually accounted for about a third, and, on occasion, for nearly a half, of the total prison population. Thus, Hylton's data on trends in the 'average daily count in institutions' omits a potentially substantial component of the Saskatchewan prison population.

Hylton's omission of federal inmates in Saskatchewan must be considered serious. Preliminary inquiry into an alternative source of information indicates that: 1 / in 1962, the first year examined by Hylton, the count of federal inmates in Saskatchewan actually exceeded that of provincial ones; 2 / subsequently, during some periods when the provincial prison population was increasing, the federal one was decreasing; and 3 / in general, during the period of Hylton's study, the federal prisoner population in Saskatchewan appears to have been proportionately larger than it is typically in Canadian jurisdictions (see Statistics Canada/Dominion Bureau of Statistics, *Correctional Institutions Statistics*, Cat no. 85-207, Annual, 1962–79).

Trends in a province's overall prison population may be as much related to trends in the federal penitentiary population in the province as they are to those in the population of provincial community corrections programs. Hylton claims that programs administered by the federal government for offenders 'could not reasonably be regarded as part of the provincial correctional system' (1981a: 202). This point about administration obfuscates the issue, especially given that the process whereby offenders are sentenced to under or over two years originates in the courts, which – ideally – should also be considered in any study of the relationship among institutional sentences and alternatives. Can one claim to have studied the effect of community programs on imprisonment when apparently upwards of 40 per cent of the standing prison population have been excluded?

Hylton's omission of the federal population is probably not so much related to the administrative separation of federal and provincial prisoners in the province as to his general point about the 'difficulty of obtaining data' (1981a: 202). Apparently, for the period of his study, the federal facilities in Saskatchewan were also used for some federal inmates from the Yukon and the Northwest Territories because there were no federal penitentiaries in those jurisdictions. During the 1960s, the Saskatchewan inmate population may also have included offenders from the neighbouring province of Alberta. The difficulties of reliably estimating the federal population of inmates from Saskatchewan would have been exacerbated by these factors. Here, I do not propose to complete Hylton's analysis by gathering and examining all of the relevant figures. Doing so would require a major research initiative, and one that – given the administrative complexities of identifying Saskatchewan offenders in the federal prison – might be impossible to complete. Nor, from the very preliminary inquiry that has been undertaken here, am I asserting that the incorporation of the federal prisoners from Saskatchewan would necessarily contradict Hylton's major conclusions. The point to be emphasized is that, whatever may be the trends in the overall Saskatchewan prison population from 1962 to 1979, they have not been fully documented.

Even if one were to accept Hylton's dubious proposition that information on the provincial prison population, and thus only on imprisonment for less than two years, is adequate for a study of decarceration, there are still important omissions from his data – most notably, consideration of remand and other non-sentenced admissions to prison. Arguably, non-sentenced admissions should form an important component of an analysis of prison and community-program populations. The length of time spent on remand can affect both the nature and the length of sentence chosen by judges. Moreover, non-sentenced admissions can be a substantial and variable proportion of total admissions to prisons. In Ontario, for example, non-sentenced admissions constituted 34 per cent of total admissions to prison in 1971, but only 14 per cent in 1982. As Hylton's data concern 'sentence admissions,' and as he makes only passing reference to a small number of inmates in police cells without discussing the situation of other remand prisoners, the reader has no idea of the size of the remand sector of the prison population either at a specific time or longitudinally.

The omission of non-sentenced admissions obscures the meaning of the category 'average daily count in institutions' as presented by Hylton. It also confuses the inferences he draws about the length of sentences longitudinally. Based on his observation that sentenced admissions increased by 58 per cent between 1962 and 1979, and that average counts increased by 54 per cent, Hylton states that, 'on average, individuals were retained in correctional institutions for about the same length of time in 1962 as in 1979,' and that the system therefore 'expanded by institutionalizing more offenders for about the same period of time' (1981a: 199). What Hylton has apparently done here is juxtapose admissions data, which include sentenced admissions only, with data on average counts, which seem to include all inmates, sentenced and non-sentenced, in the institutions.

More accurate estimates would have been provided by analysing total admissions in conjunction with total counts; and, by analysing sentenced admissions in conjunction with counts of inmates serving sentences. The first method would show the average length of time spent in prison by all inmates, and the second would identify the average length of sentence served. These data would also facilitate an examination of trends in admissions, and in the length of time incarcerated, for remand inmates. As it stands, Hylton's combination of sentenced admissions data with overall-count data does not allow for precise deduction about trends in the overall, the remand, or the sentenced population.

Even if, for the sake of argument, one were to assume that Hylton's statement that the 'system expanded by institutionalizing more offenders for about the same period of time' was correct, his subsequent remark is also problematic. Hylton goes on to say that 'this finding is all the more remarkable when it is recalled that a number of programs (including the CTR [Community-Training Residence] program) were developed in part to *reduce* the length of time offenders remained institutionalized' (1981a: 199, emphasis added). In fact, assuming that alternative programs would be used primarily for those who would have shorter prison sentences in the first place, the effect of a 'successful' use of alternatives should be rather to *increase* the proportionate length of time served by those remaining, as only those receiving longer sentences would still be going to prison in such a situation. Although individuals transferred to alternatives would experience a reduction in or elimination of the length of time served in prison, if the development of alternatives was the only reform taking place, average prison sentence lengths would increase. The situation whereby a successful reduction in prison admissions would most likely result in an increase in the average length of sentences still to be served is one of the basic empirical points frequently overlooked in the literature.

In summary, Hylton's analysis of the prison population in Saskatchewan is incomplete. While he documents the growth of community programs in the province, the nature of their relationship to traditional institutions is by no means clear. Indeed, in a note that discusses institutions in the United States, Hylton points out that 'decreases in one part of the [prison] system may be compensated for by increases in the other parts, but this may not become evident if only part of the social control apparatus is examined' (1981a: 213). Conversely, *increases* in one part of the prison system may be compensated for by decreases elsewhere. In the case of Saskatchewan, to what extent was the increase in the provincial system accompanied by a decrease in the federal one? Were there times when sentenced admissions were increasing and non-sentenced admissions decreasing? Perhaps the complex research needed to answer these questions would demonstrate that Hylton is correct in his statement that the 'utilization of correctional institutions did increase in the period from 1962 to 1979' (ibid: 207). However, in the absence of more detailed documentation of the process his assertion must be considered propositional rather than factual.

In light of these methodological problems, the adoption of Hylton's conclusions by other analysts must also be considered problematic. Statements such as Cohen's (1985: 47) that Saskatchewan 'institutions now process more offenders than at any time in the province's history and *all trends indicate* that this expansion is increasing' (emphasis added) represent an overgeneralization from limited data.

A RE-EXAMINATION OF CHAN AND ERICSON'S RESEARCH

Chan and Ericson's (1981) research has also been a frequent source for analyses of net-widening. Having pointed to the growth of alternative programs in the province of Ontario, and in Canada as a whole, the authors contend that this growth has not been associated with any decrease in imprisonment: 'none of the evidence appears to support that fewer people are being imprisoned today' (ibid: 42).

Chan and Ericson also obfuscate trends in the prison population. One way in which this occurs is through their making observations based on absolute numbers that do not accord with those based on the stronger indicator of rates. They report that, 'in Canada, both federal and provincial prison populations are at an all-time high' (1981: 39). This finding is true in terms of *absolute numbers*. However, the data for the Canadian prison population from 1955 to 1977 that they cite in support of this statement show that it clearly does not apply in terms of *rates per 100,000 population*, which, in total, stood at 95.9 in 1955, reached a high of 105.5 in 1962, and decreased to 98.4 in 1977 (ibid: 77). Indeed, per 100,000 population, the imprisonment rate for Canada as a whole was higher in about a third of the years under consideration than it was in 1977. While increases in absolute numbers are an important concern for policy makers and administrators, for analysts of penal trends, particularly in a country such as Canada that has experienced significant postwar population growth,[1] rates are a better indication of changes in the relative size of prison populations.

Specific to the Canadian provincial (i.e., sentences of less than two years) imprisonment rate, Chan and Ericson go on to say that the 'incarceration rate appears to have dropped in the early seventies but is now climbing rather steeply back to the late 1960 level' (1981: 39). Their data (p. 77) indicate that, per 100,000 population, the rate was lower in

1977 than for more than half of the previous years. Only in the federal (i.e., sentences of two years and over) prison population is an overall trend of increase evident. Although Chan and Ericson emphasize stability and growth of the prison population in their narrative, their data equally support the finding that the Canadian prison population per 100,000 was lower overall in 1972–7 than in 1955–60, with a decrease occurring in the provincial population that was greater than the increase in the federal one. For 1955–60, the average federal imprisonment rate per 100,000 population was 34.4 and the provincial rate 60.9, for a total rate of 95.3. For 1972–7, the federal rate was 39.6, the provincial 50.4, and the total 90.0 (p. 77).

Further obfuscation has occurred as other writers, who accept the conventional wisdom about the continuance and growth of prison populations, have made statements based on Chan and Ericson's analysis that go beyond the data presented by them and are conducive to being misread. Consider, for example, Cohen's (1985: 46) statement about the situation in Canada, based on his understanding of Chan and Ericson's research: 'after a slight drop in the early seventies incarceration *rates* began to climb back to the late sixties level, and, by 1982, *rates* (in federal *and* provincial prisons) were showing an all-time high, both in the standing population and those flowing through the system' (emphasis added).

A series of misunderstandings, ambiguities, and overgeneralizations are evident in this brief summary. Chan and Ericson's original statement about a drop in the early 1970s is specific to the provincial population, but Cohen generalizes it to the total prison population. He also expresses his point about an 'all-time high' in terms of rates, and this statement is likely to be misread by those unaware that Chan and Ericson were discussing absolute numbers. Cohen again overgeneralizes in his statement about an all-time high in 'those flowing through the system.' The relevant data presented by Chan and Ericson (1981: 41–2, 78) are in absolute numbers, not rates, and apply only to the federal prison population; they present no equivalent admission and release data for the provincial population. Cohen's phrase 'by 1982' is perplexing, as he cites no Canadian data source other than Chan and Ericson, and their data do not go beyond 1978.

More fundamental confusion – with implications for understanding and use of the concept of 'net-widening' more generally – arises in the context of Chan and Ericson's discussion of the comparative size and growth of prison and probation populations. Chan and Ericson's analysis is based on a graph that is reproduced as figure 4.1 here.

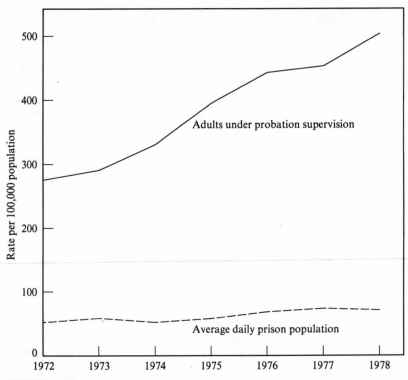

FIGURE 4.1
Ontario: adults under probation supervision and average daily prison
population. Reproduced from Chan and Ericson (1981: 44)

The data in figure 4.1 are central to Chan and Ericson's argument
that community programs act as supplements rather than alternatives to
incarceration, with incarceration itself tending to remain stable or to
increase. This figure is the only one in which they present imprisonment
and community alternative data in tandem. Clearly the graph illustrates
a striking case of net-widening: it reveals substantial growth in probation
in Ontario between 1972 and 1978, and probation generally appears to
be far greater numerically than imprisonment. Quantitatively, Chan and
Ericson observe that 'the rate of adult persons under probation supervision has risen from 275.4 to 503.7 per 100,000 population from 1972 to
1978,' and that, during the same period, 'the rate of incarceration has
risen from 52.1 to 71.1 per 100,000 population' (1981: 42, 45).
An examination of the appendix containing the statistical tables

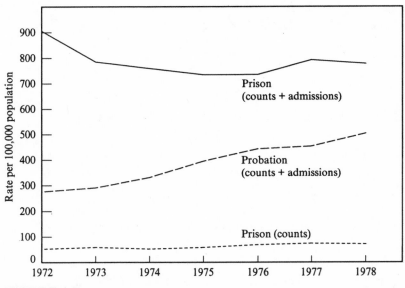

FIGURE 4.2
Ontario: prison counts plus admissions; probation counts plus admissions;
and (provincial) prison counts, 1972–1978

(1981: 80–1) on which Chan and Ericson's graph (1981: 44) relies shows
that Chan and Ericson are not comparing similar categories. Specifically, in their analysis, 'probation supervision' includes *both* counts and
admissions, that is, 'total under supervision at start of the fiscal year
[counts] and those placed under supervision during the fiscal year
[admissions].' However, their category 'average daily prison population'
includes only counts (and the figures presented are those for the end of
each fiscal year rather than averages).[2]

As a matter of heuristic interest (to be explained momentarily), it is
interesting to observe that, when the corresponding information on
prison admissions is tabulated (tables 4.1 and 4.2), and graphed (figure
4.2), a very different picture emerges. Where Chan and Ericson's graph
of probationers and prisoners suggests that probationers are numerically greater, the opposite situation is evident here. Further, while Chan
and Ericson's graph suggests an overall trend of increase in prison population (being 36 per cent greater in 1978 than in 1972), presenting the
data in a consistent way suggests a trend of decrease from 1972 to 1976.
Although there is some increase in the last two years, the 1978 figure of
772 counts and admissions per 100,000 is somewhat lower than that of

TABLE 4.1
Ontario: trends in adult probation, 1972–1978

Fiscal year	Count at beginning of fiscal year	Admissions during year	Total	Population	Rate per 100,000 (total) population
1972	10,943	10,270	21,213	7,703,100	275.4
1973	11,530	11,225	22,755	7,833,900	290.5
1974	12,577	13,691	26,268	7,938,900	330.9
1975	14,565	17,386	31,951	8,093,900	394.8
1976	17,099	19,323	36,422	8,225,800	442.8
1977	18,576	18,851	37,427	8,264,500	452.9
1978	20,768	21,413	42,181	8,373,500	503.7

Source: Chan and Ericson (1981), Table 12, p. 80, with 'Total Persons under Supervision' broken down into count and admission components

TABLE 4.2
Ontario: trends in prison population, 1972–1978

Fiscal year	Count at end of fiscal year	Admissions during year	Total	Population	Rate per 100,000 (total) population
1972	4,079	65,664	69,743	7,703,100	905.4
1973	4,747 (revised)	56,754	61,501	7,833,900	785.1
1974	4,202	56,701	60,273	7,938,900	759.2
1975	4,723	54,721	59,444	8,093,900	734.4
1976	5,643	54,791	60,434	8,225,800	734.7
1977	6,138	59,362	65,500	8,264,500	792.5
1978	6,008	59,072	65,080	8,373,500	777.2

Sources: Count and population figures from Chan and Ericson (1981), Table 13, p. 81; admissions figures from the annual reports of the Ministry of Correctional Services

905 in 1972 (a 15 per cent decrease overall). In short, when the imprisonment data are presented through the counts and admissions categorization Chan and Ericson apply to the probation data, the results can be used to challenge their assertion that the prison population had remained stable or increased as probation expanded.

Chan and Ericson's incorporation of prison admissions data in their presentations of trends is primarily of heuristic interest because count and admissions data each refer to substantially different phenomena. Any summation of them, therefore, is methodologically questionable, as it does not provide a very useful overview of correctional trends.

One way of illustrating the potential problems arising from a summation of admissions and counts data when documenting correctional trends is to make an analogy with an attempt to document trends in two peoples' incomes. In this case, each person's total income for the year can be considered as the equivalent number of admissions; and each person's total amount in the bank on 31 December, the year end, can be considered as the equivalent of counts. We will assume that, over a three-year period, both of these people have an annual income of $12,000. However, the first person – Priscilla – tends to spend her money rather quickly. At the end of the first year, only $100 remains in her account. By contrast, the second person – Prudence – is more parsimonious. At the end of the first year, she still has $3,000 in her bank account.

We will further assume that, over the next two years, each of these individuals continues her pattern of spending and accumulation. After three years, trends in Priscilla's and Prudence's incomes could be tabulated as in table 4.3, and graphed as in figure 4.3.

Next, imagine that some readers of this research tend to be bored by the mundane details of the underlying statistics. They proceed straight to the graph, where they presume that the major point of the analysis lies. Clearly, such readers are vulnerable to making an interpretation that not only was Prudence's income initially larger than Priscilla's, but that it also increased at a far greater rate. Such readers could easily miss the point that the main difference between Priscilla and Prudence was not in their annual income – which was equivalent and constant for both – but in the rate at which they actually spent their money over time. In short, the graph that emerges from the methodological strategy of combining income (the equivalent of 'admissions') and balance on a given day (the equivalent of 'counts') does not provide a very helpful overview of these peoples' individual, or comparative, incomes. The fundamental point about the equality of their annual incomes is obscured.

In the corrections context, summations of admissions and count data are of similarly little use in the analysis of penal trends. But, the reasons are not as readily apparent. Exploring them requires a more detailed inquiry into the vagaries of data on both imprisonment and probation. On that basis, it will be revealed that the longer length of probation compared to prison sentences needs to be taken into account in making comparative assessments.

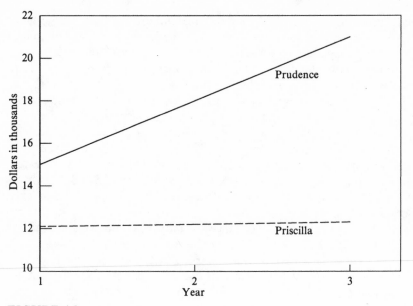

FIGURE 4.3
Comparative financial trends

TABLE 4.3
Comparative financial trends

	Priscilla			Prudence		
	Year 1	Year 2	·Year 3	Year 1	Year 2	Year 3
Income for year	12,000	12,000	12,000	12,000	12,000	12,000
Year-end count	100	200	300	3,000	6,000	9,000
Total plus year-end count	12,100	12,200	12,300	15,000	18,000	21,000

In sum, Chan and Ericson's graph depicting net-widening and penal expansion is questionable on grounds of consistency and validity. More important, however, the inadvertent oversights it reflects give rise to some more fundamental issues of methodology in analyses of net-widening. Specifically, what are the ways in which data on probation and imprisonment can be compared? Is the manner in which prison and probation have been compared in quantitative arguments about net-widening methodologically satisfactory?

Issues in Comparing Data on Probation and Imprisonment

Any comparison of probation and prison data requires careful attention to the nature of admissions and count data with respect to each of these categories. The necessity for such attention can be illustrated by further considering the relevant Ontario data for the period 1972–8 dealt with by Chan and Ericson. When the respective count and admissions statistics for probation and imprisonment are separated, and graphed (figures 4.4 and 4.5), some of the basic differences between these two types of disposition become clearer.

Most notably, while there is little difference during these years between probation admissions and counts (indicating that the average probation term lasted approximately one year), there is a vast gap between admissions and counts in the case of imprisonment (indicating that a substantial proportion of admissions are for very short periods). In order to support the argument of net-widening, including a stable or increasing imprisonment rate, the most effective way (and, in this instance, the only way) to reorganize the data is to present the counts of those on probation and in prison.

The methodological strategy of combining probationer and prisoner counts facilitates the most dramatic statements about penal expansion made in the critical literature. It enables Hylton (1981: 203), for example, to state that 'the rate per 100,000 population under supervision of the Saskatchewan correctional system increased from 85.46 in 1962 to 321.99 in 1979 – an increase of 277 percent in 18 years' (see also Mandel 1991: 184–5). While such observations about counts are highly effective in furthering the net-widening argument, in light of the differing nature of prison and probation dispositions it is doubtful that . such juxtaposition is methodologically appropriate.

The fact that the average sentence to probation is longer than the average prison sentence has crucial consequences for any attempt to examine count data. One way of illuminating these consequences is to consider the effect of alternative community programs on the correctional population (that is, probation plus imprisonment) in a hypothetical jurisdiction. In this hypothetical jurisdiction, I will assume that, initially, only the disposition of imprisonment exists; that there are 50,000 admissions a year; and that admissions are constant throughout the year (i.e., there is an average of about 137 admissions to prison per day, yielding the total of 50,000 admissions per annum). Then, a dramatic reform takes place. The alternative of probation is newly intro-

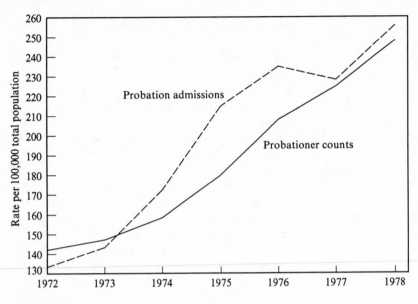

FIGURE 4.4
Ontario: admissions to probation and probationer counts, 1972–1978

duced, and is used precisely as intended by reformers seeking to reduce the use of imprisonment: that is, it is used in such a way as to replace the disposition of a prison sentence in certain instances, and is not used at all for people who would not have gone to prison in the first place.

In order to clarify the differences between prison and probation counts, further assumptions include that, in this hypothetical jurisdiction, the average prison sentence (both before and after reform) is 31 days, or about a month, while the average probation term (when introduced) is 365 days, or a year; that there is a constancy over time in the conviction rates, in the number and type of offender subject to a penal disposition, and in the population of the jurisdiction. The major question to be addressed is: What changes in correctional population counts result from a 'perfect' development of alternatives to prison in this hypothetical jurisdiction?

What I wish to point out is that 'net-widening,' in terms of correctional population counts, is *by definition* a feature of community alternatives to imprisonment. In this case, in the years prior to reform, if the jurisdiction had been sentencing 50,000 offenders a year to imprisonment, the average daily prison population (i.e., count) would have been

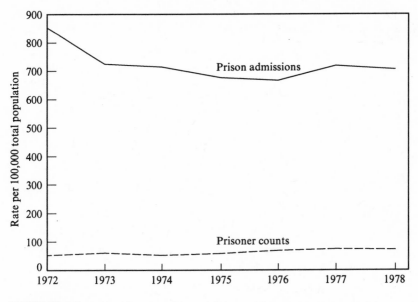

FIGURE 4.5
Ontario: admissions to prison and prisoner counts, 1972–1978

about 4,247. But, subsequent to the first year of reform, when deinstitutionalization had now been successfully accomplished in 50 per cent of sentencing dispositions, with the other half being sentenced to the newly introduced alternative of probation, the average daily penal population would increase to 27,123. Specifically, there would be 25,000 probationers and 2,123 inmates in the system on any given day. In short, this 50 per cent reduction of prison population through the substitution of probation as an alternative would have increased the penal population count by 539 per cent. Meanwhile, despite this enormous increase, not one 'extra' person would have been brought into the system. In what sense numerically does this result reflect 'net-widening'? Would analysts of community corrections argue that, in such a situation, reform had not been accomplished in practice? Table 4.4 sets out the calculations underlying this analysis.

The growth of the penal population, even in this hypothetical case, is attributable to the fact that – given the longer length of probation compared to prison sentences – the 'average' probationer is about twelve times more likely than is the 'average' prisoner to show up in the count statistics. One of the few ways in which deinstitutionalization through

TABLE 4.4
Net-widening in a hypothetical jurisdiction: I

	Admissions (1)	Average length of sentence (2)	Total days under sentence (3)[a]	Average daily population count (4)[b]
Before reform				
Prison	50,000	31	1,550,000	4,247
Probation	0	0	0	0
Total				4,247
After a year of reform				
Prison	25,000	31	775,000	2,123
Probation	25,000	365	9,125,000	25,000
Total				27,123

(% increase of 27,123 over 4,247 = 539)
(% decrease of 2,123 from 4,247 = 50)

Note: As these calculations indicate, the average daily count for each disposition is estimated in the following way: The total number of admissions per year is multiplied by
the average length of days spent under sentences during the year. Dividing this total by
365 – or the number of days in the year – provides the average daily population count.
a Col. (1) x Col. (2).   b Col. (3) ÷ 365

the use of probation could occur without net-widening in terms of counts
would be if for every new probation sentence imposed, judges actually
sent only one out of every twelve prison candidates to prison and let the
other eleven convicted offenders go free! Another way would be for the
probation disposition itself to be radically restructured, such that probation terms became equivalent in length to prison terms: the average probation term imposed in lieu of imprisonment would be reduced to about
a month. This reduction would, of course, have enormous implications
for other probation dispositions. One could hardly give one-month probation terms to probationers who would otherwise have gone to prison,
while continuing to impose far longer probation terms on other probationers convicted of lesser offences and unlikely to be imprisoned at all.
Meanwhile, even with such a radical reduction in the length of probation,
no reduction in correctional counts would be accomplished. Rather, the
correctional count would merely remain stable.

Moreover, it should be recognized that, in this hypothetical case, for

TABLE 4.5
Net-widening in a hypothetical jurisdiction: II

	Admissions (1)	Average length of sentence (2)	Total days under sentence (3)[a]	Average daily population count (4)[b]
Before reform				
Prison	25,000	42	1,050,000	2,877
	25,000	20	500,000	1,370
Probation	0	0	0	0
Total				4,247
After a year of reform				
Prison	25,000	42	1,050,000	2,877
Probation	25,000	365	9,125,000	25,000
Total				27,877

(% increase of 27,877 over 4,247 = 556)
(% decrease of 2,877 from 4,247 = 32)

a Col. (1) x Col. (2).   b Col. (3) ÷ 365.

the purposes of clarity, I have been conservative in assuming that the average prison sentence would remain at about one month after reform. Specifically, by assuming a continued average prison sentence of thirty-one days, I have implied that not only did the jurisdiction substitute probation for imprisonment in 50 per cent of cases, but that it also *shortened* the sentence lengths of the remaining prisoners. As mentioned earlier, a more realistic expectation is that the average length of sentences would *increase*, given that those with the shortest prison sentences would be more likely to receive the alternative of probation. In fact, if 50 per cent of inmates prior to the hypothetical reform had average sentences of twenty days, and the other 50 per cent an average of six weeks (yielding an overall average sentence length of about one month), the average inmate count after reform would be 3,877 inmates, and the total correctional count would be 27,877. Therefore, in this case, resting on more plausible assumptions, securing a mere 32 per cent decrease in the prison population would entail a 556 per cent increase in the overall penal population count. Table 4.5 sets out the relevant calculations.

Even this second hypothetical case makes conservative assumptions. Bottomley and Pease (1986: 107) have estimated, on the basis of actual sentencing and imprisonment data for England and Wales in 1983, that sentences 'up to and including six months account for 51% of receptions but only 17% of population.' Therefore, 'to attempt to reduce the sentenced prison population by a mere 17%, over half the custodial decisions of the courts would have to be substituted by non-custodial decisions.' Meanwhile, the overall correctional population count would have to increase substantially.

Documentation and analysis of trends in corrections must include two fundamental points. First, even without any new people coming into the system, relatively small reductions in prison population counts necessitate large changes in sentencing practices. Second, increases in correctional count populations are an inherent feature of even 'true' community alternatives to imprisonment. Critical analysts have assumed that the phenomenon of net-widening as illustrated through count data, means that more people are actually *coming into* correctional systems. For example, Chan and Ericson (1981: 55) summarize their findings as they relate to other studies on community corrections:

> No doubt the picture presented here is still somewhat sketchy. More data on the use of community alternatives would have been useful to illustrate the extent of decarceration in this country. Statistics on sentencing patterns over the years would have helped to clarify the influx of prisoners. However, regardless of how many more details we add to the present picture, its central message is unlikely to change: people are not directed from, but into and within the system. (Greenberg 1975; Blomberg 1977; Cohen 1979a: 349)

Whatever might be discovered about the movement of people within the system (as, for example, with the use of day release passes), the contention that community alternatives are invariably associated with more people coming into the system is problematic. When the detail of admissions to prisons is considered in relation to Chan and Ericson's Ontario data, the picture does change somewhat. The increase in probation admissions per 100,000 population was accompanied by some decrease in prison admissions (see figures 4.4 and 4.5).

Furthermore, when the data on prison *plus* probation admissions in Ontario are considered, the total for 1978 (961 per 100,000) is lower than that in 1972 (986 per 100,000 population). Given that there is a decline in the overall rate of people coming into prison and probation when these two years are compared, in what sense quantitatively can the 'net-widening' hypothesis be supported in Ontario for this period?

In summary, re-examination of Canadian critical literature on community corrections reveals two interrelated set of problems in analyses of 'net-widening.' First, it has been too readily assumed that prison populations are predominantly subject to maintenance and increase. Evidence of growth in sectors of the prison population has been generalized to the whole prison population. Indicators of decrease in imprisonment have been glossed over in favour of supporting the theme of expansion. The size of prison population, and longitudinal trends within it, require closer attention in future studies.

Second, questionable approaches have been taken in juxtaposing data on probation and imprisonment. Quite apart from the dubious methodology of taking these penal dispositions in tandem without considering sentencing trends more generally (see Bottoms 1983; Matthews 1987), the substantive differences between imprisonment and probation data – notably with respect to counts – have received insufficient attention. That a growth in correctional counts reflects a growth in the numbers of people coming into the correctional system is one of the problematic impressions fostered by this omission. Greater precision in the mundane task of documenting penal trends is a prerequisite for their analysis and explanation.

Critical analysts of community corrections internationally have shared a remarkable consensus about their failure in reducing imprisonment, and about their association with 'net-widening.' The frequent reference to the Canadian situation raises questions about the empirical bases of similar observations in other jurisdictions. Has the association of alternatives with net-widening and penal expansion been satisfactorily documented elsewhere? Even a brief consideration of studies from other countries further highlights methodological problems in documentation and theorizing of trends in imprisonment, alternatives, and net-widening.

The Case of the United States

Analysts of the failures of decarceration make frequent reference to the occurrence of net-widening and penal expansion in the United States. Identification of the extraordinary growth of prison population there since the mid-1970s represents a crucial point in such analyses.

The u.s. prison population certainly is remarkably large, as becomes evident through comparisons with those of Canada and European countries. For example, in 1985, the United States had a prisoner count of 292 per 100,000 population. This was far higher than Canada's prisoner count of 111 per 100,000 population in 1983–4, and the average prisoner count of fewer than 70 per 100,000 population in the member states of the Council of Europe during the mid-1980s (Tournier 1986). By the early 1990s, the U.S. prison count had reached more than 400 per 100,000 population (Christie, forthcoming).

Arguably, analysts of decarceration have too readily seen such indicators of U.S. expansion as fitting with the net-widening thesis. In face of the scale of imprisonment, they have overlooked basic problems in, and complex aspects of, documentation of U.S. prison population. Analysts have also insufficiently addressed questions about the relationship between the growth of alternatives and of imprisonment. Again, by keeping issues of imprisonment as a core problematic to be explored, a preliminary identification can be made of some weaknesses of the net-widening argument.

Documentation of trends in the U.S. prison population has often been incomplete. The U.S. rates cited above include jails as well as state and federal prisons. Some studies of decarceration, however, have included only data on state and federal prisons (e.g., Scull 1977: 47). Data on jail population have been excluded.

This omission of jail population can be a substantial one as the jails – which include many prisoners sentenced for up to a year, as well as remand and other inmates – have frequently accommodated over one-third of the total prison population. Moreover, trends in jail populations have sometimes differed from those in state and federal ones. For example, comparing 1974 with 1978 – at which time state and federal prison counts were increasing – some estimates cite an average jail population count in absolute numbers of 160,000 in 1974, and the lower figure of 153,162 in 1978 (Cottle 1979: 319; Davies 1985: 5). As in other countries, the focus on dramatic aspects of expansion has diverted attention from the occasional diminution that has occurred.

In general, adequate documentation of trends in the U.S. jail population is faced with a range of problems. The most basic of these is that a count is not taken on an annual basis. Rather, there is a census every five years. Further, some jurisdictions (e.g., Minnesota) have taken such liberties as defining jail inmates as part of the community correctional, rather than prison, population. A similar array of technical, administrative, and organizational complexities confound identification of trends throughout the penal system. For example, as Scull (1977: 44) himself observed in his initial analysis of decarceration, with 'the persistence of a relatively high degree of fragmentation and decentralization in the criminal justice apparatus, with decision making being so widely dispersed among a variety of competing and overlapping administrative unity – counties, cities, states and at the federal level ... arriving at even a rough estimate of the number being diverted out of the institutional sector becomes a virtual impossibility.'

The difficulties in identifying trends in the u.s. jail population are important, not only because jails include a substantial component of the total prison population, but also because these short-term prisoners are among the most likely to be affected by any developments of alternatives that do occur. Yet, some of the research on decarceration omits trends in the use of jails. For example, studies of the deinstitutionalization of mental patients, in exploring whether many of these people might have been transinstitutionalized into correctional institutions, have limited their focus to data on state mental hospitals and state prisons (Biles and Mulligan 1973; Grabosky 1980; Penrose 1939; Steadman and Morrissey 1987). In omitting jails, they have failed to consider the correctional sector that ex-patients are most likely to encounter. In light of this lack of attention to jails in analyses of the experiences of ex-mental patients, Steadman and Morrissey (1987: 244–5) rightly question:

> Is it not ... logical if the mentally ill are now entering the criminal justice system, that it is the gaol rather than the state prison in which they will be most visible? It is hard to get into United States prisons today. First-time offenders or minor criminals cannot fit. These are the classes into which persons unable to get into mental hospitals as a result of deinstitutionalization would most often fall ... Research which includes only the state mental hospitals and prison as the focal organizations (and even work that includes the local gaol as a separate component) is clearly inadequate.

Apart from jails, another complexity of the u.s. prison population that is frequently overlooked is the widely varying rate of imprisonment among states. For example, on 15 February 1978, the prisoner count for state prisons and jails, in the country as a whole, stood at 195 per 100,000 civilian population. But, the counts for individual jurisdictions differed greatly. They ranged from exceptionally high figures of 594 in the District of Columbia, 382 in Georgia, 260 in Florida, and 345 in Nevada, to the comparatively low ones of 69 in Vermont, 58 in Hawaii, 56 in Rhode Island, and 45 in North Dakota (National Institute of

Justice 1980: 14). How, one wonders, should general statements about the development of alternatives being accompanied by high imprisonment rates be interpreted in light of these diverse situations? There is a need for greater specificity about trends in imprisonment, alternatives, and net-widening in different parts of the United States. As Michalowski and Pearson (1987: 271) have observed: 'patterns and practices of punishment ... in the United States with its 50 different prison systems, vary noticeably from one political jurisdiction to another. Thus, while aggregate national statistics can provide clear and useful summary data, they may obscure important variations among states. For this reason, future prison research should include more in-depth analysis of the individual states as well as studies of national aggregates.'

Overall, while the decarceration literature emphasizes prison and penal expansion in the United States, there has been little analysis of precisely how alternatives have been associated with net-widening in specific jurisdictions. In turn, this observation gives rise to crucial issues about the sources of growing imprisonment.

The fact that the 1960s and early 1970s were a period of declining imprisonment rates in the United States has been given little attention in recent literature on decarceration. The relative neglect is all the more serious, as, during that period, albeit primarily in conjunction with the ascendancy of rehabilitation, the use of community programs was growing. The predominant focus has been on the period since the mid-1970s when, along with the demise of rehabilitation, the discourse of community programs as 'alternatives' became more prominent. The point that tends to be emphasized is that, in conjunction with the growth of alternatives, imprisonment rates increased. These developments are seen as interconnected, and as indicative of net-widening.

What this argument overshadows, however, are other penal developments, and ones that may be more significant in the growth of imprisonment in the United States. In particular, the decarceration literature has paid insufficient attention to the ideologies and consequences of the 'justice model.' For, while the ideology of community correctional alternatives has been prominent since the mid-1970s, that of just deserts has arguably been far more so. Moreover, while the justice-oriented debates of the 1970s saw liberals convene with conservatives around such issues as determinate sentencing, implementation of related policies has tended to take severe and punitive, rather than reductionist, directions (Greenberg and Humphries 1980). It may well be that the growth of prison population in the United States is associated with the lengthening of sentences, reduction of administrative discretion; and general emphasis on deterrence and incapacitation characteristic of the implementation of the justice model, rather than with the purported consequences of community-correctional programs. Indeed, the implementation of the justice model has been associated with the reduction, and even abolition, of community alternatives facilitating release from prison, rather than with their expansion. For example, by 1987, following disenchantment with rehabilitation and a movement towards determinate sentencing, eleven states had abolished discretionary parole release (Canadian Sentencing Commission 1987: 239).

In sum, knowledge of prison and penal trends in the United States continues to be rudimentary. Broad generalizations about net-widening have been made on the basis of aggregate trends in imprisonment, and without much information being presented on the implementation and experiences of alternatives. The impact of wider penal developments on trends in imprisonment has been insufficiently considered. Many basic questions, therefore, remain to be addressed. For example, what part did the growth of community corrections play in the decrease in U.S. imprisonment that was taking place prior to the mid-1970s? What have been the purposes, nature, and consequences of community alternatives since the mid-1970s, when the ideologies and practices of just desserts have been more prevalent? Is it possible that some community-correctional initiatives have helped to constrain the more general tendency of growth in imprisonment?[3]

The Case of Britain

The critical literature on net-widening also makes frequent reference to the case of Britain, and especially to England and Wales. Again, however, the literature is methodologically problematic. Despite frequent and generalized references to the jurisdiction, the overall extent of development of community programs in Britain remains unclear. For example, in Scull's initial discussion of decarceration, he stated that, 'no decarceration programs of comparable scope and intensity [to those in the United States] have as yet been implemented in England' (1977: 56). Although net-widening of the penal population is a major theme of his 'Afterword' to the second edition of *Decarceration*, while Scull (1984) discusses the growth of the prison and borstal population in England

and Wales, he does not discuss the growth of community programs. In his more recent commentary on decarceration (1991), Scull does not address British developments at all.

Cohen's analysis is similarly uninformative. He cites official statistics on imprisonment, but, in relation to alternatives, says that 'little research of equivalent sophistication' to that in North America is available in the form of specific case-studies (1985: 45, 48). Cohen implies that trends similar to those in North America exist in Britain, but they have not been equally documented. He particularly points to an increase in the incarceration of younger offenders, and posits the 'Intermediate Treatment' community program as fitting the general pattern of negative or equivocal results in reducing custody.

Such critical summaries of knowledge about, and trends in, imprisonment and alternatives should be read with caution. Extensive empirical literatures on specific penal measures in Britain, such as suspended sentences and community service orders, and on their relationship to the use of imprisonment do exist (e.g., Bottoms 1981; Pease 1985; Pease and McWilliams 1980; Sparks 1971; Young 1979). Moreover, while there is evidence that the younger sector of the British penal population experienced by far the most dramatic growth from the mid-1950s until the late 1970s (see Matthews 1987: 349), this trend dramatically changed during the 1980s: the number of juvenile offenders (age fourteen to sixteen) who were 'sentenced to custody for indictable offences fell from 7,700 in 1981 to 4,000 in 1987, a reduction of about a half in six years' (HMSO 1988: 7). By 1988, the number had dropped to 3,200 (Allen 1991: 31). While demographic factors partly account for this striking decarceration, changing legislation, policies, and practices – including with respect to community corrections – were also influential (see Allen 1991; Rutherford 1988).

Meanwhile, other, and more long-term, aspects of decarceration that have occurred in Britain have tended to be glossed over in the literature in favour of an emphasis on indicators of expansion. As noted, the proportionate decline in judicial use of imprisonment compared to other sentencing dispositions that was evident until the late 1970s has been little discussed (Bottoms 1983; Downes 1988: 57).

Critical analysts of 'net-widening' in Britain have also failed to address the striking reduction in imprisonment that did occur in England and Wales between 1880 and 1940 (Downes 1988: 7). This is a serious omission as the development of probation and other alternative measures appears to have played an important part in this decarceration (Sutherland 1934; Rutherford 1984). By neglecting such situations, critical analysts have missed opportunities to explore those factors that have been conducive to decarceration at various times.

Similarly, little attention has been paid by critical analysts to the apparent removal of some offenders from imprisonment by virtue of their subjection to other penal measures. Thus, for example, where a program such as community service orders is discussed in any detail, the tendency is to emphasize that, in about half of the cases in which they are used, the offender would probably not have been imprisoned anyway (e.g., Menzies and Vass 1988). This approach to summarize research findings detracts attention from the point that, in the other half of cases, community service orders have apparently been used in lieu of imprisonment. In seeking to criticize such programs, attention to their accomplishments has been minimal.

However, and as alluded to earlier, some British commentators have suggested important modifications and directions for future inquiry. Matthews (1987) has moderated his position that community programs are 'invariably' associated with net-widening, and has analytically and empirically pointed to the complexity of penal trends. Matthews (1989) has also outlined elements of a 'realist' approach to reducing imprisonment. Vass and Weston (1990) have followed Rodger (1988) in questioning the 'dispersal of discipline' thesis. Through their analysis of a probation day centre, they argue that alternatives may at least sometimes be successful in diverting some offenders from custody. Bottoms (1983), while recognizing growth in the numbers of those imprisoned since the 1930s, has sought to place this development in the context of broader and historical penal trends. He has emphasized the proportionate decline in the use of imprisonment as a sentencing disposition, and has suggested that the growth of the fine was far more significant than that of community correctional programs in England and Wales from the 1930s to 1980. Peter Young (1986) has observed that community corrections have not been extensively used in Britain, and has concurred with Bottoms's observations about the use of fines. Expressing his wish that Cohen 'had tempered his imagination by a much closer scrutiny of empirical developments' (ibid: 223), Young (forthcoming) has undertaken a detailed inquiry into the place of the fine in the penal system. The proportionate decline of the fine during the 1980s (Bottoms 1987) should not be allowed to obscure this century's more longitudinally evident trend of substantial increase in its use for both summary and indictable offences.

Meanwhile, other jurisdictions that have had low or decreasing prison populations have been given far less attention in the critical literature. There are some important exceptions to this, notably in the case of The Netherlands (e.g., see de Haan 1990; Downes 1988; Rutherford 1984). Literature concerning West Germany (Feest 1988; Graham 1990) and Australia (Chan and Zdenkowski 1986a; Walker, Collier, and Tarling 1990) has also called attention to aspects of reduction.

Nevertheless, such studies have not been used in directly confronting wider critical tenets about net-widening and penal expansion, and the conventional wisdom has remained partial in its emphasis on Anglo-American – especially North American and British – jurisdictions. More often than not, critical analysts from other countries who have addressed issues of the interrelationships of imprisonment alternatives have stressed those aspects they see as according with the conventional wisdom of the Anglo-American literature (e.g., in the case of The Republic of Ireland, see McCullagh 1988; in the case of The Netherlands, see de Jonge 1985; in the case of West Germany, see Deichsel 1988; in the case of Australia, see Muncie and Coventry 1989; in the case of Norway, see Mathiesen 1983, 1986; and Larsson 1990). These tendencies in the exportation and importation of assumptions about net-widening reveal that North America and Britain have retained a position of prominence in the 'free trade' of critical criminological ideas, although the quality of their product leaves much to be desired.

Overall, even a brief reconsideration of international contentions about net-widening suggests that methodologically problematic claims have not been peculiar to the Canadian case. Many assertions have been ahistorical, and have overgeneralized from limited data. Specific community programs have sometimes been charged with failing to reduce the use of imprisonment, without sufficient empirical details being provided to enable readers to make their own assessments. Indicators of the reductionist effect of some alternatives as reflected in proportionate decreases in the use of imprisonment in sentencing, and in their use in some cases for people who would have otherwise gone to prison, have been largely overshadowed by a relentless emphasis on indicators of expansion.

In sum, the predominant approach of net-widening analysts has been to point to the maintenance and increase of imprisonment, and to posit alternatives as not only failing to counter, but also fostering, this trend. Yet, documentation of trends in imprisonment, and of substantive processes of net-widening, has been sketchy. Moreover, inherently problematic assertions about the quantitative occurrence of net-widening have been made and gone unnoticed. The very concept of net-widening, and the ways in which it has been used, have arguably obscured as much as revealed trends in imprisonment and alternatives. Critical knowledge has been partial.

Re-examining Issues and Practices of Decarceration

The following study of penal trends seeks to redress some of the characteristic imbalances of decarceration literature. My focus is on the Canadian province of Ontario. Given the earlier presentation of this jurisdiction as experiencing net-widening, it provides a useful case for further re-examining and exploring analytical issues in the study of postwar penal trends.

This study also embodies a distinctive approach, which has been informed by my identification of problematic aspects of other decarceration literature. Most generally, I seek to follow Cohen's (1987: 369) advice that we maintain a 'sensitivity to success (however ambivalent),' along with an 'experimental and inductive attitude.' Where many assumptions have been made about growth in alternatives being accompanied by that in imprisonment, here, the size of prison population is retained as a core problematic to be explored. Rather than limiting my analysis of postwar imprisonment to its expansionist aspects, I ask: What have been overall, and subsidiary, trends in imprisonment? What have been its reductionist, as well as its expansionist, features?

Further, where critical studies of alternatives to prison have typically focused on community corrections (such as probation, halfway houses, and community service orders), I here also inquire into the use of other penal sanctions, particularly the fine. In this way, rather than paying attention only to those sentencing alternatives that have been most prominent in public and academic discourse, I present a fuller account.

Where critical analysts have highlighted the presumption that community programs would be used in lieu of imprisonment as a key feature of reformist correctional discourse, I also take this as an important problematic to be explored. Rather than adopting a perspective that contrasts the failures of community corrections with their purported intentions, I address questions that more deeply explore the intentions of those supporting community programs: Why, in Ontario, did community correctional discourses and practices become prominent? What factors underlay, and what purposes were furthered, by these programs?

Finally, where other studies tend to make generalizations about imprisonment from the vantage of alternatives, I adopt the analytical tactic of keeping documentation and explanation of trends in imprisonment central. Although my objective is to explore the interrelationships of imprisonment and alternatives, as well as their situation in the context of broader penal trends, my primary vantage-point is that of the prison. As will become clear, even a determined focus on imprisonment – which is supposedly concerned with more serious aspects of crime – leads the analysis beyond prison walls into the realm of mundane everyday behaviour and the regulation of petty violations. But, by keeping the prison analytically central, trends and developments there are brought more clearly into view.

In conclusion, the following research has the immediate objective of documenting prison, alternative, and penal trends in Ontario during the postwar period. It has the methodological objective of overcoming at least some of the problematic aspects of other studies of decarceration. In turn, these objectives combine with the wider analytical endeavour of forming analytical frameworks that clarify what has been going on, and, in doing so, acknowledge the complex and contradictory aspects of penal reform.

5

Decarceration
in Postwar Ontario

Ontario Postwar Correctional Discourses and Practices

> Inmates were really treated as though they were less than human. To me,
> it was quite shocking to go in and see how people were treated [in the
> 1950s] ... Inmates were not allowed to speak unless they were spoken to
> ... an inmate couldn't go up to an officer with an everyday request, he'd
> sort of have to stand to attention and hope that he would catch an
> officer's eye.
>   Punishments were very harsh in those days. The strap was still a
> common form of punishment. (Don Sinclair, former correctional official
> in Ontario, interview with author, 1987)

> By the late 1960s the department's changes in policy, personnel and
> structure were irreversible. Modernization had been achieved. Whatever
> problems the future might bring, the bad old days were gone forever.
> (Oliver 1985: 190)

What were the major tendencies in Ontario prisons and corrections during the postwar period? Here, I address this question, first, by reviewing
major discursive and policy shifts in corrections; and, second, by documenting key empirical trends in the use of imprisonment. As will
become clear, the postwar period was one of distinctive transformation
in Ontario corrections.

In discussing Ontario correctional history, my major focus is on
provincial corrections. The main sector of the prison population
referred to, therefore, is that of those serving sentences of under two
years. The reason for this focus on provincial, rather than federal, corrections, is that – as is made clear later in the chapter – the most strik-

ing changes in the use of imprisonment during the postwar period were those related to shorter sentences.

A full account of Ontario corrections from the mid-century remains to be written. Nevertheless, postwar correctional discourses in Ontario can roughly be characterized in terms of three phases. During the 1950s, there was an emergent reformism, with correctional officials and reformers expressing support for rehabilitation. During the 1960s, officials expressed their commitment to rehabilitation far more vociferously, and fostered an aura of progressivism. During the 1970s, and into the early 1980s, reformist enterprises continued, with the ideology of community corrections superseding that of rehabilitation.

In short, in Ontario, as in other Western jurisdictions during the postwar period (see chapter 2), there was a movement from emphasizing how imprisonment itself could be improved, to looking beyond prison walls and emphasizing the advantages of community-based programs.

THE 1950s: EMERGENT REFORMISM

... the inescapable conclusion is that, with a few notable exceptions, Ontario's reform institutions are not living up to their name. (Stewart 1954: 6)

In the early 1950s, corrections in Ontario primarily consisted of institutions. The province's department of Reform Institutions had responsibility for four reformatories, five industrial farms, seven training schools (for juveniles under sixteen years of age), and eight district jails. The department also had some supervisory responsibilities for thirty-five county and two city jails. The federal government administered several federal penitentiaries in the province. Where community-based programs were concerned, probation in Ontario – as will be discussed below – was relatively underdeveloped and used. The Ontario Board of Parole, having fewer than ten members and limited jurisdiction, was similarly limited in its personnel and operations.

Various accounts indicate that, during the 1950s, Ontario prisons were certainly vulnerable to identification as being in need of a range of reforms. Some of the problematic aspects of the prisons were described to me in interview by Don Sinclair. Sinclair had been employed by Ontario corrections, at increasingly senior levels, for a total of thirteen years between 1956 and 1974 (culminating with the most senior correctional post of deputy minister).

According to Sinclair, during the 1950s Ontario correctional institutions were run in a 'quasi-military' manner. A similar militarist ethos has been observed elsewhere. Indeed, according to Morris (1968: 81), 'almost all the prison systems in the world have attempted to organize their personnel along the lines of a military unity, a practice almost certainly originating from the fact that ex-soldiers and ex-sailors provided in the nineteenth century the only pool of suitably qualified labour for the tasks of maximum custody.'

In Ontario, while the number of prison guards who were ex–military personnel is unclear, and while it has been observed that 'many of the guards were farmers trying to pick up a little extra cash' (Oliver 1985: 175), it is clear that the Department of Reform Institutions had a military orientation. One aspect of this was the practice whereby, 'in lieu of other criteria, promotions to the higher positions in the Ontario reforms field until the late 1950's tended to favor men with military training and outlook' (Mann 1967: 30).[1] The appointment of Colonel Hedley Basher as deputy minister from 1952 until 1959 was 'typical' (ibid) of this tendency.

According to Sinclair, under Colonel Basher's directions, institutions such as the Guelph Reformatory[2] were 'run on military lines.' The staff 'just took orders. Their ranks were run the same as military ranks; they were called corporals, and sergeants ... it was very like being in the army.' Mann's (1967) study of Guelph confirms that, in 1961, the custodial staff 'included 235 privates, 14 corporals, 9 sergeants, 8 lieutenants, [and] one captain.' Moreover, as Mann (ibid: 30–1) elaborated:

> The impact of the institution's physical structure upon the inmates is highly reinforced by the military-type characteristics of the supervisory and administrative personnel. Guards and officials with few exceptions are regularly dressed in military-type khaki apparel, are accorded military title and are expected to deport themselves with military precision and formality ... With disciplined military men at the top and other military accoutrements including titles and uniforms, it is natural that inmates will be handled by the barking of orders and the external disciplines of a military-type system.

Yet, despite the militaristic and authoritarian control of both staff and inmates, Ontario's prison system was not always totally effective in maintaining order. For example, in 1952, a riot occurred at the Guelph Reformatory and 'became the most notorious such occurrence in the province's history' (Oliver and Whittingham 1987: 239). Resulting in damages of about $1 million, the riot was instrumental in the Department of Reform Institution's decision to establish Millbrook – an 'impersonal maximum-security facility ... intended principally for trouble-makers and recidivists' – in 1956 (Oliver 1985: 175; *Hansard,* 25 March 1957, 1518).

Conditions in the prisons run by the Department of Reform Institutions were tough. Prisoners slept without mattresses. At institutions such as Guelph, candy, toiletries, and other such 'luxuries' were prohibited; only one letter a week, one page in length, was allowed; visits were similarly limited; work was boring; little reading material was available. All components of the daily routine, from eating in silence to the way one spoke to guards and slept in bed, were governed by a detailed series of rules (see, generally, Mann 1967).

By all accounts however, the physical conditions in the province's jails – which accommodated remand and short-term prisoners – were particularly bad. As one author (Hooper 1964: 453) recalled on the basis of visits to all of Ontario's jails during the late 1940s: 'Apart from all the antiquated buildings and facilities observed on those occasions, the most striking memory is of the dingy jail cells and corridors, stench, overcrowding, and almost always – inactivity. It was difficult to convince oneself that a single prisoner might benefit from confinement in such an unwholesome and stultifying atmosphere and confinement.'

In addition to problems with inadequate ventilation, sanitation, and lighting, and some cells being 'unbelievably small' (Stewart 1954: 136), various administrative difficulties were also being experienced. Some jails were frequently overcrowded, while others had 'insufficient inmates to justify their existence' (ibid: 164).[3] Staffing was also a problem, with many institutions experiencing high turnovers. According to Sinclair, particularly in the more rural areas, the jails were often staffed by 'people who were on the city's welfare rolls so long, that in order to get them off the welfare rolls, and save the city money...they found them jobs in jails.' Ontario prisons, it appears, have been associated with forced labour in more ways than one.

In light of such conditions, a select committee of the Ontario legislature concluded in 1954 that 'the existing city and county jail system is outmoded and unworthy of the people of Ontario' (Stewart 1954: 136). Historian Peter Oliver (1985: 175) concurs that at least some of the jails were 'a disgrace to the province.' In Don Sinclair's recollection, the jails were generally 'an unholy mess.'

Nevertheless, while a range of problems with Ontario's prison system in the 1950s were readily apparent, and while politicians of the day remained relatively unconcerned about the conditions to which prisoners were subjected,[4] some developments had also taken place that fostered an emergent reformism in corrections. The establishment of the Department of Reform Institutions in 1946 had been very important. Formerly, the province's penal institutions had been administered through a branch of the provincial secretary. As the provincial secretary had other responsibilities – such as the administration of Ontario's lottery – attention to prisons as a distinct entity had been hindered. By contrast, from 1946, with penal institutions now having their own ministerial department, their potential to become more of a political and administrative priority was enhanced.

The formation of the Department of Reform Institutions combined with other political developments accentuating the need for criminal-justice and correctional reform. The postwar period saw growing concern about juvenile and adult crime. In the late 1940s, both provincial and municipal governments appointed committees to examine delinquency (Brownell and Scott 1950; Goldring 1950). In 1952, the riot at Guelph Reformatory stimulated the reform climate within the Department of Reform Institutions as 'shocked officials began to cast about for new policies' (Oliver and Whittingham 1987: 239). In 1953–4, the Ontario Legislature, motivated by perceptions of increases in both adult and juvenile crime, as well as by the riot at Guelph, initiated a detailed investigation of the province's correctional system (Stewart 1954).

The reformist aspirations of the Department of Reform Institutions were expressed in its formulation of the 'Ontario Plan.' Elements of the plan were outlined in annual reports during the late 1940s, and were constantly reiterated and expanded during the 1950s. The plan's policy proposals for corrections included classification of prisoners; creation of smaller and specialized institutions; expansion of academic study programs; inauguration of formal vocational training; and, where employees were concerned, 'increased care' in their selection, and the provision of training. Notably, the plan also included 'permanent employment of specialists to apply the best penological and scientific methods,' with the duties of these employees including systematic and intensive efforts 'to rehabilitate prisoners.' In short, the emergent reformist ethos involved affirmation of rehabilitation and its principles.

The extent to which this reformist ethos affected the actual operation of prisons during the 1950s remains open to question. Administration of the local jails continued to be beyond the ambit of the Department of Reform Institutions. While the department did develop some facilities and services said to be treatment-oriented, it also established punishment-oriented Millbrook Reformatory, and endorsed the use of corporal punishment in the institutions. In 1954, the Ontario Select Committee examining custodial institutions commented that officials of the Department of Reform Institutions 'differed on details of exactly what constituted the Ontario Plan' (Stewart 1954: iv). The committee further commented that the Department of Reform Institutions 'has admirable aims, as expressed in its "Ontario Plan," but realization of these aims has barely been started' (ibid: 6).

Mann's observation of the Guelph Reformatory in the early 1960s also indicates that commitment to rehabilitation was more rhetorical than real. According to him: 'while paying earnest *lip service* to rehabilitation, owing to its traditions, personnel and size, the actual structure at Guelph Reformatory was oriented principally to three objectives, (1) security... (2) convenience and efficiency of operation, and (3) the maximizing of income from the industrial shops' (Mann 1967: 37; emphasis added). More generally, Oliver (1985: 175) has observed that, in the decade and a half following the Department of Reform's establishment in 1946, 'there was not much progress.'

None the less, while practices in the institutions overall may have changed little during the 1950s, the proposals expressed in the Department of Reform Institutions' 'Ontario Plan' were important indicators of the growing importance of the ideology of rehabilitation in corrections. The notion of rehabilitation provided officials with a resourceful rationale in advancing arguments for new institutions, programs, and policies and procedures. It also provided critics and reformers with a useful reference point in highlighting current inadequacies and problems in the prison system.

Emergent reformism and growing commitment to rehabilitation in Ontario during the 1950s was most clearly expressed in the establishment of the province's probation service. Although an amendment to the federal Criminal Code in 1921 had provided for probation supervision of adults, and the 1922 Probation Act had provided for the appointment of officers in Ontario, by the early 1950s only four areas had used these provisions (Boyd 1978; Coughlan 1963; Hogarth 1971). In 1950, there were only fourteen probation officers in Ontario (Oliver and Whittingham 1987: 245).

The initiative towards the development of probation was taken by the Department of the Attorney General in 1950. At that time, probation officer Dan Coughlan was approached by the department, and asked if he would be interested in developing and heading a probation service. Coughlan had been trained as a social worker, had served in both the British merchant marine and the Canadian navy, and had also been ordained as an Anglican priest (Oliver and Whittingham 1987: 246). His fervour in advancing the cause of probation while serving as a juvenile probation officer had been commented on in the recent report on juvenile delinquency commissioned by the attorney general (Brownell and Scott 1950). Referring to Coughlan, the report stated that he 'has given five hundred speeches in three years and has visited every school, lawyer, minister, doctor and service club in Wellington County' (ibid, quoted in Oliver and Whittingham 1987: 245).

Coughlan accepted the offer. The probation service was established in 1952. Following this, Coughlan enthusiastically continued his efforts at selling the idea of probation as director of the service. Oliver and Whittingham (1987: 245) report Coughlan's claim that over the years he spoke 'close to 6,000 times in public, all the way from groups of 4,000 strong such as the annual banquet of the Canadian bar, down to little groups of ten or eleven up in the far north.' Moreover, Coughlan ensured that his missionary zeal permeated the probation service more generally: for his twenty years as director, he retained a monopoly over appointments, and evidenced a preference for clergymen and veterans over other candidates (ibid; Outerbridge 1979). As William Outerbridge (1970: 191) – one of Coughlan's colleagues – has expressed the early spirit of the service: 'Most of us in probation developed a concept of ourselves as among the agents of enlightenment and humaneness in the field of corrections.'

The enlightened and humane nature of probation was highlighted by comparison with imprisonment. Moreover, and similarly to reformers elsewhere, proponents argued that not only did probation have the virtue of being more humane, but it was also less costly, and more effective in accomplishing rehabilitation, than imprisonment. As Oliver and Whittingham (187: 251) report in 'a typical Coughlan effort... he offered a compelling case built primarily on comparisons between Britain and Canada. The British use of probation, he reported, had achieved a 75 per cent rehabilitation rate and had allowed them to close down more than half of their prisons; by contrast, "the prognosis for eventual rehabilitation ... through incarceration is at most 40 per cent." In terms of costs, probation carried a bill per person of $50 a year, imprisonment in a penitentiary, $2,000.'

The effort to expand probation gathered political force when diverse sources – including Donald McDonald, provincial leader of the Canadian Co-operative Commonwealth Federation (a left-leaning party), Rotary Clubs, and the press – advanced similar arguments to those of the civil servants (Oliver and Whittingham 1987: 252–3). From the outset, both the popularity and scope of probation grew: where there had been about 1,500 adults on probation in 1949–50, the number had risen to about 9,980 by 1960–1 (Whittingham 1984: 208); where there had only been 14 probation officers in the province in 1950, by 1960 there were 150 (Oliver and Whittingham 1987: 245). In sum, both in prisons and in the field of corrections more generally, the 1950s saw an emergent reformism, with an emphasis on rehabilitation.

THE 1960S: THE RISE OF REHABILITATION

During the 1960s, reform activity accelerated, and facilitated the coming of age of rehabilitation in the province. As Glenn Thompson – who was involved in corrections in increasingly senior positions from 1960 until 1974 (culminating in his serving as deputy minister) – expressed it in interview, the 1960s 'almost got hyperactive in changing things.'

Within the Department of Reform Institutions, the primary facilitators of this activity were reform-minded minister Allan Grossman (1963–71), and his compliant deputy minister Leo Hackl (1965–72). This powerful duo went on a 'big rehabilitation jag.' They hired additional psychological, psychiatric, and social-work professionals, and generally sought 'to spread the treatment gospel throughout all the institutions' (interview with Don Sinclair). The department annual reports re-emphasized the principle of the 'Ontario Plan,' and were replete with descriptions of new buildings designed in a manner conducive to rehabilitation; of advances in staff training programs; and of the growing range of therapeutic, educational, and other services being provided.

Aspects of prevailing institutional conditions, and of senior officials' perceptions about what should be changed, are evident in historian Peter Oliver's biography of minister Allan Grossman. While Oliver's account adulates Grossman, he none the less skilfully portrays the reformist spirit that pervaded the upper levels of the corrections bureaucracy under Grossman's direction. For example, Oliver (1985: 184) recounts that

the Grossman regime rejected many old practices; existing practices were justified or ended. Grossman reacted angrily when he learned that an inmate in one institution had been strapped to his chair so that his hair could be cut short. 'When this came to my attention it seemed to me another example of destroying someone's self-respect. Why shouldn't a guy keep his hair or beard long? The problem was that it could be done to excess or become a matter of hygiene, so I put in the rule that hair and beard could be kept at the length they were when the inmate came in unless it was creating a hygienic problem.'

The intersection of concern with humaneness with that about reha-bilitation is also captured in Grossman's account of another reform he supported within the institutions (quoted in Oliver 1985: 184):

'Whenever I visited an institution I tried to speak with as many inmates and staff as possible. On one visit to Brampton, when I met with the student council, they said they'd like to get some deodorant.
'That's one of the things that used to hit you right on the nostrils when you went into the institutions, body odour. It was a surprise to me that they'd never had deodorant, and when I asked the officials why not, nobody could give me any reason. This was the sort of change you dare not talk about in public. Can you picture the headlines, "Government orders deodorant so inmates will smell sweeter." The most important part of rehabilitation is self-respect. I ordered deodorant to be supplied but not publicly announced.

One of the interesting features of Grossman's narrative is its sugges-tion that, while public-culture discourse may have emphasized the more therapeutic and scientific aspects of rehabilitation, within the control culture of the prisons principles of rehabilitation provided a rationale for ameliorating some of the degrading aspects of institutional life. More-over, such amelioration was not always publicly proclaimed. Later cri-tiques of rehabilitation were often to overlook such mundane but important accomplishments that the ethos facilitated, and this tendency would again be reflected in critical literature on alternatives.

In keeping with his beliefs, first, that people were sent to correc-tional institutions *as*, and not *for*, punishment; and second, that pro-motion of self-respect is a key to rehabilitation, other initiatives supported by Grossman included providing all of the institutions with mattresses, discouraging the use of corporal punishment, providing can-teens and modest pay for prisoners, enhancing medical care, and sup-plying prisoners with more information about legal (e.g., bail and legal aid) procedures and their rights. Steps were also taken in improving pay and training for custodial staff. On the broader policy front, and in addition to recruiting staff committed to rehabilitation, Grossman established a research section, worked towards improving conditions in the jails by promoting plans for a provincial takeover, and also facilitated plans for the development of a temporary-absence program for inmates. Where juvenile delinquents under the jurisdiction of the department were concerned, Grossman undertook legislative reform said to be aimed at improving both the rehabilitation and the civil rights of children (see generally Oliver 1985: Chs. 10 and 11).

Again, the impact that these reformist enterprises had on general conditions within the institutions remains open to question. Within the department, some correctional officers were resistant to change and opposed reform. Grossman and his officials also came under attack from external sources. For example, from the mid-1960s, opposition members of the legislature focused on problems with the facilities, procedures, and staffing of training schools for juvenile delinquents.[5] Where adult institutions were concerned, the book *Society behind Bars: A Sociological Scrutiny of Guelph Reformatory* by W.E. Mann (who had formerly been a chaplain at Guelph) was published in 1967. The picture it presented of the conditions that had prevailed in 1960–1, and that Mann assumed had continued, was not exactly complimentary. In 1964, conditions at the Mercer Reformatory for women became a political issue when – following a critical grand jury report – the press and opposition members drew attention to its antiquated facilities and lack of medical and other services. In 1965, following a disturbance at Millbrook, political and press attention was also focused on conditions there.

Despite such criticisms, there is little doubt that, by the end of the 1960s, the department had successfully fostered a progressive aura. According to Oliver (1985: 208), over a decade after Grossman's departure as minister in 1971, correctional staff still referred to his regime as 'the golden age of Corrections in Ontario.' Many of the reform activities coalesced with the passage of the Department of Correctional Services Act in 1968. This act took some major organizational steps, and greatly broadened the jurisdiction of the newly titled department. For example, with the local jails now having been taken over by the province, the Department of Correctional Services assumed responsibility for them. Altogether, the act replaced eighteen pieces of previous legislation, and 'provided greater scope for the rehabilitative commitment of the Department' (Ministry of Correctional Services, n.d.). With probation having continued to rapidly expand under the aegis of the attorney general's department during the 1960s, a spirit of reformist optimism prevailed.

THE 1970S AND EARLY 1980S:
THE ASCENDANCY OF COMMUNITY CORRECTIONS

The progressive aura of the department was sustained by its officials through the 1970s and into the 1980s. Early in the 1970s the agency's endeavours were threatened by outsider critiques of imprisonment, and by the department's loss of responsibility for young offenders (i.e., under sixteen years of age) when they were transferred to the Ministry of Community and Social Services. However – and as I shall discuss in some detail in chapter 9 – these threats were largely overcome through the ministry's timely acquisition of new and different responsibilities for community correctional programs, and by their superseding the discourse of rehabilitation with that of community corrections.

The agency's movement towards community corrections did not involve an explicit rejection of the objectives of rehabilitation. Rather, it initially followed from an accentuation of offenders' 'reintegration' with the community as part of their rehabilitation. In this shifting direction, the temporary-absence program, which had been provided for by the 1968 act, and the 1969 Federal Criminal Law Amendment Act, was a key component. The temporary-absence program allowed for prisoners to get out of the institutions for up to fifteen days, on the basis of educational, medical, humanitarian, or rehabilitative reasons. Temporary absences, therefore, were not initiated as an alternative to penal sanction to be used *in lieu* of imprisonment. Rather, they constituted a program to be operated from the prison in enabling offenders' transition to the community. In 1971, a community program coordinator was appointed to facilitate the program, as well as to encourage the work of community volunteers in the department.

In 1972, the ministry's potential for involvement in 'community' matters increased dramatically. Until this time, administration of probation had remained under the attorney general, and was thereby separate from that of prisons. Now, however, this responsibility was transferred to the Ministry of Correctional Services. As it had already acquired responsibility for the local jails, the ministry now assumed centralized control over corrections, vastly expanding its staff and organi-

zation and instituting a wide range of correctional operations that provided potential platforms for reform activity. Overall, the early 1970s
was an eventful period: some old jails were being closed, and modern
facilities were being established; temporary-absence programs were
being developed; staff training was intensified, and initiative encour-
aged; emphasis on volunteers' involvement in corrections was growing;
institutional and community corrections were brought together under a
single administrator. Enthusiastic correctional officials overseeing these
developments increasingly stressed the importance of 'community' and
'reintegration.'

As the 1970s progressed, community corrections gathered strength
in both the custodial and the non-custodial sectors. By the end of the
decade, on any given weekday, about 1,000 sentenced persons – approximately 20 per cent of the prisoner count in provincial prisons – could
be found 'coming and going from various Ministry of Correctional Services institutions and Community Resource Centres on different types
of Temporary Absence Programs' (McFarlane 1979: 316); the operations of the provincial parole board had expanded; a total of thirty
Community Resource Centres – a form of halfway house – were in
operation (*Annual Report* 1980: 10); the use of probation had again
grown from 9,691 admissions in 1970 (a rate of 187 per 100,000 population) to 29,775 in 1980 (a rate of 459 per 100,000); almost 10,000
offenders had been involved in community service order programs; bail
verification, victim–offender reconciliation, victim assistance, and restitution programs were in the process of being implemented (ibid); almost
3,800 volunteers were involved in the work of the ministry (ibid: 22).
The formation of a separate 'Community Programmes' division within
the ministry in 1978 had helped to formalize, and add organizational
impetus to, this remarkable growth of community corrections.

One particularly significant aspect of the development of community corrections in Ontario is the change in the state's relationship with
'community,' 'private,' or 'voluntary' agencies. At the beginning of the
decade, if such agencies – for example, the John Howard Society, the
Elizabeth Fry Society, or the Salvation Army – received any money at
all from the Department of Correctional Services, the sums involved
were relatively small, and usually took the form of grants. By the end of
the decade, however, ministry disbursements to non-state organizations
had vastly increased. Moreover, most of this money was distributed
through contracts, or in the form of fees for services in community corrections. Where, for example, in the 1976 fiscal year the amount of

money being given to community agencies by the ministry still totalled only $116,416 and took the form of ex gratia grants, just five years later the amount of money given to outside agencies by the ministry amounted to $2,384,000 – an increase of nearly 2,000 per cent – and took the form of contract payments for community corrections (Roe 1981: 55). The advancement of community corrections was accompanied by the increasing involvement of community organizations in the provision of correctional programs. In short, in Ontario, community corrections have fused with, and fuelled, practices of privatization (see Ericson, McMahon, and Evans 1987).

Community corrections continued to be at the forefront of the ministry's reformist discourse and practices during the 1980s. The ministry 'Goal Statement,' for example, listed its first principle as: wherever practical, correctional programs should be community-based.' Annual reports emphasized how, on any given day, the vast majority of offenders for which the ministry was responsible were under community correctional, rather than institutional, supervision. During the 1986 fiscal year alone, $3.5 million were spent on the 'expansion' of community programs in addition to what was already being spent on them (a sum not specified in the report) (*Annual Report* 1986: 11). In presentations to community groups such as the Elizabeth Fry Society, correctional minsters and their officials similarly emphasized the community aspects of their endeavors.

By 1987, the ministry held a total of 212 community correctional contracts with non-state agencies. Of these, 155 were non-residential. The non-residential contracts involved a wide range of programs, including alcohol awareness, bail supervision, community service order, counselling, driving while impaired, employment, family violence, fine option, native restitution, victim–offender reconciliation, and other 'miscellaneous' programs (*Annual Report* 1987: 55–7). A diverse range of organizations were contracted to service these programs. In addition to the John Howard Society, Elizabeth Fry Society, and the Salvation Army, who had long been involved in corrections, the Lions Club, the Rotary Club, native chiefs and bands, Operation Springboard, Reaching Out Inc., Community Development Enterprises, Welcome-Port Hope Optimist Club, Hiatus House Inc., Blakeney Consulting Services, Catholic Family Development Centre, Pembroke and Area Correctional Council, and numerous other agencies were put under contract. Residential contracts also involved a sometimes mesmerizing range of agencies and locations, including, for example, Magwa Gami Gamig in

Wikemikong, Harmony House in Kirkland Lake, and Bunton Lodge in Toronto (ibid: 58).

These community correctional developments in effect transformed the role of the probation service. With probationers increasingly being supervised by community agencies, the probation service was divested of its traditional concern with casework. It became a 'service administered by specialists in which the probation officer is the broker' (Hatt 1985: 313). The role of probation officers in Ontario became that of program management (Carey 1978: 5). I argue later that this managerial orientation of probation reflects a similar development in the wider ethos of the Ministry of Correctional Services. Moreover, issues of management – fiscal, administrative, and ideological – are crucial in explaining the emergence, as well as the still evolving characteristics, of community corrections in Ontario.

Again, the actual impact of these changes on the conditions experienced by prisoners, and by offenders in community programs, requires further inquiry. What is clear, however, is that, during the 1970s and into the 1980s, the discourse of outsider reformers and critics shifted in a direction similar to that of correctional authorities themselves. The purported advantages of community corrections became a primary focus. Critiques of imprisonment became linked with calls for alternative approaches. By the mid-1980s, critical attention to issues of imprisonment tended to highlight the problem of overcrowding and its consequences, with the development of alternatives being posited as a crucial part of the solution.

This theme – where overcrowding is seen as the problem and alternatives as the solution – was even taken up by correctional (i.e., prison) officers themselves. In 1983, the correctional officers' union OPSEU (Ontario Public Service Employees Union) produced a report entitled 'A Crisis Behind Bars: Ontario's Correctional System.' According to the union (OPSEU 1983: 1), 'the situation in Ontario's correctional facilities is calamitous. These institutions are grossly overcrowded, lack adequate programs for inmates and are an administrative nightmare. Life for both the inmates and correctional staff is becoming increasingly dangerous and stressful, and is now at a point of serious crisis.'

Having documented attendant problems, the union recommended that the government 'reform our criminal justice system with respect to sentencing, remands and bail restriction. Alternatives to jail, including community service and restitution programs, must be expanded' (ibid: 21).

The following year a report issued by Bob McKessock, a Liberal member of provincial parliament echoed and elaborated similar concerns. According to McKessock, overcrowding in the province's jails and detention centres was a key factor in explaining deplorable conditions in the prison system. Further, despite the Ministry of Correctional Services' public emphasis on community programming, the agency's commitment to alternatives was, he claimed, in practice, very limited. According to McKessock (1984: 1–2, 13):

> the Ministry has, to a large degree, reneged on its responsibilities. Indeed, one has only to refer to the remarks of both Ministry officials and other concerned actors to see that the Ministry of 'Correctional' Services is not as concerned with true change as with the perception of change. Nor would it be unfair to say that it has abandoned its aspirations of reducing the criminal population in its institutions, or of helping them to alter their behavior, and has settled comfortably into the role of warehousing these people. Sadly, the sign at the driveway entrance to the Barrie Jail well summarized the state of corrections in Ontario today: it reads simply, 'DEAD END'... At one time the Ministry of Correctional Services was regarded as a dynamic actor in the field of corrections and alternatives. No longer.

With respect to overcrowding, McKessock argued that keeping institutions full beyond their capacity was in superintendents' and the ministry's interests: inmates were needed to cook, clean, and otherwise meet the operational needs of the institutions. When counts were low it was difficult for superintendents to put inmates into programs as they were needed to carry out a variety of chores. In particular, 'low risk' inmates who would be most suitable for rehabilitative and community programs became the subject of a competition among the ministry's different organizational interests, with institutional needs for maintenance winning out over others.

The observations took on added poignancy in light of McKessock's (1984: 5–6) observations that

> if we were to believe the rantings of the Ministers of the Attorney General and of Correctional Services, jails and provincial correctional centres are filled with vicious, hardened and habitual criminals. No one else. Our tour of these same institutions revealed quite the opposite. In fact, while jails do detain so-called hardened inmates, they also contain a mixture of the following 'types'; innocent people, petty criminals,

mentally retarded, borderline retarded, alcoholics, the poor and desti-
tute, young offenders, first offenders, short-term offenders.

It is evident that prisons are acting as catch basins catching the
victims who fall through the cracks in the social welfare system.

In documenting the problems following from overcrowding and
related conditions – especially with respect to women, natives, young
offenders, the mentally ill, the impoverished, and other groups –
McKessock repeatedly emphasized the need for serious commitment to
alternatives. He advocated that reduction of the prison population
become a long-term priority for the ministry, that long-range policy
planning of alternatives be undertaken, and that the use of existing
alternatives be increased (ibid: 2, 3, 4). In doing so, his reform perspective accorded with that articulated by a wide range of insider and outsider reformers during the 1970s and into the 1980s.

In sum, Ontario provincial correctional discourses and policies during the postwar period initially emphasized rehabilitation, and subsequently community corrections. Meanwhile, similar shifts also occurred
in federal correctional agencies for prisoners serving two years and
longer. The Archambault (1938) and Fauteux (1956) reports paved the
way for the development of rehabilitation. Following Fauteux, a
national parole board was established in 1959. Classification and treatment programs were developed within federal prisons, including
Ontario ones.

The federal movement towards community corrections was marked
by the Ouimet Committee report of 1969. Again, this report did not
reject rehabilitation per se but 'suggested that treatment efforts for
many offenders might more profitably be pursued within a community
setting than inside correctional institutions' (Ekstedt and Griffiths 1984:
52). Later reports did reject rehabilitation, suggesting modification in
institutional practices and advocating community corrections with
involvement by the private sector (Law Reform Commission, 1975;
MacGuigan 1977; Task Force on the Creation of an Integrated Canadian Corrections Service 1977; Task Force on the Private Sector in
Criminal Justice 1977). Following such recommendations, federal prisons moderated their regimes, placing an emphasis on the responsibilities
of offenders rather than on their rehabilitation. Through policies of
'cascading,' suitable offenders transferred to less secure environments.
By 1983–4, the Correctional Service of Canada 'held contracts with 175
privately-owned, non-profit halfway houses and after-care agencies at a

cost of 10.5 million dollars' (Ministry of the Solicitor General of Canada 1985: 18).

With the ascendancy of community corrections, one of the characteristics of official and public-culture discourses on corrections is that – as within criminology – issues of imprisonment itself often become secondary. Even when imprisonment is specifically discussed, it is usually difficult to get a sense of what the overall trends are, and have been. For example, while overcrowding in some of the province's jails and detention centres was an issue in the early 1980s, and has continued to be an issue into the 1990s, it is also true that overcrowding in some of the province's jails was an issue in the 1950s. An examination of empirical trends in imprisonment facilitates the development of a clearer longitudinal picture. It will also facilitate more precise inquiry into the complex interrelationships between institutional and community corrections.

Trends in Ontario Prison Population

What trends in imprisonment were occurring alongside the discursive and policy shift from rehabilitation to community corrections in postwar Ontario? The trends are by no means self-evident from a general review of the changing ideologies and practices of correctional officials. Indeed, while annual reports on corrections in Ontario have been heavily laden with data on various aspects of imprisonment, the size of prison population and longitudinal trends have rarely been a major theme of such reports.

Nor has this lack of attention to trends in imprisonment been restricted to the public-culture presentations of ministry officials. In my interviews with those who were senior officials prior to the mid-1980s, their notable lack of knowledgeability about trends emerged. With the exception of the occurrence of crises in overcrowding, correctional officials had only a rudimentary knowledge of changes in the size of prison population. As Don Sinclair – who subsequent to his involvement in Ontario corrections became involved in justice data enterprises both provincially and federally – expressed it, in the corrections business 'deplorably little attention is paid to sheer numbers.' Dennis Conly – formerly of the federal Canadian Centre for Justice Statistics – also identified the lack of interest of correctional officials in quantitative trends. According to him, while provincial officials were 'drawn very much to the Centre [which was established in the 1970s] because it was creating something in the bureaucracy ... and there was a lot of travel, a lot of meetings,' at the same time, there was 'not very much looking at data.' The major interest, it seemed to him, was in the 'politics of the enterprise' of generating data. Calls for more information were frequently made by people, 'who you know full well haven't really looked at what was already got.' I later address more specifically how correctional officials – despite their limited knowledge – were able to make generalized statements about correctional trends in support of their political and organizational interests.

In presenting the data on imprisonment, I have chosen 1951 as a base year, since, as we have seen, Ontario's probation service effectively began in 1952. A comparison of trends in imprisonment and the major correctional alternative of probation is thereby facilitated. A methodologically pragmatic reason also underlies this choice. While the imprisonment data published by the Ministry of Correctional Services and its predecessors are of relatively good quality from the 1950s (Conly 1986: 11; Hann et al 1983: 8), those of previous decades are not. In the words of Andrew Birkenmayer – former manager of Research Services with the Ministry of Correctional Services – provincial correctional data for Ontario from the mid-1920s until the later 1940s 'make no sense.'

I have chosen 1984 as the concluding year of the statistical analysis since, by that time, community corrections more generally had been firmly established in the province. Again, a methodologically pragmatic reason also underlines this choice. The implementation of the Young Offenders Act in 1985 involved the age at which one was considered to be an adult offender being raised to eighteen from sixteen. With accompanying changes in the categorization of data by the Ministry of Correctional Services, it becomes difficult to compare accurately statistical trends with those for earlier years.

I present the data in rates per 100,000 adult population. Where Ontario adult population (i.e., those age sixteen and older) stood at 3,296,200 in 1951, it had more than doubled, to 6,926,500, in 1984. With such a substantial population growth, standardizing the data in this way provides a clearer perspective on the relative size of prison population over time.

DECREASING ADMISSIONS AND COUNTS

The major trend in imprisonment in Ontario from the 1950s to the 1980s is that of a striking decrease. Such a trend is rather different from

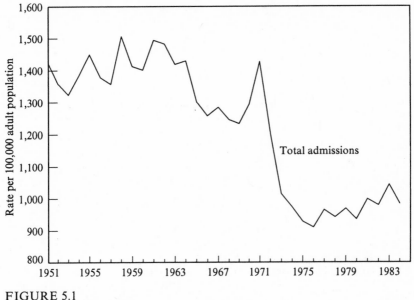

FIGURE 5.1
Ontario: total admissions to prison, 1951–1984

what critical literature on decarceration would lead us to expect. At this point, however, rather than further engaging assertions of the decarceration literature, I chart the contours of the decarceration that has occurred in Ontario.

Where total admissions (i.e., sentenced and non-sentenced) to Ontario federal and provincial prisons are concerned, there were 1,422 per 100,000 adult population in 1951. In 1984, the equivalent figure was 984, which represents a reduction of 31 per cent for these years (see figure 5.1).

Admissions data are only part of the picture of trends in imprisonment. The situation of counts – that is, the prison population on a given day – must also be considered. For, it could be the case that, although admissions were decreasing, the length of stay of those going to prison was increasing. Such a scenario could result in a growth in counts simultaneous with a decrease in admissions.

In Ontario, however, the postwar period also saw a substantial decline in the prisoner counts taken once yearly. In 1951, the count stood at 168 prisoners per 100,000 adult population. In 1984, the equiv-

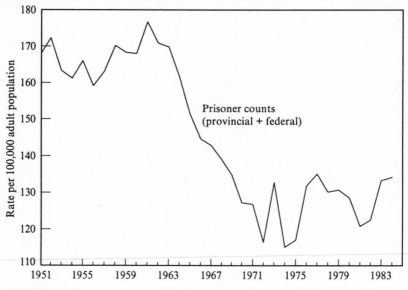

FIGURE 5.2
Ontario: total prisoner counts (provincial plus federal), 1951–1984

alent figure stood at 134. This represents a 20 per cent decrease in the probability of an Ontarian being in prison when these two years are compared (see figure 5.2).

Several important analytical observations can be made on the basis of these data. First, it can be seen that the greater part of these decreases in both admissions and counts occurred in the 1960s and early 1970s. After this period, prison population was relatively stable, albeit far lower than that of the 1950s. It appears, therefore, that decarceration in Ontario occurred primarily during the heyday of rehabilitation. The advent of community-correctional discourses and policies in the 1970s marked the culmination, rather than the initiation, of decarceration. I argue later that, although this phenomenon initially appears paradoxical, it signposts the underlying rationales for correctional officials' support for community corrections.

Second, these aggregate admissions and count data provide some clues about the major areas of decarceration within the prison population. The fact that the percentage decrease in admissions is greater than that in counts suggests that, while there were fewer admissions over time, those who were admitted were experiencing longer periods of imprisonment. This proposition is supported by data that separate

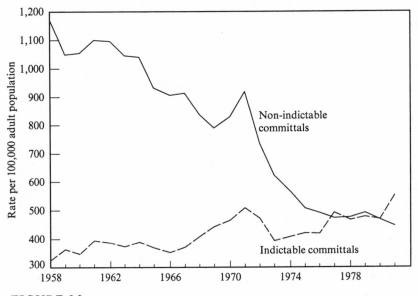

FIGURE 5.3
Ontario: committals to prison for non-indictable and indictable offences,
1958–1981

admissions into those for the more serious indictable and those for less serious non-indictable offences (see figure 5.3). As figure 5.3 reveals, admissions to prison for indictable offences increased during the postwar period. However, admissions for non-indictable offences were far more numerous at the outset, and subsequently declined. In short, the overall decrease in admissions to prison is explained by that in non-indictable committals, which would normally be associated with shorter periods of imprisonment.

The proposition that decarceration has been concentrated among those spending short periods in prison is further supported by more detailed examination of trends in prisoner counts. Specifically, when the count data are broken down into their federal and provincial components, it can be seen that the trends in each are by no means synonymous (see figure 5.4). The counts of federal prisoners (serving two years and more) evidence stability and some increase. However, counts of provincial prisoners (serving under two years) both were more numerous and experienced decrease. The overall decrease in prisoner counts, therefore, is explained by that in the provincial, or shorter-term, sector of the prison population.

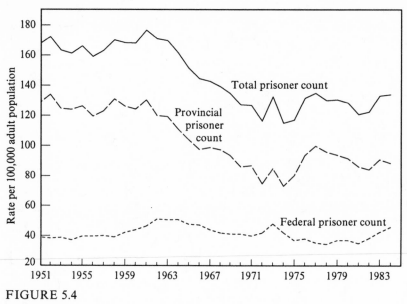

FIGURE 5.4
Ontario: prisoner counts, provincial and federal, 1951–1984

Taken together, these data reveal that Ontario decarceration occurred through a decrease in provincial-sector committals for non-indictable offences. It appears, therefore, that the contrasting trends observed for the federal and provincial prison populations may have also applied *within* the provincial population itself. That is, overall decarceration may have derived from that in the very shortest terms of imprisonment. An examination of the subgroup of sentenced prisoners, and of trends in the lengths of sentences, supports this proposition.

DECREASES IN SHORT-TERM SENTENCES TO PRISON

Among the data published by the Ministry of Correctional Services and its predecessors are those on the lengths of sentence for admitted prisoners. Fortunately, aggregate data on sentenced admissions to Ontario federal penitentiaries are also included, which facilitates some comparative analysis of all sentence lengths. When discussing these sentencing data, I compare 1951 with 1981. Owing to a change in the ministry's data-recording procedures, the figures for 1982–4 are somewhat inflated. The extent of this inflation cannot be specified. However, it is generally likely

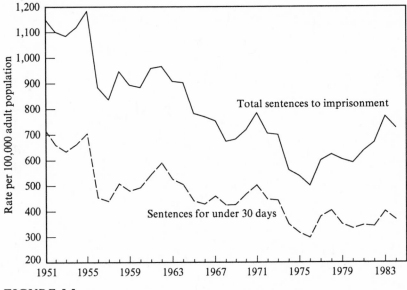

FIGURE 5.5
Ontario: total sentences and those under thirty days, 1951–1984

that the longer the sentence, the greater the amount of inflation.[6]

Turning first to data on all sentences to imprisonment, along with those on the very shortest sentences (under thirty days), several key trends become apparent (see figure 5.5). As would be expected, total sentenced admissions have generally decreased. Where there were 1,149 sentenced admissions per 100,000 adult population in 1951, there were 638 in 1981 – a comparative decrease of 56 per cent.

More surprising, perhaps, is the revelation that, throughout the period, the very shortest sentences have accounted for at least half of all sentenced admissions, and, at times, for up to two-thirds of all sentenced admissions. Moreover, during the period a substantial decrease also occurred in these short sentences. Where there were 714 sentenced admissions for under thirty days per 100,000 adult population in 1951, by 1981 such admissions had declined by 46 per cent, to 346. Clearly, much of Ontario's decarceration derived from that in the shortest terms of imprisonment.

This point is further illustrated by examining data on sentences of under six months (figure 5.6) and by contrasting these trends with those for six months and over (figure 5.7). As figure 5.6 reveals, sentences of

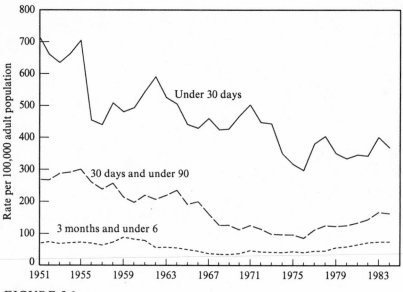

FIGURE 5.6
Ontario: length of prison sentences under six months, 1951–1984

thirty days and under ninety have also experienced substantial decarceration. By contrast, the somewhat longer sentences of three months and
under six months predominantly evidence stability.

More striking contrasts are evident when the data for six months
and over are considered. As figure 5.7 illustrates, for sentences of six to
twelve months, twelve to twenty-four months, and two years and longer
in Ontario federal penitentiaries, there is little sign of longitudinal
decrease. On the contrary, while some fluctuation has occurred, the predominant trends in these longer sentences have been of stability and
increase.

Another means of displaying the trends in sentence lengths is to
compare sentences of under ninety days, three to six months, and longer
than six months at different times, both in terms of rates per 100,000
adult population and in proportion to each other (table 5.1).

The fact that the rate of prison terms under ninety days decreased
substantially between 1951 and 1981 is further illustrated in table 5.1.
Again, the shortest sentences can be seen to be the most numerous and
decreasing. By contrast, longer sentences are far less numerous, and dis-
play tendencies of stability and increase. In proportionate terms, where,

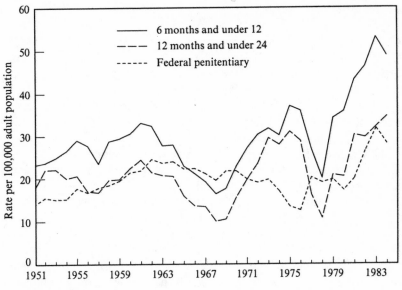

FIGURE 5.7
Ontario: length of prison sentences six months and over, 1951–1984

TABLE 5.1
Ontario: trends in sentence lengths, 1951, 1960, 1970, 1981

	Rate per 100,000 adult population			Proportionate length of sentences		
	Under 90 days	3 to 6 months	Over 6 months	Under 90 days	3 to 6 months	Over 6 months
1951	982.1	69.5	55.3	88.7	6.3	5.0
1960	689.7	82.4	74.4	81.5	9.7	8.8
1970	579.5	37.1	60.2	85.6	5.5	8.9
1981	479.5	64.8	93.3	75.2	10.2	14.6

Source: Derived from the annual reports of the Ontario Ministry of Correctional Services and its predecessors
Note: Data for 1951, 1960, and 1970 exclude indeterminate sentences.

in 1951, sentences under ninety days constituted 88.7 per cent of all prison sentences, by 1981, they had decreased to 75.2 per cent. Where, in 1951, sentences of more than six months constituted 5.0 per cent of all prison sentences, by 1981, they had increased to 14.6 per cent.

Decarceration in Ontario

During the postwar period, decarceration occurred in Ontario, as is evident in terms of both admissions and counts. In the early 1980s, the proportion of Ontarians being imprisoned was clearly lower than it had been in the 1950s.

This decarceration has not been evenly distributed across different sectors of the prison population, but has been confined to those receiving shorter sentences, of under ninety days. By contrast, imposition of longer sentences has tended to remain stable or to increase. The large volume of shorter sentences, and the scale of their decrease, has yielded the aggregate decrease in imprisonment.

These trends in imprisonment are remarkable as, apart from Scull's (1977) early work on decarceration, the critical literature (including that referring to Ontario) has generally emphasized the tendency of imprisonment to remain stable and increase. Overall trends in Ontario imprisonment do not evidence such an expansionist tendency. At the same time, had I chosen to follow the conventional wisdom, and to highlight expansion, selected aspects of the data are amenable to such an endeavour. For example, I could have focused on stability and growth in longer sentences, or pointed to growth in terms of absolute numbers without taking account of Ontario's population increase. Such strategies, however, would have provided a partial or misleading picture of trends in imprisonment.

Another such strategy would have been to select the period 1975–84, to have reminded the reader that this was the phase when community correctional discourses and policies became most prominent, and to have highlighted the tendency of imprisonment to remain stable or increase during this time. This strategy would provide strong support for contentions about the expansionist tendencies of both prison and alternatives. However, while such an approach has been widely accepted, it is also partial. It glosses over the fact that probation as the major community correctional disposition had been in use in Ontario long before the mid-1970s. A more complete examination of both imprisonment and community corrections therefore requires a longitudinal study from the 1950s, when probation was incepted. What is less obvious, moreover, is that a more satisfactory examination of trends in imprisonment also requires attention to the disposition of the fine, which has been less prominent throughout the period.

As documentation thus far reveals, trends in imprisonment – specifically, those in the shortest sentences – that are usually considered trivial are potentially significant. Proposals to reduce imprisonment generally through reductions in short-term sentences are often criticized because these sentences are perceived to make a minimal impression on prisoner counts. The logic is that, for example, twelve admissions for one-month sentences have the same effect on prisoner counts as just one admission for a year. In order to reduce prisoner counts, therefore, it is argued, an emphasis on the reduction of the length and imposition of longer sentences is required. While these arguments are logical, they gloss over what can be achieved through reduction in the shortest sentences in some jurisdictions. Apart from humanitarian gains that might follow the reduction of short-term imprisonment, in places where the volume of these sentences is extremely high to start off with such reductions can also have an impact on prisoner counts. Precisely this situation applied to postwar Ontario. Very short-term sentences existed on such a large scale, and experienced such a substantial decrease, that a reduction in terms of counts *did* ensue.

The questions now arising are: Why did this reduction in short-term sentences occur in postwar Ontario? Was it influenced by developments in the use of alternatives? Was it related to changes in penal reform discourses and policies? Addressing these deceptively simple questions brings us more deeply into the labyrinth of penal data, discourses, policies, and practices. In this exploration, I turn first to Ontario community corrections, and especially the most extensively used program, probation.

6

Explaining Decarceration: Trends in Probation and Community Corrections

Probation and Issues of Penal Expansion

> Is it not better to throw out the lifebuoy of probation than to allow a man or woman to sink in the jail cesspool? (Kidman 1947:86)

> ... the practice of probation remains at the heart of efforts to deploy alternatives to incarceration. (Oliver and Whittingham 1987: 225)

According to decarceration analysts, probation has not reduced imprisonment, but has brought new people into the correctional system. Given this net-widening effect of probation, critical analysts have argued that it is not more humane, economical, or effective than imprisonment. Although reformist dissatisfaction with prisons provided strong arguments in favour of probation's development, probation has failed to ameliorate the pains of imprisonment. In short, for critical analysts, probation has been justified under the false pretense of its being an alternative to imprisonment.

The net-widening argument has been advanced, in the case of Ontario, by Chan and Ericson (1981). According to them, from 1972 to 1978 the use of probation increased substantially, with some increases also occurring in imprisonment. I have already disputed Chan and Ericson's claim that more people were coming into the correctional system during that period on the grounds that their use of count data was methodologically problematic. Moreover, examination of admissions data indicated that the numbers of those coming into the system had not increased.

The longer-term trend of decarceration in Ontario reaffirms the necessity for caution in making claims that net-widening has occurred.

However, the possibility that it has occurred during the postwar period must not be dismissed. At issue, therefore, are the following questions: To what extent was the more longitudinal decrease in imprisonment in Ontario accompanied by an increase in probation? Is it possible that probation has been used in lieu of imprisonment? What changes in penal control have actually taken place with the development of probation and other community programs?

Probation and the Absence of Net-widening

The core charge of net-widening analysts against probation is that it has yielded a *quantitative* expansion of penal control: with the development and expansion of probation more people are brought into the correctional system. In evaluating this charge the best indicator is that of admissions, since admissions identify the numbers of people passing through the entrance points of the system. Here, in documenting prison admissions, I focus on total rather than sentenced admissions as time spent on remand can often be a factor affecting subsequent judicial decisions about what sentence to impose. Several studies of remand indicate that only a half or less of Canadian remandees subsequently received a prison sentence (Canadian Centre for Justice Statistics, 1986: 47; Madden 1978; Madden, Carey, and Ardron 1980; Stanley 1977). It appears, therefore, that many judges consider time on remand as 'sentence' time. Here, I also focus on data from 1961 as this is the point at which probation data became systematically available.[1]

Initial consultation of the relevant data suggests that probation may well have served as an alternative to imprisonment in Ontario (see figure 6.1). Specifically, in rates per 100,000 adult population, decreasing admissions to prison have been accompanied by increasing probation admissions. At a minimum, the basic point can be made that probation has apparently not been associated with an increase in admissions to prisons in the province. No doubt advocates of probation could use these data to support a claim that probation in Ontario has been a 'successful' alternative.

Those sceptical of such claims might argue that, although imprisonment has been reduced, the overall net may still have been widened if total admissions to prison and probation had increased. That is, the decline in imprisonment might have been numerically outpaced by the increase in probation. The way to explore this possibility is to add prison and probation admissions.

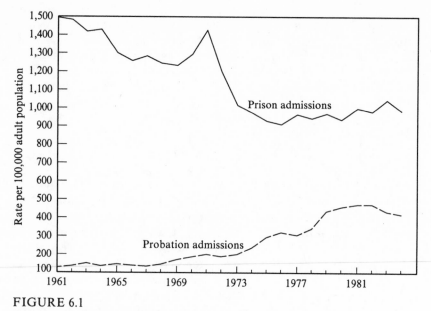

FIGURE 6.1
Ontario: admissions to prison and probation, 1961–1984

When prison and probation admissions are summed, the proposition that the system's overall intake increased appears to have little validity (see figure 6.2). In terms or rates per 100,000 where there was a total of 1,622 prison plus probation admissions in 1961, in 1984 the rate was a bit lower, at 1,402. There is no indication that the growth of probation has expanded intake into the correctional system.[2] Rather, the trend is one of stability and occasional decrease.

In light of these findings, and in contrast to the more usual emphasis on net-widening, the question of whether there are other indications that probation in Ontario has not been associated with net-widening and the expansion of penal control can be raised. Several sources of information further suggest that the uses and enforcement of probation have been reductionist rather than expansionist.

First, there is evidence that at least some judges do view probation as an alternative to be used instead of incarceration. For example, a study by Jackson (1982: 17) of judicial attitudes to community sentencing options in Ontario revealed that, when judges were questioned as to what sentence they would have considered if the option of probation was unavailable, 'jail ... was the most frequently listed sentence of

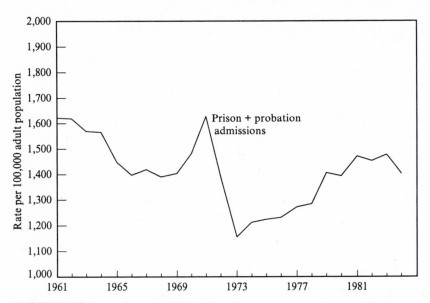

FIGURE 6.2
Ontario: prison plus probation admissions, 1961–1984

those who responded.' Presumably, judges expressing this view might actually use probation instead of prison in some cases.

Second, a historical study by Whittingham of a sample of Ontario probationers, indicates that, during the 1950s, 24 per cent of terms were for less than one year, and 69 per cent, for one to two years. Whittingham (1984: 10) compares these data with those collected in 1977 and presented by Renner (1978) identifying 59 per cent of probation sentences as being for less than one year, and 38 per cent for one to two years. It appears, therefore, that the average length of probation sentences decreased between these years. That is, the growth of probation has been concentrated in shorter, rather than longer, probation terms.

Third – and most important, given the fragmentary nature of studies supporting the previous points – a number of sources suggest that procedures for dealing with breaches of probation have been relatively rarely used, and often do not result in incarceration. This argument is significant because, in identifying the *means* through which net-widening is said to occur, critics of community corrections frequently refer to the consequences of violating the conditions of programs. Specifically, it is pointed out that correctional programs often entail conditions of residence, abstinence from alcohol, and so forth. If offenders violate these conditions – through behaviour that does not necessarily constitute criminal activity in itself – they may be doubly penalized by being punished not only for the original offence, but also for breaching or violating conditions.

This type of argument is advanced by Boyd (1978) in his examination of probation in Canada. Boyd's point of departure is the 'substantial power' wielded by probation officers, particularly with respect to potential breaches of conditions. He elaborates the legal context of breaches, noting that they can lead to charges under the summary offence of 'failure to comply.' Ensuing penalties include fines of up to $500 and/or six months of imprisonment, in addition to sentencing for the original offence (ibid: 355). Boyd finds it 'especially troubling' that breaches potentially cover a wide range of non-criminal behaviour. Additional punishment might be imposed without the commission of another offence (ibid: 356). For Boyd, 'probation can be well understood as something of a totalitarian regime' (ibid: 372).

Although the *threats* associated with probation officers' exercise of power are substantial (a point to which I shall return below), they are not often carried out in practice. Indeed, Boyd himself acknowledges that failure-to-comply charges are proceeded with in only 3.9 per cent of all cases. Moreover, only a very small proportion are associated with a penalty being imposed for the original offence: 'sentencing on the original offence takes place in less than 0.3 per cent of all cases' (Boyd 1978: 377). How much, one wonders, can such a low rate of sentencing for original offences increase prison population, particularly if probation has been used as an alternative to imprisonment in some cases? While the probation disposition clearly embodies the potential for the creation of wider and denser nets through the revocation process, substantial quantitative indicators that this has occurred are lacking.

Whittingham's study is also pertinent. He reports that 'considerably higher levels of reporting and charging of probation violations were also observed in the 1950s' than appeared to be the case subsequently (Whittingham 1984: 11). He suggests that this 'marked lack of probationer's success in this earlier period may in part be attributable to more stringent controls being then employed on these individuals by the likely self-conscious fledgling service' (ibid: 13). Whether or not this is the reason, the longitudinal decline in the follow-up of probation violations is difficult to reconcile with critical arguments about the perpetual expansion of penal control.

Reluctance to enforce probation conditions, and to respond to violations, is also evident in a study of fifty-three cases by Jackson, Webster, and Hagan (1982). According to the authors: 'of those individuals completing probation in this study, 56 percent completed satisfactorily, with the remaining 44 percent *completing despite non-adherence to conditions or unco-operative behavior during the period*' (ibid: 273; emphasis added). For example, in five of eight cases in which the judiciary imposed specific conditions, such as receiving psychiatric treatment or obtaining particular employment, 'the conditions were not enforced. They were not adhered to by the offender, but probation was not revoked.' Similarly, in cases where general reporting conditions were not complied with, probation was still 'allowed to terminate' (ibid: 274). Probation was not completed in only six of the fifty-three cases. These non-completions were not ascribed to any failure to comply by probationers. Rather, in each of the six cases, the reason given for non-completion was 'reoffence.'

What happens in those cases where probationers are brought back to court following breaches or violation? Again, the indications are that the response is often lenient rather than harsh. Thus, Jackson (1982: 19) comments that some of the judges she interviewed 'are disturbed by the practice of placing again on probation those who have already breached.' In interview, Don Evans – who started working in probation in 1967, was involved in the development of community corrections, and became Executive Director of Community Programs in the Ministry of Correctional Services in the early 1980s – also remarked on judges' tendencies to impose probation as a penalty for violating a probation order. According to Evans: 'Judges didn't seem to take too much excitement about probation [i]f it was violated, because sometimes people would get probation for violating probation ... I don't know how often it happened, but there are enough instances to make you wonder: some people would have five probation orders.'

Taken together, the observations that probation officers have been reluctant to enforce probation conditions and formally follow up on breaches, and that members of the judiciary have also been reluctant to imposes prison sentences for breaches of probation, cast further doubt on critical assertions about probation's quantitatively widening the net.

My interpretation of this reluctance in penalizing probation violations runs contrary to the conventional wisdom of the community-corrections literature. Examination of the usual interpretation – as expressed by Evans himself – reveals some of its limitations.

Following Evans's observation that probation violators were responded to by the judiciary with the reimposition of probation, he went on to observe: 'judges obviously had no intention of this guy going to prison!' In saying this, Evans's suggestion was that neither at the original point of sentencing to probation, nor at the point of subsequent violation, did the judiciary intend to send individuals in this situation to prison. This argument obviously fits with the critical proposition that probation is not an alternative to prison, but is used for another category of offenders who would not have gone to prison in the first place. The implication, therefore, is that probation is an 'add-on' to imprisonment. This conclusion seems logical.

However, the problem that arises is that, if the other potential tendency were to be observed – that is, if it was found that judges were likely to incarcerate probation violators – this tendency would also fit with the net-widening argument. Violators not only would have endured probation, but would now also be subject to imprisonment. The question is: What actions could probation officers and judges take in circumstances of violation that would not provide support for the analysis of critics of net-widening? It seems that, whatever action they take, the argument of net-widening is upheld. For this reason, the argument seems overly functionalist and instrumentalist.

By contrast, I have argued here that low revocation rates in Ontario may be an indication that probation does not invariably yield quantitative expansion of the correctional system. This is not to suggest that low revocation rates should always be seen in this way. Rather, in light of the decrease in imprisonment, such an interpretation seems reasonable.

A series of observations, therefore, suggest that the development of probation in Ontario has not been associated with the quantitative expansion of the correctional system; some judges apparently do view probation as an alternative to imprisonment; the length of probation term and the probability of revocation have declined proportionately since the 1950s; and officials have shown reluctance both in pursuing violators and in penalizing them through imprisonment. Each of these observations gathers persuasive force in light of the overall trend whereby, as the use of probation has increased, that of imprisonment has decreased, while, at the same time, the number of people coming into the correctional system overall has remained relatively stable. It appears that probation may well have constituted an alternative to imprisonment in Ontario.

But what about community programs other than probation? Have they brought new people into the system of correctional control? In Ontario, they have not. Surprising as it may initially seem, my analysis of admissions to prison and probation included admissions to community corrections in general.

Elaboration of how Ontario corrections operate clarifies the basic point that admissions to prison and probation include those to residential, vocational, and other community programs. In Ontario, as in most jurisdictions, there are two main routes into community programs. People enter, either because they have been given a community-correctional sentence by the courts or because they have been released to community programs by the prison. One way – albeit crude – of conceptualizing these two ways of getting into community corrections is to describe those who enter directly via the courts as 'front-door' admissions, and those who enter via the prisons as 'back-door' admissions.

The situation of front-door admissions to community corrections in Ontario is quite distinctive. The expansion of programs that are accessed this way has not occurred through the legislative creation of new sentencing dispositions separate from other ones. Rather, it has occurred through the Ministry of Correctional Services' development of new programs, and through judicial specification of participation in community programs as a condition of a probation order. Community corrections accessed through the front door, therefore, are typically adjuncts to probation. One might say that – in contrast to other jurisdictions where new community correctional programs represent the construction of additional front doors – in Ontario, probation itself is the front door providing access to other community programs.

Developments in community service orders in Ontario are a good example of this wider organization of community corrections. In England and Wales, there is specific legislation authorizing community services orders as a sentencing disposition. An offender can be sentenced directly to a community service order. By contrast, in Canada, community service orders were initially developed by some judges who, during the mid-1970s, interpreted 'section 663(2)[h] of the Canadian Criminal Code which allows "other reasonable conditions" to be attached to a probation order as permitting csos [community service orders]' (Menzies 1986: 159). Once the Court of Appeal had approved this strategy, judges 'had a major new non-institutional sentencing option' (ibid: Nadin-Davis 1982: 458 et seq; Ruby 1987: 251–2). In Ontario, judicial use of the option, and the Ministry of Correctional Services' fostering of community service order programs, proceeded apace. (For a comparison of the development of community service orders in Ontario, and in England and Wales, see Menzies and Vass [1989].)

Front-door admissions to other community programs in Ontario, and in Canada more generally, have been organized in a similar way. For example, where victim–offender reconciliation is concerned, 'there is no provision in the *Criminal Code* for victim–offender reconciliation programs *per se*' (Canadian Sentencing Commission 1987: 352). A study of one such program found that it had been decided that referrals 'would be through a stipulated condition of probation' (Dittenhoffer and Ericson 1983: 316–17). Participation in restitution, 'driving while impaired,' and multifarious other community programs have also been typically organized as conditions of probation (Canadian Sentencing Commission 1987: 253; Jackson 1982: 259). The data presented on probation admissions also include front-door admissions to other community programs.

Meanwhile, back-door admission to community programs – that is, those who enter community corrections via the prison – have already been accounted for through the data that have been presented on prison admissions. Taken together, prison and probation admissions incorporate those to Ontario's wide range of community programs.

The implications of prison and probation constituting the major points of entry to Ontario community corrections are basic but crucial: given that no quantitative net-widening was evident when prison and probation admissions were summed longitudinally, it can be inferred that community-correctional programs have not been associated with net-widening in terms of the numbers coming into the system. As illustrated, in 1961 – prior to the expansion of community programs – prison plus probation admissions were at a slightly higher rate than was the case in 1984, following their development. Critical generalizations about the consequences of alternatives to prison in bringing more people into the correctional system are difficult to sustain in the case of Ontario.

Yet, while contentions about net-widening have been central to critical analyses of community corrections, other criticisms must also be considered. Most notably, community corrections have been seen as yielding stronger and different nets of penal control. These concepts raise another set of issues about community corrections. Are Ontario community-correctional nets of control different from previous ones? Are they stronger? How should the impact of community corrections on penal control be characterized?

Community Corrections and Changes in Penal Control

> Whether prisons were built in the middle of cities, out in the remote
> countryside or on deserted islands, they had clear spatial boundaries to
> mark off the normal from the deviant ... Those on the outside would
> wonder what went on behind the walls, those inside could try to imagine
> the 'outside world.' Inside/outside, guilty/innocent, freedom/captivity,
> imprisoned/released – these were all distinctions that made sense.
>
> In the new world of community corrections, these boundaries are no
> longer as simple. The way *into* an institution is not clear (it is just as
> likely to be via a post-adjudication diagnostic centre as a police car) the
> way *out* is even less clear (graduated release or partial release is just as
> likely as full freedom) nor is it clear what or where *is* the institution.
> (Cohen 1985: 57)

My analysis of *quantitative* trends in corrections in Ontario casts much
doubt on the core charge of net-widening made by critical analysts of
community corrections. By contrast, analysis of *qualitative* aspects of
Ontario community corrections reaffirms critical claims that stronger
and different nets have been developing. While advocates of alternatives
might take heart from the finding that community corrections do not
inevitably bring more people into the correctional system, the kinds of
control involved in the development of alternatives arguably give much
cause for concern. For, as is particularly clear where Ontario probationers are concerned, community corrections have been associated with a
growth in the state's mechanisms and capability in exerting control.

Turning, first, to the issues of different nets, there is little doubt that
community corrections in Ontario have signalled a substantial transformation in correctional control. In the early 1950s, Ontario corrections essentially consisted of prison and probation. The experience of
being in prison differed from that of being on probation. Put simply,
while probationers remained in wider society, prisoners were removed
from it. The typical prison was an institution in every sense of the word:
it was organizationally, architecturally, and spatially distinct and separate from other social environments.

By the mid-1980s, corrections had radically changed. This situation
is reflected, for example, in the location and appearance of some prisons. While there are still many large and separate institutions (now
rarely referred to by officials as prisons), with the development of community corrections, there are also many smaller institutions in neighbourhood locations. Moreover, many of these newer buildings are

indistinguishable from neighbouring ones. In Ontario, an ordinary-looking house on a residential street might be one of the Ministry of Correctional Services' 'community resource centres,' accommodating inmates serving sentences of under two years. Or, it might even be a federal 'community corrections centre,' which is considered to be 'a penitentiary within the meaning of the Penitentiary Act' (Correctional Service of Canada n.d.).

These spatial and architectural changes are just one aspect of what critical analysts have aptly described as the 'blurring' of boundaries involved in community corrections. This blurring is also evident in the operational uses of community correctional residences. For example, while most residents of community resource centres are sentenced inmates, any given individual might find himself or herself living in one, initially as a condition of bail, later as a sentenced inmate on a temporary-absence pass from prison, and, later again, as a condition of parole.

With this blurring of institutional and community boundaries, difficulties arise in identifying and depicting the extent of penal control to which different inmates are subject. How, for example, does one meaningfully compare the situation of a resident of a community resource centre, who is not allowed out of the house, with that of an inmate who lives in a large and antiquated prison but is released on a daily basis to work a full-time job? How does one characterize the situation of a person who is sentenced to prison – through a judicial or prison officials' recommendation – and is immediately released on temporary absence? More generally, how does one compare the situation of those sentenced to prison and transferred to community corrections with that of some probationers who might have conditions of residence, curfew, and abstinence from alcohol, as well as being prohibited from seeing certain people and going certain places? As Cohen (1985: 57) has observed, with this blurring of boundaries it is 'by no means easy to know where the prison ends and the community begins or just why any deviant is to be found at any particular point.'

However, while blurring of community and institutional boundaries is one good indication that corrections in the late twentieth century have been different from those at mid-century, this does not necessarily reveal that – in the experience of those being controlled – corrections are more severe than was previously the case. Critical analysts have tended to assume that whatever is new and different in corrections is somehow worse, or more ominous, than what went before. Qualitatively, this judgment is expressed through the concept of stronger nets. As was true for net-widening, however, the issue of net-strengthening should be explored rather than accepted as a given. At issue, therefore, is what is usually meant by the concept of 'stronger nets.' Have Ontario community corrections strengthened the net of penal control?

According to Cohen (1985: 44), stronger or denser nets have been developed, because, with community corrections, 'there is an increase in the overall intensity of intervention, with old and new deviants being subject to levels of intervention (including traditional institutionalization) which they might not have previously received.' From this definition, it is clear that the perception of community corrections as representing stronger nets is interwoven with an assumption of net-widening itself: community corrections are stronger or more intense largely because they are used for new deviants, with imprisonment continuing much as before. But, as has been documented, this scenario does not apply in Ontario during the postwar period. Given that the use of imprisonment decreased, one important component of the phenomenon of stronger nets is therefore absent.

Nevertheless, with this important qualification in mind, the modified question should still be asked: Did community corrections yield an intensification of penal control for the relatively stable proportion of Ontario's population that continued to come into the correctional system?

Answering this question is no easy matter. The wide range of community corrections that do exist in Ontario, the blurring of boundaries that they entail, and the lack of consistency in official reports on community corrections, all impede analysis. For example, it is impossible to chart longitudinally trends in the use of different community programs in a similar manner to that which has been done for imprisonment and probation. Nevertheless, reflection on the significance of community corrections, first, from the perspective of sentenced inmates, and, second, from that of probationers, suggests that their consequences in terms of stronger nets have not been uniform throughout the correctional system. In brief, while those sentenced to incarceration undoubtedly experience strong nets of control as a result of community corrections, it is by no means clear that such nets are qualitatively stronger than more traditional forms of imprisonment. By contrast, where probationers are concerned, it is far clearer that community corrections have greatly increased the potential for their being subject to increased formal intervention.

Community Corrections and Changes in Incarceration

The changing correctional situation of inmates can be illustrated
through an examination of the community-correctional program of
community resource centres, which are operated by the Ministry of Correctional Services and to which offenders serving less than two years may
be transferred. As noted, these correctional residences are often situated
in neighbourhood locations and might initially appear to be not only
spatially, but also socially, far removed from the traditional prison.
Their geographic location and the 'community' title might suggest that
these centres are indeed a community alternative to prison. Such a suggestion has often been prominent in the ministry's public-culture discourse on the centres. Nevertheless, revealing that these centres can also
be understood as comprising a modernized version of the traditional
prison does not necessarily require a deconstruction of correctional discourse, but rather a closer examination of the discourse itself. Consider,
for example, correctional minister Frank Drea's statement to members
of the Ontario legislature (Ontario *Hansard*, 30 May 1977, 2997):

> I do want to emphasize that the community resource centre, the CRC, is
> not a halfway house. It is for sentenced inmates. It is a jail. In terms of
> discipline it is under the direct control and under the direct operating
> authority of the superintendent of the institution to which it is attached.
> It may be separated physically, but it is none the less attached. The
> privileges and the responsibilities that go with a halfway house for ex-
> offenders is [*sic*] simply not present in a CRC, regardless of how flexible
> our program is in there.

That community resource centres in many ways replicate the features of more traditional prisons is reflected in their social separation
from the community, broadly defined. For example, in a study by Sone,
which was commissioned by the ministry, he (1976: iv) concluded that
'the Centres are not really trying to reintegrate the men into the community.' As Sone (ibid: i) elaborated: 'on three levels the CRCs were
making very little use of community resources. First, the men rarely
obtained passes for use of community recreational facilities. Second,
Alcoholics Anonymous and Canada Manpower were the major community agencies to which men were referred, but apart from the problems these agencies dealt with, men with other difficulties were rarely
referred to treatment agencies. Third, most CRCs chose to maintain very
low profiles in the community.'

The 'passes' alluded to by Sone are an important indicator of the centres' strict regulation of residents' opportunities for contact with the outside world. Most houses do not issues passes to inmates for the first one or two weeks. During the early 1980s, for example, in the case of the Red Lake Community Centre, there was 'an initial "settling period" where no passes are issued for 30 days' (Ontario Ministry of Correctional Services 1982: 94). When passes were issued, they were rarely for long. In Madeira House, for instance, one weekend pass is issued every 3 weeks on the authority of the parent institution' (ibid). Meanwhile, as is true of prisons, it has been difficult not only for inmates to get out of the centres, but also for their visitors to get in. For example, at Ke-Shi-la-lug, a community resource centre run by the Ontario Native Women's Association, visitors were allowed only on a once-weekly basis, with the duration of a visit being limited to two hours (ibid: 88). Again, as was true of prison, inmates could receive their visitors only in designated areas of the residence.

The issuing of both short leisure and weekend passes also reflects the coercive resources available to the centres in controlling inmates. Passes can be withheld, for example, on the basis of 'infractions' of house discipline. Potential infractions include 'late waking up,' 'not doing chores,' the 'use of alcohol,' and a late return from a previous leave (Madden and Hermann 1983). Infractions also include the omission on the part of inmates of 'not finding employment' (ibid), a situation that, in some instances, is beyond the individual's control. Meanwhile, inmates can also find that passes and other privileges are withheld on the basis of less easily identifiable infractions, based on staff evaluations of their 'attitude and behaviour.' For example, in Gerrard House, operated by the John Howard Society, 'attitude and behavior are monitored by staff daily and are the final determining factor for granting or restricting of passes and other privileges. Emphasis is placed on rewarding appropriate behavior and not on the fact that a resident avoids getting into trouble' (Ontario Ministry of Correctional Services 1982: 35).

This monitoring of inmates' behaviour and demeanour also extends to their participation in programs, which, from an outsider's perspective, might appear to be voluntary. For example, during the 1980s, at Kawartha House, run by the Salvation Army, an Alcoholics Anonymous meeting was being held once weekly, and 'all residents with an alcohol related offence *must* attend.' Similarly, at Onesimus House, which is attached to an Evangelical Fellowship, 'those with alcohol problems are *required* to attend a minimum of two A.A. [Alcoholics Anonymous] meetings a week or to become involved in a new program called Alcoholics Victorious.' The paradox of coerced volunteerism is even more apparent at La Fraternité, an 'independent' community resource centre where 'all residents who are unemployed or waiting for admission to an educational program *must* participate in La Fraternité's *Volunteer* program (Ontario Ministry of Correctional Services 1982: 67, 70, 91; emphasis added).

In sum, despite their neighbourhood location, community resource centres are mini-institutions. While they are smaller in size than traditional prisons, while they are more ordinary in appearance, and while they may be staffed by private organizations rather than by state personnel, their policies and procedures resemble those of imprisonment. In the case of these centres, the charge of critical analysts that 'many varieties of the more or less intensive and structured "alternatives" are virtually indistinguishable from the real thing' (Cohen 1985: 58) is supported.

At the same time, caution needs to be exercised in linking this charge to that of new community programs for sentenced inmates as constituting stronger or denser nets of penal control than those involved in traditional imprisonment. While residential and other community programs for sentenced inmates certainly represent strong nets of control, on what basis does one claim that these are any stronger than those which have previously been involved in imprisonment? Are, for example, the residents of community resource centres being subjected to stronger control than prisoners who spend most of their time locked in a traditional cell? While major changes have taken place in the experience of incarceration, it is not necessarily the case that it has become stronger or more pervasive than before community corrections. Much more research is needed on those who have experienced these changes in Ontario. Meanwhile, and particularly in light of decarceration in the province, it can be argued that, while forms of incarceration have changed, it is not at all clear that they have yielded wider or stronger nets of penal control.

Community Corrections and Changes in Probation

As has been documented, community corrections in Ontario – other than in the case of prisoners – have been developed primarily through transformations in the disposition of probation: community programs have typically been established as conditions of probation. Here, and in contrast to the situation for prisoners, it is far clearer that community corrections have tended to strengthen the net of penal control. They have been add-ons, not as an unintended consequence, but throughout their legislative and administrative development. In the case of Ontario front-door admissions to community corrections, therefore, several paradoxes are apparent. First, while the growth of community corrections was not associated with a widening net of correctional admissions, the new programs have been a substantive adjunct to probation as a form of penal control. Second, despite the rhetoric of alternatives used both by correctional reformers and by their critics, in practice there has been no question of, for example, community-service or victim–offender reconciliation programs per se being an alternative that could be used directly instead of imprisonment. Both before and during the community-corrections era, the correctional sentencing options open to Ontario judges have been those of prison and probation. Overall, while probation may have contributed to a reduction of imprisonment in Ontario, with the development of community corrections, probation itself has become a far more severe sanction that it was previously.

One way of illustrating the substantive changes that have occurred in probation is to consider how probation officers' roles have changed with the development of community corrections: probation officers have experienced a 'movement away from the client-centered counselling model in favour of a case-management model for probation supervision' (Ekstedt and Griffiths 1984: 82). The client-centred principles of one-to-one intervention and counselling, with probationers being individually supervised by probation officers, have given way to the case-management approach. This managerial approach 'is based on the assumption that other community agencies can contribute to the supervision of the probationer and the realization of any special conditions imposed by the court in the probation order. The primary responsibility of the probation officer is to "manage" the entire case-load with attention to the involvement of individual probationers with other agencies where appropriate' (ibid: 93–4).

This change has been possible because – in accordance with the Ontario Ministry of Correctional Services' twin priorities of community corrections and privatization – much of the work of organizing, administering, and overseeing the compliance of individual probationers with their conditions has been shifted to private-sector agencies such as the John Howard Society, the Salvation Army, and the Elizabeth Fry Society. With this formalization of the ministry's relationships with the private sector, the scope of the probation service has expanded enormously. By 1975, it was already being estimated that such privatization strategies could secure a 400 per cent workload increase, with only a 45 per cent staff increase in probation and parole (Roe 1981: 55; Daniels 1980: 1); by 1980 the community-service-order programs alone had 'more than 450 employees as well as hundreds of volunteers being directly involved in the operation of these programs' (Roe 1980: 3). Since then, private-sector participation in the exercise of probation sanctions in relation to community service orders, victim–offender reconciliation, restitution, driving while impaired, and other programs has continued to grow (see Ontario Ministry of Correctional Services, Annual Reports). While precise data on the numbers of state and non-state personnel involved in administering probation are not available, it is clear that their rate of growth has exceeded that of probationers.

In keeping with these developments, probationers have been subject to a growing range of penal controls. During the 1950s, probation involved the offender occasionally meeting with, and reporting to, his or her probation officer, and being bound by the general conditions of probation orders, as well as, no doubt, being subject to a variety of informal local controls. Today, however, many probationers, in addition to the purview and surveillance of the probation officer, and through the more specific and specialized community-correctional conditions of probation orders, encounter members of the Salvation Army and John Howard and Elizabeth Fry societies, as well as the numerous church, business, native, and other community groups and volunteers charged with penal processing. It is difficult to conceive that the growth of the Ministry of Correctional Services' community satellites has not entailed the evolution of increasingly pervasive modes of penal control.

Victim–offender reconciliation programs provide one illustration of the strengthening net of probation that has ensued from the development of community corrections. By 1986, there were thirteen victim–offender reconciliation projects in operation in Ontario. A study by Jackson (1982: 21) revealed that, when judges were questioned as to what sentence they would pass in the absence of these projects, the alternative most frequently cited was probation. As the victim–offender programs operate in conjunction with probation, the implication is that it is used by judges to strengthen that disposition. Further, Dittenhoffer and Ericson's (1983) study reports that, while three of six judges interviewed in a southern Ontario city 'felt that VORP [the victim–offender reconciliation program] was an alternative to jail, at least at certain times,' five of the six stressed the 'punitive aspect' of the program, and two judges felt that jails are not punitive enough, and that sentencing alternatives would be unnecessary if they were' (ibid: 337, 336). In short, interviews with judges support the point that, although probation and community programs are sometimes used as alternatives to prison, community programs themselves are used to intensify the severity of probation as an alternative disposition.

Dittenhoffer and Ericson's study of the operation of one of the victim-offender reconciliation projects illuminates how severe modes of punishment can lie behind benign and conciliatory public-culture presentations of community corrections. In the program studied by them, operating procedures were in marked contrast to stated goals. For example, while the program design emphasized the need for voluntary participation by both victims and offenders, the fact that it was a condition of probation for the offenders, and the assertive approach of the agency in securing victims' participation, undermined this principle. Moreover, while the program design emphasized the ideal of reconciliation rather than restitution, in the program's operation restitution came to the fore. Indeed, in the program's training manual for volunteers, 'it is explicitly stated that the word "reconciliation" is never to be used in gaining the support of the victim and that a discussion and payment of losses are given as the essential reasons for a meeting' (1983: 332). Overall, although restitution was supposed to be important only in that it facilitated reconciliation, in fact, in the forty-seven cases studied (ibid: 239), 'a significant amount of money was usually to be paid by the offender [averaging $462 per offender] (only three offenders escaped payment to victims) and the alternative of personal service was never once realized. Frequently, there was no victim/offender meeting throughout the process. Most significantly, one in five cases required the reimbursement of insurance companies.'

Ominous tendencies are also evident in the case of community service orders. They, too, increase the range and intensity of formal conditions of probation. Yet, the program has ideological appeal across the political spectrum. Within corrections, it enjoys the support of judges, correctional officials, and numerous private-sector groups who have become involved in the provision of community-service-order programs in Ontario (see Menzies 1986). Much of the appeal of community service orders derives from their perceived reparative effects. But, as Axon (1983: 7) has observed in her study of community service orders in Canada, 'what Community [Service] is, in fact, is unpaid work done by the offender in the community. Whether or not this unpaid labour constitutes reparation is another matter entirely.'

The appeal of community service orders – as with community corrections more generally – also derives from their emphasis on community. As Cohen (1983: 110) has observed, the word 'community' is not only 'rich in symbolic power, but it lacks any negative connotations.' Different, competing, and even contradictory assumptions can be brought together under the ambiguous concept of community. Leaving aside the problematic issue of how 'community' should be defined, the extent to which offenders are members of the community that benefits from their own unpaid labour is doubtful. Studies of community service orders in Ontario, and in Canada more generally, suggest that those subject to the program are often young, unemployed males, who are first-time offenders, do not belong to clubs or organizations, and have had 'poor education with few prospects of obtaining anything but "dead end" jobs' (Axon 1983: 15; see also Menzies and Vass 1989; Renner 1978). What would be of benefit to these offenders, it seems, are better opportunities to become members of the community's paid labour force, rather than being subjected to forced labour.

At the same time, one segment of the wider community has clearly benefited from, and been remunerated through, community service orders: private-sector groups have derived financial as well as ideological benefits from the development of programs. They pressured the Ministry of Correctional Services to develop community-service-order programs and to make contracts with them for operating the programs. Following from this, community service orders have done more to provide jobs for those affiliated with the John Howard Society, the Elizabeth Fry Society, the Salvation Army, and other groups, than for offenders. In the process, the incomes of these groups increased. They and their quasi–civil service staff benefited from the perception that community service orders 'helped humanize the correctional system while providing them with worthwhile jobs' (Menzies 1986: 167). In a variety of ways, and similarly to the situation of community-service-order programs elsewhere, 'in reality, the service which the offender gives is not to an abstract "community" but rather to those agencies and individuals who are willing to be involved with offenders' (Pease and McWilliams 1980: 61, quoted in Axon 1983: 14). Overall, community service orders strengthen the net of penal control not only by formally extending probation conditions, but also in expanding the range of non-state agencies becoming involved in – and financially dependent on – the exercise of control.

I later elaborate the penal accomplishments of community corrections in more detail. First, though, in order to more fully understand the decarceration that has occurred in Ontario, it is necessary to return to issues of the interrelationships of imprisonment and alternatives. We have seen that community corrections, particularly in the case of probation, have had some arguably undesirable consequences in strengthening the net of penal control. At the same time, by the mid-1980s, probation and community corrections were not associated with net-widening in terms of those coming into the correctional system. The question that arises is: Does the growth of probation actually account for the decrease in imprisonment that occurred in Ontario during the postwar period?

Probation as Explaining Decarceration: Cautionary Observations

Several analytical and empirical observations suggest a need for caution in identifying the growing use of probation as the major factor in explaining decreasing imprisonment in Ontario. First, and as Matthews (1987: 347) has pointed out, much of the critical literature on community corrections has engaged in 'mystification,' as it 'observes the simultaneous expansion of community corrections and incarceration and uses one to explain the other.' In the present context, to highlight the concomitant decrease in imprisonment and increase in probation – in the absence of other considerations – would be to reproduce rather than to transcend such mystification. The nihilistic impossibilism of much of the literature would merely be replaced by an equally unsatisfactory stance of naïve optimism.

Empirically, a major reason for caution in identifying probation as the major alternative contributing to reduction of the prison population arises from closer examination of figure 6.1. Specifically, when 1961 to 1984 is considered, it is clear that the greatest substantive decrease in imprisonment occurred during the early part of the period, while the greatest substantive increase in probation occurred during the latter part. Summing the totals of prison and probation admissions (figure 6.2) reveals that, in rates per 100,000 population, while there was an overall trend of decrease from 1961 to 1973, afterwards there was a gradual increase. Some of the implications of these observations become clearer when the relevant data for the first and last years, and for 1973 (being the lowest point reached), are tabulated (see table 6.1).

As table 6.1 reveals, although net-widening does not occur when 1984 is compared with 1961, if 1973 is taken as the base year, an

TABLE 6.1
Ontario: prison and probation admissions (rates per 100,000 adult population), 1961, 1973, 1984

	Total prison admissions	Probation admissions	Prison + probation admissions
1961	1,494	128	1,622
1973	1,015	201	1,216
1984	984	419	1,403

increase in the overall total of those coming into prison and probation can be observed. In other words, if a study was to take 1973 as its point of departure, some expansion of those coming into the correctional system would be apparent.

The implications of this are twofold. First, when 1973 is taken as the point of departure, some quantitative net-widening is evident: the imprisonment rate remained stable, while that of admissions to probation approximately doubled. There is an increase of about 15 per cent in total admissions to prison and probation when 1984 is compared with 1973.

Second, and correspondingly, the data indicate that the decrease in Ontario imprisonment between the early 1950s and the early 1980s is primarily accounted for by that which took place prior to 1973. Decarceration, therefore, took place before the greatest expansion in probation and other community correctional programs. An anomalous scenario emerges: during the 1970s in Ontario, the growing emphasis on community corrections roughly coincided with the end of decarceration, and with the development of tendencies toward quantitative net-widening.

These observations raise further questions about the interrelationships of trends in imprisonment, community corrections, and the phenomenon of net-widening. In explaining trends in imprisonment itself, however, the immediate question at issue is: If trends in probation only partly explain Ontario decarceration prior to 1973, what other factors have been relevant?

7

Explaining Decarceration: Trends in Fines and Fine Defaults

In further exploring the sources of decarceration in Ontario, one potential line of inquiry would be to examine trends in imprisonment as they relate to those in crime rates, unemployment, psychiatric hospitalization, and other factors outside the penal system. Substantial literature already exists on such interrelationships, albeit with its findings tending to be contradictory and inconsistent (see W. Young 1986).

Arguably, the deterministic approach of these studies is unappealing. They tend to see imprisonment rates as resulting from external factors that are largely beyond immediate political control (W. Young 1986). Their orientation is such as to produce overly functionalist and ahistorical analyses, with the complex dynamics and processes of social change being given inadequate attention. Here, by contrast, I prefer to focus on developments that are internal, rather than external, to the penal system. This is not to say that more structural factors are not relevant or important. Rather, my objective is to illuminate how changing penal discourses, policies, and practices actually affected the prison population, as well as how broader structural conditions both shaped and were shaped by the activities of penal agents and agencies.

This approach – of keeping other penal practices and trends as primary in explaining those in imprisonment – leads to the key contention that changes in the disposition of the fine were fundamental in yielding decarceration in Ontario. As the nature of this interrelationship between fines and imprisonment is by no means immediately apparent, the best way of documenting it is to retrace the process through which it was discovered from data on penal trends.

Methodologically, my orientation accords with that outlined by

Glaser and Strauss (1967). Although their discussion is focused on strategies for qualitative research, it is also helpful for that involving a substantial quantitative component. Glaser and Strauss advocate that analysis be 'grounded' in data, and that theory be generated from the data. In short, the idea is to avoid an orientation that starts with a theory and seeks supporting data (an orientation, it will be observed, that has come to characterize critical literature on decarceration). Rather than adopting a 'preconceived theoretical framework' (ibid: 65), the data are approached in a manner informed by previous theorizing, but also sensitive to other theoretical possibilities.

This theoretical sensitivity facilitated the emergence of the disposition of the fine as an important focus of inquiry. During the postwar period in Ontario, the sentencing disposition of the fine was used far more frequently than any other disposition. Fines numerically overwhelmed other dispositions, even when they are taken in combination. Where in 1951 fines for indictable and summary offences were used at an estimated rate of 19,754 per 100,000 adult population, the estimated rate of use of other dispositions (i.e., suspended sentences with and without probation, imprisonment, death) was only 624 per 100,000. In 1971, where fines were used at an estimated rate of 17,505 per 100,000 adult population, that of the use of other dispositions was still far lower, at 1,417 per 100,000.[1] A similar situation applies in Canada overall, as well as in Britain, West Germany, the Netherlands, and many other – if not all – Western countries (Newton 1981).

The phenomenon whereby the fine is the disposition applied in well over 90 per cent of criminal cases derives from its being used for traffic offences, and particularly from its association with petty traffic infractions where the penalty of a fine is routinely applied. However, even when the category 'traffic' is subtracted from estimates of the frequency of the imposition of fines compared to other dispositions, the total of fines is still substantially higher than that of the other sentences. Specifically, excluding the category 'traffic' yields an estimated rate of 2,922 per 100,000 adult population in 1951, and an estimated rate of 3,593 in 1971, which still far exceed the corresponding rates of 624 in 1951 and 1,417 in 1971 for other dispositions. In sum, one reason for paying attention to fines in analysis of penal trends is that, although when viewed in the aggregate they are overwhelmingly associated with minor traffic offences, even when this category is excluded they still greatly outnumber the use of other dispositions.

Anthony Bottoms (1983) is one of the few analysts who has recognized the potential theoretical and empirical significance of the fine (see also P. Young 1986, 1989; Carlen and Cook 1989). Bottoms offers the important observation that, while fines are predominantly associated with petty offences, they are also used for more serious indictable offences, and their use may therefore have some bearing on imprisonment. According to Bottoms, while the rate of imprisonment may have continued to grow in England and Wales between 1938 and 1980, its *proportionate* use as a sentence for indictable offences has declined. This result stems from the proportionate growth, not in the use of probation, but rather in that of fines.

While these considerations contributed to my sensitivity to the issue of fines, the immediate and most important reason for deciding to emphasize them in analysing Ontario trends derived from my identification of a major discrepancy between sources of data on imprisonment. Initial awareness of this revealing puzzle arose in the context of raising, and addressing, the basic question: What *court* sentencing trends – that is, sentencing decisions taken by the judiciary – account for Ontario's postwar decarceration?

Discrepancies between Court and Correctional Data on Imprisonment

The question as to what trends in sentencing to imprisonment might account for trends in Ontario's postwar prison population may initially appear spurious or trivial. Given that, in rates per 100,000 adult population, short sentences to imprisonment have decreased, while longer sentences have either remained stable or increased, it is logical to expect that court sentencing data would evidence parallel trends. Specifically, one would expect the court sentencing data to indicate that sentences for summary-conviction offences reflect a substantial decrease, while those for indictable offences reflect stability and increase. However, when the relevant data from court sources are graphed, the *opposite* trends are revealed (see figure 7.1). In rates per 100,000 adult population, court sentences to imprisonment for summary offences have greatly increased, while those following indictable conviction, although comparatively more stable, evidence some decrease.

One limitation of these court sentencing data is that they are available only until 1973. Because of disputes between federal and provincial governments, the lack of commitment to collecting such data, and difficulties in trying to automate court sentencing data, Ontario was in the remarkable position of being unable to provide comprehensive sen-

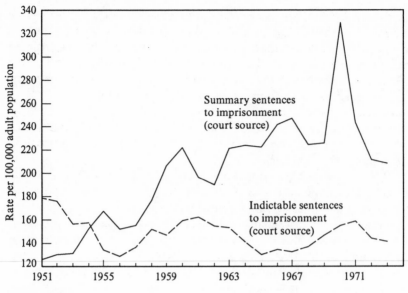

FIGURE 7.1
Ontario: court sentences to imprisonment, indictable and summary,
1951–1973

tencing data after 1973. This situation obviously impedes analysis of
sentencing trends in the latter part of the period with which we are concerned. Nevertheless, some important insights can be derived from
available data.

Fortunately, for this particular study of penal trends, the lack of
court sentencing data after 1973 is not as serious a problem as might be
expected. What I am exploring here is primarily the decarceration that
occurred, and, as has been documented, most of the trend of decrease in
imprisonment was concentrated in the period prior to the mid-1970s.
First, both total and sentenced admissions to prison declined between
1951 and 1973. Second, total prisoner counts declined during the same
period, with provincial prisoners accounting for the decline, and federal prisoner counts remaining stable and increasing somewhat. Third,
within the provincial prison population during this time, shorter sentences to imprisonment declined substantially, and longer sentences evidenced stability and increase. Therefore, while the absence of court
sentencing data in Ontario from 1974 to 1984 certainly constitutes a
serious impediment to detailed analysis of trends during that period,
and thereby the period when the trend of decrease appears to have

ended, it does not prohibit examination of the predominant trend of decrease since the 1950s.

What can be made of the discrepancy between trends in sentences to imprisonment between 1951 and 1973 as suggested by court sources compared to those indicted by correctional sources? An exact congruence of data from each of these sources would not be expected. Differing units of count, vagaries in counting, and possible variation in meanings (e.g., in defining indictable, non-indictable, and summary) all complicate comparison. However, there should be a reasonable degree of similarity in accounts from different sources concerning the same trends. The anomalies here are that the correctional data suggest that committals for non-indictable offences were greatly decreasing, but the court data suggests that sentences to imprisonment on summary conviction were greatly increasing. Also, the correctional data suggest that committals for indictable offences tended towards an increase, but the court data on sentences to imprisonment on indictable conviction suggest that they tended more towards stability and some decrease. These anomalies are more readily apparent when the differing trends for each of indictable and non-indictable categories as indicated by court and correctional sources are graphically portrayed (see figures 7.2 and 7.3).

As is clear in figures 7.2 and 7.3, the discrepancy is far greater for non-indictable than for indictable offences. Where indictable offences are concerned, several considerations suggest that the discrepancy between the correctional and court data is relatively unproblematic. First, the correctional data refer to total (i.e., including unsentenced) rather than only sentenced admissions. The discrepancy between these and the court data on imprisonment, therefore, is partly accounted for by remand admissions. Second, much of the difference also derives from that in the unit of count: while correctional data use the number of sentences as the unit of count, the court data are based on the number of persons convicted. Both of these features of data organization comparatively inflate the correctional source figures, which is consistent with the general trend of the anomaly.

Where summary-conviction prison sentences are concerned, the scale of the difference between correctional and court data is far greater. Moreover, it is difficult to find an explanation for any major discrepancies in the data from these sources, because it is less likely that remand admissions are associated with non-indictable offences than they are with indictable ones. Further, in contrast to the situation of sentencing data for indictable offences, the unit of count from the correctional and

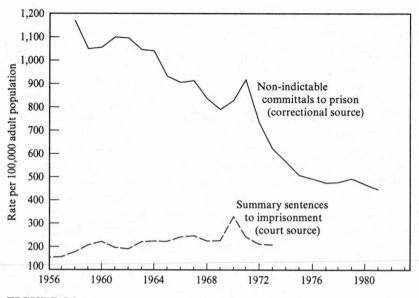

FIGURE 7.2
Ontario: non-indictable committals to prison, 1958–1981, and summary-
conviction prison sentences, 1956–1973

court sources is relatively similar: court data on sentencing for summary offences use convictions rather than persons as the unit of count,
which closely accords with the unit of counts of sentences used by correctional sources.

One possible reaction to these discrepancies between court and correctional data would be to discount the court sentencing data in the
belief that they are not reliable. However, when court and correctional
statistics with respect to probation are examined, the two different
sources are in close accord. As noted earlier, it is generally agreed that
correctional sources are among the most reliable of justice statistics, and
they certainly provide the most detailed information on the dispositions
of probation and imprisonment. Given that correctional and court data
are in accord on the probation disposition, the court statistics on
imprisonment warrant further consideration.

If it is accepted that the court data on sentencing are, in fact, reasonably reliable, then the discrepancy between court and correctional
sources concerning imprisonment for non-indictable offences merits
further inquiry. As figure 7.2 indicates, the scale of the discrepancy is
very large, but it also diminished somewhat over time: by the early

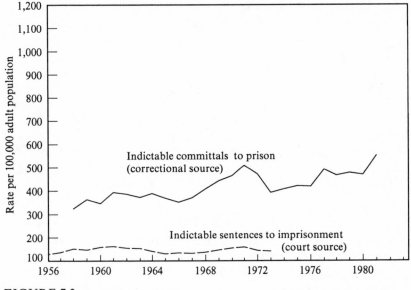

FIGURE 7.3
Ontario: indictable committals to prison, 1958–1981, and indictable-conviction prison sentences, 1956–1973

1970s, while there was still a large gap between the court and correctional source accounts, the gap was smaller than had been the case in the late 1950s. What might account for this vast, but longitudinally diminishing discrepancy? Might there have been any particular groups of convicted offenders who were not registered by the courts as subject to imprisonment, but who ultimately did go to prison and were included in the correctional data on imprisonment?

It is in response to such questions that the issue of fines becomes crucial. Arguably, the differences between the two data sources are largely accounted for by the number of fine-default committals to prison in Ontario. To explain, the categorization of those who were initially sentenced to a fine, and who were subsequently committed to prison by reason of default – that is, on the basis of a failure to pay the fine – is very different for correctional and court sources. The court data sources would categorize those initially sentenced to a fine under the classification of 'fine.' Offenders who then defaulted on the fine through failure to pay it, and who were committed to prison, would still appear under the classification of 'fine' in the court sentencing data.

By contrast, Ontario correctional data sources categorize those committed to prison because of fine default under the classification 'sentenced admission.' In other words, by not distinguishing between fine-default admissions to prison and those directly sentenced to imprisonment, correctional source identification of the number of prison sentences is higher than that of the court source.

These characteristics of data organization, taken together with the observation that the numerical differences between the sources has been both large and decreasing over time, lead to the key hypothesis: a decrease in the rate of fine-default admissions to prison in Ontario largely accounts for the overall decline in imprisonment that occurred during the postwar period. An examination of various accounts of fines and fine defaults persuasively supports this hypothesis.

Non-payment of Fines and Imprisonment

> The attention of your Commissioners has frequently been drawn to the large number of persons who are annually committed to jail for the non-payment of fines. The number shown by the Canadian Criminal Statistics [i.e., court data sources] for 1936 to have been sentenced to jail with the option of a fine was 9,593, but statistics were not available to show how many of these served sentences in jail ... Imprisonment for non-payment, when the convicted person has not the means to pay is, in fact, imprisonment for poverty. (Archambault 1938: 167–8)

The most logical way to examine the proposition that fine-default admissions represent the major portion of the discrepancy between court and correctional data on imprisonment would be to examine statistics on fine-default admissions to prison from 1951 to 1973. Unfortunately, as these basic and important data are not available from either court or correctional sources, such a procedure is not possible. Issues relating to fine-default admissions to prison, therefore, must be approached in indirect ways.

Historically, one important indication of the phenomenon of large numbers of fine-default admissions to prison in Ontario, and in Canada more generally, is repeated attention to this as an issue in reports of government commissions and other reformers. Typically, reports identify fine-default admissions as being voluminous, then identify the unjust aspects of imprisoning fine defaulters. For example, according to the Fauteux Commission (1956: 16), 'imprisonment of the offender by reason of his inability to pay a fine imposed for a breach of the criminal law is basically unsound. It is, in effect, imprisonment for debt.'

TABLE 7.1
Ontario: sentenced and fine-default admissions to prison, 1982–1985

	Sentenced admissions	Fine-default admissions	% Fine-default admissions
1982	44,867	14,474	32.3
1983	52,491	19,313	36.8
1984	50,248	17,991	35.8
1985	49,682	16,053	32.3

Source: Derived from annual reports of Ontario Ministry of Correctional Services, 1982–5

The dual observations of the apparent scale and of the unjust nature of fine-default admissions have repeatedly been followed by proposals to remedy the situation (e.g., Archambault 1938; Stewart 1954; Fauteux 1956; Ouimet 1969; Canadian Criminology and Corrections Association 1970; Law Reform Commission 1974, 1977; Canadian Sentencing Commission 1987). Yet, although the 'imposition of a "semi-automatic" prison term for fine default has been the subject of relentless criticism in the sentencing literature' (Canadian Sentencing Commission 1987: 380), until recently such reports failed to provide statistical details about those admitted to prison in this way. Therefore, while this reformist literature facilitates identification of fine-default admissions to prison as an issue, it is of limited use in attempting to chart statistical and historical trends in imprisonment for fine default.

Commencing in 1982, the annual reports of the Ontario Ministry of Correctional Services have provided some relevant information. These data reveal the substantial volume of fine-default admissions occurring in the province in the latter part of the period with which we are concerned: from 1982 to 1985 fine defaulters accounted for approximately one-third of all 'sentenced' admissions to prison in Ontario (see table 7.1).

Moreover, data available for Ontario and other Canadian provinces during the early 1980s reveal that fine-default admissions sometimes accounted for the majority of 'sentenced' prison admissions in some jurisdictions. For example, on Prince Edward Island in 1982–3, fine-default admissions accounted for 58 per cent of sentenced admissions to prison (Canadian Centre for Justice Statistics 1983, 1984). Within Ontario, in the area of Kenora, from 1 December 1981 to 30 November 1982, fine-default admissions accounted for 71 per cent of total admissions to district jail (Jolly and Seymour 1983: 10).

Data on the incarceration rates of fine defaulters in Canada during the early 1980s also reveal that these rates can vary widely across provinces. Prince Edward Island's rate of 75 per cent in 1982–3, for example, was far higher than those of Saskatchewan (26 per cent), Manitoba (20 per cent), British Columbia (18 per cent), the Northwest Territories (10 per cent), as well as than the Canadian average (37 per cent) (Canadian Centre for Justice Statistics 1983: 95).

In short, a variety of preliminary observations suggest that the proposition that fine-default admissions may account for the major portion of the discrepancy between Ontario correctional and court data sources is worth pursuing. Both historical and more recent inquiries into the penal system have pointed to problems associated with imprisonment for fine default. In the early 1980s, in Ontario, fine-default admissions to prison were standing at over 30 per cent of all sentenced prison admissions. Also during the early 1980s, much variation in incarceration for fine default was evident across Canada. It may well be the case, therefore, that substantial changes in rates of fine-default admissions to prison took place in the province of Ontario itself during the postwar period.

Liquor Offences and Fine-Default Admissions to Prison

> Drain the 'drunk tank.' (Title of policy statement by the Canadian Criminology and Corrections Association 1970)

> As recently as the 1950s, despite the great support for the idea that alcoholism is a disease, the Skid Row inebriate was still being treated as a criminal. Those that benefited from the popularization of the disease concept were alcoholics of other social classes; it was they who received the sympathy and treatment services. This anomaly helped to create pressure for changes to alleviate the lot of Skid Row alcoholics. (Drigo 1984: 7)

If fine-default admissions largely account for the discrepancy between court and correctional data sources, what factors explain the decrease in fine-default admissions to prison that appears to have occurred during the postwar period? Obviously the lack of longitudinal data specifically concerned with fine-default admissions to prison impedes attempts to address related issues.

Nevertheless, in explaining trends in fine-default admissions, it appears that data relating to the imposition and administration of fines

TABLE 7.2
Ontario: fine-default admissions for the three most highly represented charge categories, 1978–1984

	Drinking/ driving		Highway Traffic Act		Liquor		Total	
	N	(%)	N	(%)	N	(%)	N	(%)
1978–79	1,517	(9.2)	3,027	(18.5)	5,548	(33.8)	16,401	(100)
1979–80	1,373	(8.4)	2,858	(17.6)	5,534	(34.0)	16,266	(100)
1980–81	1,358	(9.0)	2,104	(13.9)	5,090	(33.7)	15,091	(100)
1981–82	1,431	(9.9)	1,927	(13.3)	5,064	(35.0)	14,474	(100)
1982–83	1,876	(9.7)	2,624	(13.6)	6,729	(34.8)	19,313	(100)
1983–84	1,740	(9.7)	2,586	(14.4)	6,404	(35.6)	17,991	(100)

Source: Ontario Ministry of Correctional Services, 'Fine Default Admissions: 1978–84,' Strategic Planning Background Paper no. 68, unpublished, n.d.: Table 2

for the offence of intoxication are of particular importance. The first reason is because convictions for the offence of intoxication are more likely than are convictions for other offences to provide candidates for fine-default admissions to prison, as is revealed, for example, through data on fine-default admissions to prison kept by the Ontario Ministry of Correctional Services from 1978 to 1984. During that period, the category 'liquor' consistently accounted for approximately a third of all fine-default admissions to prison in the province (see table 7.2).

That 'liquor' violations result in a strikingly high rate of fine-default admissions to prison is evident when a comparison is made with Highway Traffic Act violations. In 1973 (the last year in which court sentencing data were published), while there were 22,276 fines imposed for the offence of 'intoxication' under provincial statutes, there were 783,928 fines imposed for violation of provincial 'Highway Traffic' statutes (Statistics Canada, *Statistics of Criminal and Other Offences* 1973: 285). Yet, although Highway Traffic Act violations vastly exceeded those for liquor, as table 7.2 documents, generally more than twice as many people ended up in prison on the basis of fine default for liquor than did for Highway Traffic violations.

Further, data published from 1983 reveal that, not only are liquor offenders more likely to be admitted to prison for fine default, but they are also the least likely group among imprisoned fine defaulters to succeed in paying a portion of their fine once imprisoned and thereby reduce their term of imprisonment by a proportionate length (see table 7.3).

TABLE 7.3
Ontario: fine-default admissions to prison, pro-rata payment of fines, 1983–1987

	Highway Traffic Act %	Liquor %	Other provincial offences %	Municipal by-laws %	Criminal Code and federal offences %	Total % paid pro rata
1983	50.2	30.3	47.6	37.5	51.4	42.9
1984	56.2	35.0	52.3	42.1	55.4	47.5
1985	57.3	35.2	55.9	46.2	53.5	48.5
1986	59.0	36.5	58.3	42.2	53.5	48.5
1987	65.6	38.4	54.6	50.3	58.7	53.0

Source: Derived from annual reports of Ontario Ministry of Correctional Services, 1983–7

Longitudinal data on the imposition of fines following conviction for intoxication (available in the court data source Statistics of Criminal and Other Offences, Dominion Bureau of Statistics/Statistics Canada) further support the hypothesis that the discrepancy between overall increased rates of incarceration suggested by court data, and decreased rates indicated by correctional sources, arises largely from decreased rates of 'sentenced admissions' for fine defaults: both in absolute numbers and in rates per 100,000 adult population, summary convictions for intoxication leading to a fine decreased substantially between 1951 and 1973 (see figure 7.4). In 1951, there were 36,586, or a rate of 1,110 per 100,000 adult population, of such convictions and sentence. By 1973, the numbers had dropped to 22,593, or a rate of 404.

It is clear from the 1980s data that the rate of fine-default admissions following from liquor convictions is higher than that of other categories of offence, but this observation reveals little about what proportion of those fined for intoxication might be expected to default in earlier decades. Fortunately, data presented on intoxication and fine default in Toronto in 1960–1 prove useful here. According to Oki et al (1976: 26) only 37.5 per cent of those fined for drunkenness were able to pay in court. In other words, 62.5 per cent were unable to pay the fine immediately following sentence, and therefore became candidates for fine-default admissions to prison.

Following from the finding that over 60 per cent of the drunkenness offenders in 1960–1 were unable to pay their fines in court, an estimate of 50 per cent of offenders defaulting on their fines in the previous decade would seem to be a conservative one. As, in the 1950s, relevant

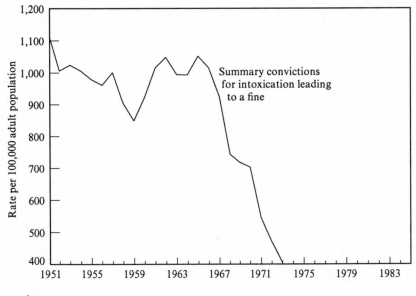

FIGURE 7.4
Ontario: summary convictions for intoxication leading to a fine, 1951–1973

legislation ordered imprisonment in default of *immediate* payment, a rough estimate of the number of fine-default admissions for intoxication can be derived (see table 7.4).

The information and estimates presented in table 7.4 lead to the startling proposition that an estimated average of 49 per cent of sentenced admissions in Ontario from 1951 to 1960 followed from an inability to pay fines in court following conviction for intoxication. In short, the imposition of fines for intoxication was a major factor in determining sentenced admissions to prison during the postwar period. This observation is also supported by juxtaposing data on the imposition of fines with data on sentenced admissions to prison (see figure 7.5). As figure 7.5 reveals, there is a striking similarity in the trend of decrease in the imposition of fines for intoxication and that of sentenced prison admissions.

Several further observations can be made of correctional and court data sources that indicate that liquor-related fine-default admissions were a major component of prison admissions during the 1950s.[2] First, that liquor-related admissions to prison were voluminous during the 1950s is supported by an examination of the subtotal of such admissions compared to the total of committals for this and all other offence categories identified by correctional data sources (see table 7.5).

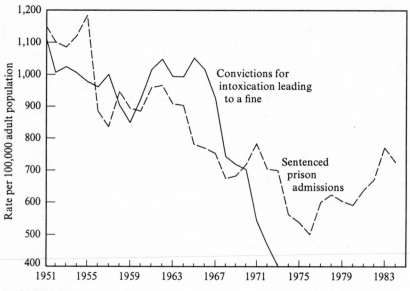

FIGURE 7.5
Ontario: intoxication leading to a fine and sentenced prison admissions, 1951–1984

TABLE 7.4[3]
Ontario: estimated fine-default admissions to prison for drunkenness, 1951–1960

	Total fines for drunkenness	Estimated inability to pay*/Fine-default admissions to prison	Total sentences to imprisonment	Drunkenness fine defaulters (%)
1951	36,586	18,293	37,879	48.3
1952	34,137	17,068	37,366	45.7
1953	35,557	17,778	37,699	47.2
1954	35,867	17,933	39,966	44.9
1955	35,649	17,824	43,130	41.3
1956	35,689	17,844	32,839	54.3
1957	38,422	19,211	32,110	59.8
1958	35,486	17,743	37,191	47.7
1959	33,987	16,993	35,783	47.5
1960	37,570	18,785	36,035	52.1

* Estimated inability to pay (immediately in court) is set at 50 per cent of total fines imposed for drunkenness.

TABLE 7.5
Ontario: intoxication and liquor committals as a proportion of total committals to prison, 1951 and 1960

	Intoxication/liquor committals	Total committals	Percentage of committals for intoxication/liquor
1951	24,193	46,858	52
1960	27,762	57,085	49

Source: Derived from annual reports of Ontario Department of Reform Institutions, 1951–60

TABLE 7.6
Ontario: intoxication and liquor offences: court sentences to imprisonment and prison committals, 1951 and 1960

	Court sentences to imprisonment	Prison committals	Estimated fine-default 'sentences' and non-sentenced admissions for liquor intoxication
1951	1,081	24,193	23,012
1960	2,434	27,762	25,328

Sources: Court sentencing data are derived from *Statistics of Criminal and Other Offences*, Dominion Bureau of Statistics (1951), p. 108, and (1960), p. 175. Prison committals data are derived from *Annual Report*, Ontario Department of Reform Institutions (1951), p. 64, and (1960), p. 49.[4]

As can be seen from table 7.5, annual reports of the correctional-agency confirm that committals for intoxication and liquor offences during the 1950s accounted for about 50 per cent of all committals to prison.

When this information is combined with that from court data sources, the more general discrepancy that has been identified with respect to sentences to imprisonment can be specified for the particular case of intoxication and liquor offences (see table 7.6).

As can be seen from table 7.6, only a small percentage of liquor admissions to prison in 1951 and 1960 arose following a direct sentence to imprisonment by the judiciary. Rather, while some liquor committals were for the purpose of remand, the vast majority of them appear to have followed from fine default.

The situation depicted here, whereby about 50 per cent of total committals to Ontario prisons in the 1950s were for intoxication and liquor offences, and apparently close to 50 per cent of 'sentenced' prison admissions were for fine defaults following from the offence of intoxication, contrasts greatly with that which applied by the early 1980s. Where, for example, in 1951, there were 24,193 committals to prison for liquor offences (52 per cent of all committals), by 1984, there were only 6,666 sentenced admissions for such offences (14 per cent of all sentenced admissions).[5]

Decreasing Fines for Intoxication and Incarceration

In Ontario, during the postwar period, decreasing fines for intoxication were most instrumental in yielding decarceration. A range of data has been presented in support of this argument. Given the complexity of the data, a summary of the major points may help to clarify them.

At the outset of this chapter, on the basis of correctional sources explored in previous chapters, it was clear that decarceration took place in Ontario during the postwar period; that this decarceration occurred prior to the mid-1970s; and that decarceration was concentrated in short-term admissions to prison, and therefore presumably in the realm of less serious offences.

In this chapter, however, through exploring the accounts of court sources with respect to imprisonment, and particularly for less serious offences, the picture of trends in imprisonment became far more complex. Specifically, compared with correctional sources, court sources revealed a far lower, and increasing, rate of imprisonment for less serious offences from the early 1950s to the early 1970s. The basis of this large, but diminishing, discrepancy, was traced to the court and correctional sources' different ways of categorizing those who were initially sentenced to a fine, failed to pay, and were subsequently imprisoned on default. As a result of the large number of cases of imprisonment for fine-default involved, and their decline during the postwar period, Ontario experienced what might otherwise appear to be a strikingly anomalous situation: from the early 1950s to the early 1970s, when the courts were actually increasing the rate at which people were being directly sentenced to prison for less serious offences, the substantial decrease in fine-default admissions to prison that was also occurring resulted in an overall trend of decarceration.

While this decrease in the rate of fine-default admissions to prison probably also applied in relation to other offences, the decrease in relation to the offence of intoxication was most important. According to annual reports of correctional sources themselves, about 50 per cent of committals to prison during the 1950s followed from liquor offences. At the same time, court sources revealed that far lower numbers of those convicted of intoxication were directly sentenced to prison. In short, the overwhelming majority of intoxication offenders going to prison during the 1950s did so, not on the basis of a direct prison sentence by the courts, but rather following their failure to pay the fines that had been imposed on them.

In the 1960s, and into the early 1970s, major changes took place in the penal processing of intoxication offenders: there was a striking decline in the imposition of fines for intoxication. Meanwhile, a similar trend of decline occurred in the overall rate of sentenced admissions to prison as documented by correctional sources. It appears, therefore, that Ontario's postwar decarceration was largely driven by changes in the penalizing of intoxication offenders.

By the early 1980s, the size and composition of Ontario's prison population differed greatly from that of the 1950s. Sentenced admissions to prison had decreased by over 30 per cent and liquor offences accounted for far fewer admissions than had previously been the case. These decreases, however, should not obscured the fact that, in the early 1980s, fine-defaults continued to constitute about one-third of Ontario's 'sentenced' admissions to prison, with liquor offences, in turn, accounting for about one-third of fine-default admissions.

While these data provide many insights on trends in Ontario prison population, they reveal little about why drunkenness offenders were being processed at such a high rate during the 1950s. Similarly, they reveal little about what this penal processing entailed, and how it changed in such a way as to result in fewer people being sent to prison following from drunkenness. In order to gain a deeper understanding of this source of decarceration in Ontario, it is necessary to take a closer look at the changing discourses, policies, and practices associated with the offence of intoxication during the postwar period.

8

Drunkenness Offenders and the Revolving Door

> Those guys [police officers] don't know what the fuck they're doin'. They arrest ya for no reason ... just for bein' dirty and smelly. I don't do anything to 'em. They pick on ya cause ya drink in public and not in a nice big fucken house like other people. I'm poor, they don't give a shit about me ... they care only about the rich bastard. (quoted in Drigo 1984: 21–2)

> Some fellows want to get back in again. Some fellows like myself get disgusted and drink. It's a rough life walking the streets. Jail is like an emergency shelter. (quoted in Giffen et al 1966: 75)

The huge decrease in liquor-offence admissions to prison, and particularly those for fine default, indicates that major changes took place in the processing of drunkenness offenders during the postwar period. In this chapter I document salient features of these changes. I also discuss developments in countering fine-default admissions to prison more generally. Overall, while changes in legislation, policies, and practices have substantially reduced the penalizing of liquor offenders, the problem of imprisonment for fine default for liquor, as well as other offences, has been a continuing one.

Drunkenness Offenders and the Penal System in the 1950s

It appears that the strikingly high rate of processing liquor offenders – to the point of their constituting over 50 per cent of those being committed to Ontario prisons by the early 1950s – marks the culmination of a general intensification of the penalizing of drunkenness offenders during the previous three decades. As Boritch has documented in the case of Toronto, following the repeal of prohibition in 1927, the police engaged in an 'aggressive enforcement of public drunkenness statutes': where there had been 1,313 arrests for drunkenness and vagrancy in 1921, this rate had increased to 2,496 per 100,000 population in 1955 (Boritch 1985: 261–2, 257). By contrast, the arrest rate for all 'public order' offences during this period remained fairly stable. Where, in 1921, drunkenness arrests had constituted 37 per cent of public-order arrests, by 1955 they had risen to 69 per cent of such arrests.[1]

Historically, poor and transient people have been particularly vulnerable to charges of public intoxication, and to affiliated charges of vagrancy. In the 1950s, in Ontario, however, the police tended to use charges of intoxication in preference to those of vagrancy, since convictions were virtually automatic, and police testimony was rarely called for (Giffen 1966: 156). In short, laws concerning the offence of public intoxication were most often used 'as a means of dealing with homeless, unattached drinkers' (ibid: 156). James Giffen has elaborated on how this policing focus on the poor and homeless has, in turn, been associated with the legal veneration of privacy (ibid: 154):

Anatole France has said: 'The law in its majestic equality forbids the rich as well as the poor to sleep under bridges, to beg in the street, to steal bread.' To this we may add: it also forbids the rich as well as the poor to be drunk in a public place. The distinction between a private and a public place is an old and honourable one in our legal tradition. The institution of privacy, sanctified in law, has given us considerable freedom from coercion when under our own roofs. However, when, in keeping with this tradition, the law has defined certain acts, such as getting too drunk to walk properly, as legitimate if done in private but illegal if done in public, it has loaded the dice against the lower classes. Social class and access to private places are closely related, particularly access to enough private places to cover most of one's social life. And when the law has made imprisonment a penalty for the offence, it has in some measure helped to increase the initial vulnerability by making it more difficult for the offender to keep a job, a residence, a family relationship, and other ties to private places.

Significantly, there was rapid growth in the number of transients, at least in Toronto and probably in other Ontario cities, in the immediate aftermath of the Second World War. At the same time, as many relevant social agencies were becoming more specialized in those groups for whom they were prepared to provide services, the period was also one in which 'facilities for transients were cut down.' In the absence of other accommodation, 'more and more men were thus forced to turn to police stations for shelter, creating new problems for the police' (Oki and Sirman 1970: 16). Where in 1944 there had been 943 homeless men provided with shelter at Toronto police stations, by 1948 this number had rapidly risen to 5,376 (ibid, App. 2, Table III). Such close contact with the police, and the problems it was said to have caused, must also have served to increase the vulnerability of transients to drunkenness arrests and penal processing.

During the 1950s the processing of drunkenness offenders was primarily oriented towards control and punishment. But a movement towards a more therapeutic approach was also getting under way. In this the association of chronic drunkenness offenders with the wider problem of 'alcoholism' was central. In 1959, the Hon. A. Kelso Roberts, the attorney general, formed an attorney general's committee on alcoholism, and gave it the task of formulating recommendations for new procedures in dealing with chronic drunkenness offenders (Bottomley, Giesbrecht, and Giffen 1976: 38). The committee identified the paucity of information on such offenders, and recommended that a major study be undertaken in order to provide a knowledge base for reform. Subsequently, the Alcohol and Drug Addiction Research Foundation of Ontario embarked on a series of studies directed by Professor Giffen (ibid).

This twinning of problems relating to public drunkenness charges and the quasi-medical problem of alcoholism must be considered problematic. As we have seen, public-intoxication charges primarily constituted an important means of dealing with problems of vagrancy. The assumption that most vagrants were alcoholics was far from justified. For example, one study of men on Toronto's Skid Row during the late 1960s found that only about one-third of them could be described as having an alcohol problem, and only a small percentage of these could be described as chronic alcoholics. About another third could be classified as moderate drinkers, yet many of these were also regularly subjected to incarceration following from charges of drunkenness (Whitney 1970: 76). In short, while reform developments from the 1950s reflected a moderation in punitive attitudes to those subject to charges of public intoxication, they also restricted the definition of the problems experienced by vagrants more generally to those of the small proportion who could be described as alcoholics. It is not surprising, therefore, that policies that were subsequently informed by this restricted definition of the social problem of drunkenness offenders would have little impact in countering their broader social, economic, and legal difficulties.

Despite this constraining emphasis on alcoholism and chronic drunkenness, the studies carried out by Giffen and his colleagues through the Alcoholism and Addiction Research Foundation provide valuable information on the treatment of drunkenness offenders more generally. In addition to studying the situation of 230 chronic drunkenness offenders at the Toronto jail, the researchers' work also included interviews with 50 first offenders, gathering data on 18,000 cases of intoxication in a Toronto court, and participant observation of Skid Row drinking groups and police arrest procedures.

The findings of the research illuminate how, at that time, severity was the key characteristic of the 'revolving door,' or the 'cycle of public intoxication, arrest, trial, incarceration and release' (Giffen 1966: 154). This severity was evident, first, in police practices in the apprehension of offenders. Here, Giffen (ibid: 156) makes a telling comparison with the methods typically adopted in similarly minor offences concerning traffic:

> It is instructive that in minor traffic offenses, where the police sampling method inevitably nets many more offenders with jobs and other responsibilities, the procedures for handling the cases differ markedly from public intoxication cases. Traffic offenders are generally summonsed to appear, allowed to avoid trial by advance payment of the fine, and even, in some communities, provided with a night court. In contrast, drunkenness offenders are usually arrested and held for trial rather than summonsed, and they are forced to appear in court during working hours, a system obviously attuned to a clientele that is predominantly jobless and without duties to families or other organizations.

Once in court, the penal process continued to operate with few concessions to adversarial procedures whereby the accused should be considered 'innocent until proven guilty, with the onus on the state to prove guilt according to fair (due process) procedures embodied in the principle of legality' (Ericson and Baranek 1982: 222). Rather, guilt was typically assumed. While due process in practice may be limited in protecting the interests of defendants (ibid), the lack of emphasis on related procedures in the former 'drunk court' is symbolic of the low status ascribed to those charged with public drunkenness by the judiciary and other criminal-justice agents. In Giffen's (1966: 157–8) words:

Drunk trials are probably the most simple, rapid and routinized of criminal proceedings usually taking less than a minute from beginning to end. The cast of actors is cut to a minimum; lawyers rarely appear for the accused (they appeared in less than one case in a thousand in G court); the prosecution is usually handled by a police officer; witnesses are almost never called; there are no newspaper reporters; and the few spectators are more likely to be idle onlookers than interested parties. Since the overwhelming majority of the accused plead guilty, the court has only to pronounce sentence and this is usually done according to a standard scale of punishment established by usage. Except for the occasional brief interchange, usually initiated by the accused who wants to put forward a plea for clemency, no argument is heard.

The imposition of the penalty of a fine was a key characteristic of these routine trials. In the Toronto court, as in Ontario more generally, a fine was applied in about 90 per cent of all cases (see Oki et al 1976: 20, 21). The banality of fining of offenders, and the connection between fines and imprisonment, are evident in the following narrative by one of Giffen's colleagues describing his first day of observation in the drunk court (quoted in Giffen and Wangenheim 1966: 13):

The first of the new cases shuffled in, bleary-eyed and disheveled. The clerk told him that he was being charged with being drunk and asked him how he pleaded – guilty or not guilty. The man murmured 'guilty,' whereupon the clerk asked him whether this was his fifth offence for drunkenness within the last 12 months. On his admission that it was, the magistrate sentenced him to $50 or one month in jail. The prisoner returned to the bullpen [to await transfer to prison], where he was heard to call out 'one month' to the men lined up by the door to the courtroom. The second defendant on the list had already been brought in and the clerk repeated the charge and the query as to how he pleaded, 'Guilty' was the answer. 'It's his first offence, Your Worship.' 'Ten dollars or 5 days young man,' said His Worship.' The young man said he could not pay his fine and was directed back to the bullpen while the third defendant entered the room. The same procedure was repeated; the man pleaded 'guilty,' admitted to his fourth offence and was sentenced to $25 or 5 days ... And so it went on.

These routine court procedures expedited the conclusion of individual cases and the overall court session. Giffen's colleague, having observed that the court session commenced at 9:20 a.m., remarks on how, when it adjourned: 'I looked at my watch and could hardly believe that it was only 10 minutes past 10 o'clóck. Only 50 minutes had passed since court had commenced. During this period we had participated in the lives and problems of 59 individuals from many walks of life: the young and the old, married and single, working and unemployed – of various nationalities – some with houses and families, others living in a room or a hostel and some with no home at all' (ibid: 17).

Why was the fine the penalty routinely applied by the judiciary in such cases? In large measure this fact is explained by the lack of alternatives open to them. Until 20 January 1961, under the Liquor Control Act, first offences for drunkenness carried the stipulated penalty of a fine of $10 to $50, with up to thirty days' imprisonment in default of immediate payment of the fine; second offences carried the stipulated penalty of a fine of $50 to $100, with one to two month's imprisonment in default of immediate payment; and third and subsequent offences carried a penalty of three to six months' imprisonment without the option of a fine (Giffen and Wangenheim 1966: 2).

In January 1961, although an amendment to the Liquor Control Act modified these penalties, the imposition of fines and/or imprisonment remained the major sentencing options: penalties were not supposed to be more than $50, regardless of the number of offences; recidivist offenders (with more than three offences) could be directly sentenced to prison for up to thirty days; and recidivists could also be sentenced to institutions providing treatment for alcoholics for thirty days, or, with their consent for ninety days (a provision extended to all drunkenness offenders in 1962). However, as few treatment facilities were available in the early 1960s, the numbers committed in the province as a whole remained low: in 1961 there were 502, in 1962 there were 480, and in 1963 the number committed dropped to 259 (Oki et al 1976: 57).

Moreover, to describe the fine as an alternative to be used in lieu of imprisonment was, in many cases, a fiction. As explained by Giffen (1966: 158–9):

A fine may in theory be an alternative to a jail sentence, but it is, in fact, only if the offender can pay. We found that some 40 per cent of the first offenders in G court were unable to pay their fines and that the proportion increased to 96 per cent among men up for their sixth or subsequent offence within the year. If the law allows the magistrate to give the accused time to pay his fine he is under an obligation to consent to this only where the accused is a good credit risk. Consequently, the privilege

is rarely granted to chronic offenders, and usually only to those first
offenders who have a job and an address. In effect then, *a fine is a jail
sentence for most chronic offenders* [emphasis added].

Indeed, it would appear that, in practice, a fine was a jail sentence
not only for most chronic offenders, but for the majority of those with
more than one offence: 69 per cent of second offenders were unable to
pay their fines in court. This proportion rose to 81 per cent for third
offenders, to 90 per cent for fourth offenders, to 91 per cent for fifth
offenders, and, as already specified, to 96 per cent for sixth and subsequent offenders (Giffen 1966: 38).

Similarly to the repetitive practices of arrest, pretrial detention,
court appearance, and sentencing, the subsequent imprisonment of
drunkenness offenders – and particularly recidivist ones – was also characterized by routine. Documenting some aspects of these routines of
incarceration further illuminates both the experiences of these offenders
and the factors mitigating the enthusiasm of correctional officials in
seeking their deinstitutionalization. In the Don Jail, for example, where
most drunkenness offenders in Toronto arrived following sentence, the
process did not involve as much of a status-degradation ceremony, or
culture shock, as is often the case with inmates in the process of admission (Garfinkel 1956; Becker 1963). Those convicted of drunkenness
experienced different admission procedures from those of other offenders. They were likely to be both greeted and admitted by other chronic drunkenness offenders who worked in the admitting section of the
prison. The tenor of the admission process was that the incoming recidivist offender had '"come home." His old quarters awaited him and his
old job will probably be available to him perhaps even held open for
him' (Giffen et al 1966: 9).

For a variety of reasons, drunkenness offenders played an important part in the jail workforce and thereby in the functioning of the
prison. As Giffen (1966: 163) has observed, the 'administration of the
prison is judged largely on how well it looks after custody, internal
order and self-maintenance.' In the case of the Don Jail, as in other
Ontario prisons, both the building and its clientele impeded the achieve-
ment of these goals. The institution was old and large. Physical conditions were bad. There was a very high turnover of inmates as the prison
population was made up of persons who were on remand, waiting for
transfer to other prisons, or serving sentences of under three months.
This situation was not conducive to getting the cleaning, maintenance,

and other tasks necessary to the smooth running of the prison done by inmates: those on remand were under no obligation to work, and many of those incarcerated for short periods had little interest in pleasing correctional officials by working hard.

In attempting to get work done within the jail, seventeen work crews were formed, each involving up to twenty-five prisoners. A guard or civilian employee in charge of each crew acted as an 'employer.' In the process of hiring new employees, the major requirement was that 'a man should be a "regular," somebody who can be depended upon to return frequently and for a respectable time.' Prisoners who 'make the grade acquire a recognized right to be re-hired each time they are admitted' (Giffen 1966: 163, 162).

Since many drunkenness offenders could be relied upon to return regularly, the jail workforce had become heavily dependent on their labour. Given that 'intervals spent on the outside average less than one month' (Giffen et al 1966: 25), and that sentences for recidivist drunkenness offenders were often thirty to forty days, both the frequency and the length of recidivist drunkenness offenders' sentences fulfilled the needs of the jail 'employers.' As the researchers observed (ibid): 'these men represent a remarkably stable and reliable work force for the jail. Paradoxically, the drinking behavior that makes them unreliable employees in the outside world, makes them valuable to the jail because they can be relied upon to return to the jail regularly.'

The extent of the jail's institutional dependence on drunkenness offenders was such that, if their numbers were reduced, labour-force problems ensued. Such problems occurred, for example, following the opening of the new clinic for treating recidivist drunkenness offenders in the spring of 1961. Apparently, for a short period prior to this, many chronic offenders were sentenced to the facility 'in order to populate it for the official opening.' For the Don Jail, this created a serious shortage of workers for over a month which the jail staff still talk about' (Giffen et al 1966: 4).

From the perspective of chronic-drunkenness offenders, willing participation in the workforce made sense because, although all prisoners were formally equal, the jobs were informally graded in terms of prestige, could increase the prisoner's mobility within the jail, and could bring material rewards. As Giffen (1966: 162–3) points out, 'while there is no official payment, the jobs bring with them differences in the opportunities to get tobacco, extra food, changes in clothing, more frequent showers, and in some cases better quarters. Moving to a better job is possible for those who perform well, demotion for those who abuse the opportunities of their jobs, and it is even possible, with time, to retire to the section of the jail reserved for the unemployables who have become too old to work.'

Not surprisingly, therefore, drunkenness offenders were valued by correctional officers. As one official commented: 'they're damn good workers and cause us no trouble at all. They do as they're told all the time. In fact most of them know enough so that you don't even have to tell them anything. They just come in and fit right in' (Giffen et al 1966: 10).

In summary, a variety of circumstances combined in producing a high rate of incarceration of drunkenness offenders in the early postwar period. Police arrests were at a particularly high rate in the 1950s. The penal processing of those charged was severe. The likelihood of pretrial detention was very high. Subsequent court appearance usually led to imprisonment, occasionally through direct sentence (in 3 per cent of cases in 1951, and in 6 per cent in 1961), but most often as a result of fine default. Finally, within the prison system, there was little incentive to resist the incarceration of recidivist offenders, for they provided a regular and dependable workforce that played an important part in the smooth functioning of the prison.

Changes in the Processing of Drunkenness Offenders

REFORM PROPOSALS AND STRATEGIES

By the mid-1970s the penal processing of drunkenness offenders had substantially changed. Where legislation is concerned, the moderation of penalties that took place in 1961 has already been specified: following from amendments to the Liquor Control Act, average fines were reduced, prison sentences for recidivists became optional rather than mandatory, failure to pay fines in court would no longer immediately result in imprisonment as 'time to pay' could be allowed, and the possibility of referring an individual for treatment had been introduced (Giffen and Wangenheim 1966: 24, 33).

The spirit of reform underlying these changes continued to be expressed through the 1960s. In 1965, drawing from the findings of its studies, the Addiction Research Foundation recommended to the provincial government 'that the problem of the chronic drunkenness offender be viewed within the context of a complete health approach to combat the problem of alcoholism throughout Ontario' (Bottomley,

Giesbrecht, and Giffen 1976: 39). In general, recommendations following from the 'health' approach centred on the need for the establishment of 'detoxication' facilities. At the time, it was believed that such facilities could be instrumental in reducing the problem by half (ibid: 40).

Following from these recommendations, several experimental detoxication centres were opened in the late 1960s. In 1968, the Task Force on Detoxication was created, with Professor Giffen as Chair. When this task force reported in 1969, although it recommended that public intoxication be retained as an offence, it also recommended that the Liquor Control Act be amended so that the police could take inebriates to detoxication centres or hospitals instead of laying charges (Bottomley, Giesbrecht, and Giffen 1976: 41–2).

In the late 1960s and early 1970s, pressures for reform intensified when journalists reported on jail suicides by those charged with drunkenness. As practices of jailing drunks 'gained notoriety,' the police and coroners' juries joined with the media in calling for reform (Bottomley, Giesbrecht, and Giffen 1976: 36). In 1970, the Ministry of Health initiated an interdepartmental committee on chronic-drunkenness offenders. The committee, in addition to the Department of Health and the Addiction Research Foundation, included participants from the departments of Justice, the Attorney General, Correctional Services, and Social and Family Services. The committee's report (issued in 1972) reiterated the proposals of the earlier task force: it was again recommended that the offence of public intoxication be retained, but that detoxication centres be developed where the police could bring inebriates on arrest. It was also proposed that halfway houses be established for those requiring longer stays of up to thirty days (ibid: 43).

By the time the interdepartmental committee's report was presented in 1972, an important legislative modification had already been undertaken by the provincial government. Following from the suggestions of both the task force and the interdepartmental committee, the Liquor Control Act was amended. While the offence of public intoxication was retained, the amendment empowered the police to take inebriates directly to any designated public hospital or detoxication centre without laying an information. That is, public inebriates were still to be arrested, but in place of the typical former procedure of detention in a police lock-up overnight and sentencing in court the next day, an arrestee could now be escorted to a detoxication centre with no further criminal procedures being initiated (Annis and Smart 1975: 19).

The Bail Reform Act, passed in 1971 and implemented in 1972, also facilitated the police in being less severe in dealing with drunkenness offenders. Prior to this act, pretrial release was allowed when bail conditions were met. As these conditions usually involved a cash deposit of $10 to $25, with the amount depending on 'the accused's record of previous drunk convictions,' the probability of recidivist drunkenness offenders so securing release prior to trial had been low (Oki et al 1976: 13). The Bail Reform Act sought to ease release conditions (see Koza and Doob 1975; Doob and Cavoukian 1976), and to so reduce the rate of pretrial custody. The act also supported a therapeutic approach to drunkenness offenders, as it gave detoxication centres the power to hold inebriates for up to twenty-four hours.

In sum, from the early 1960s a range of legislative reforms reflected less punitive attitudes to drunkenness offenders. Notably, the issue of drunkenness offenders being committed to prison for fine default was not a major emphasis on the public-culture reform discourse. Rather, the legislative easing of penal conditions derived more from highlighting the situation of 'skid row alcoholics' and their need for treatment. In short, the legislative trend towards decriminalizing public drunkenness derived from a quasi-medical[2] definition – rather than a social, economic, or legal one – of the problem of those typically charged with intoxication. This emphasis is clear in Bottomley, Giesbrecht, and Giffen's (1976: 46) summation of major developments: 'By the early 1970s Ontario had become officially committed to the disease concept of alcohol, had conducted an intensive investigation into the nature and treatment of the skid row alcoholic, had experimented with various types of treatment for public inebriates, and had won the legislative powers necessary both to create and finance the new treatment programs. It appeared the age of detoxication for chronic drunkenness offenders had arrived.'

MODERATION OF PROSECUTORIAL AND JUDICIAL PRACTICES

While the legislative changes described above are crucial to any explanation of the decrease in liquor-related fine-default admissions to Ontario prisons, they are also only part of the story. It is equally important to recognize that, in reducing the severity with which drunkenness offenders were dealt with by the criminal-justice system, the informal policies and practices of penal agents often *preceded* legislative directives. This tendency has been most fully documented in the Toronto area, although it appears to have also occurred in most areas of the province.

TABLE 8.1
Pretrial releases of persons charged with public intoxication, Toronto, selected years

Status	1961 (%)	1971 (%)	1973 (%)	1974 (%)
Released	17.9	32.9	48.9	84.8
Not released	82.1	67.1	51.1	15.2
Total	100.0	100.0	100.0	100.0
Number	22,864	17,307	17,939	18,318

Source: Reproduced from Oki et al (1976), Table 1.7

Such informal moderation of practices is evident, for example, at the formal entry point to the 'revolving door,' that is, police apprehension and arrest. In Toronto, police arrests for drunkenness experienced a 'significant negative trend for the period covering 1960 to 1974,' with most of the decrease occurring from the mid-1960s (Oki et al 1976: 10, 9). That this decreasing arrest rate derived more from changes in police practices than from a declining availability of candidates for arrests is illustrated by Bottomley, Giesbrecht, and Giffen (1976). According to the research, on each of four occasions between 1972 and 1975 when the police were directed to return to their earlier enforcement practices, there was a 'marked increase,' averaging over 108 per cent, in the volume of arrests for drunkenness (ibid: 10, 12).

However, it appears that changes in arrest patterns were not the most important factor in decreasing imprisonment of drunkenness-fine defaulters. In many areas of the province, arrests did not decline to the same extent as they did in Toronto. Of greater importance, both in Toronto and elsewhere, were the changes in practices *subsequent* to arrest. For example, and as facilitated by the implementation of the Bail Reform Act, the rate at which the police released those charged with public intoxication increased substantially. Following the act, 'release of the accused now became routine. Those offenders not taken to a detoxication centre were "most frequently given a summons for court appearance rather than being held for trial"' (Annis and Smart 1975: 14, 22).[3] Table 8.1 illustrates these moderations of police practices in the Toronto area. Of particular note is the growing tendency towards pretrial release, evident in the 1971 data, that is, prior to the implementation of the Bail Reform Act.

One consequence of the police's increasing tendency to grant pretrial release was a large increase in the volume of those failing to appear for trial. Where only 37 per cent of those so released in Toronto in 1961 failed to appear, by 1974 it was estimated that the rate had increased to 90 per cent (Annis and Smart 1975: 16). This tendency also reduced the rate of imprisonment of drunkenness offenders. Previously, chronic recidivists experienced arrest, charge, trial, and imprisonment in quick succession. Now, however, given the time it took for summonses and convictions to take effect, those charged with drunkenness had time to accumulate additional offences before being incarcerated (see ibid: 22). Decreasing imprisonment was also contributed to by offenders with accumulated charges, when they actually appeared in court, being typically convicted on the basis of only one of the charges (Oki et al 1976: 17).

In general, the courts also evidenced a strong and increasing tendency towards leniency, which often preceded and went beyond the boundaries of legislation. For example, Giffen and Wangenheim (1966: 24) state that, although, during the period of their study in 1960–1, the law itself became less punitive, the changes it entailed 'had only a small effect on the actual penalties meted out in G Court, since in practice the magistrates had already become much more lenient than the statute required.' The researchers explain (ibid: 24):

> The majority of multiple offenders in period ɪ [i.e., prior to legislative reform] were given sentences that for want of a better term we may call 'non-statutory.' All but one of the second offenders [in the sample of 2,919 offenders] in period ɪ were fined less than the $50 minimum set by the statute. Only 24 per cent of the defendants with three or more convictions were given the mandatory jail term; the others had the option of a fine. Two-thirds of the mandatory sentences were for less than the prescribed 3 months and none was for over 3 months. (Indeed, over half of the offenders with 6 or more convictions in a year were given the option of a fine and none of these fines was higher than $50.)

Another indication of this tendency of the court to be 'more lenient than the letter of the law' (Giffen and Wangenheim 1966) was in relation to suspended sentences. In Toronto's G Court, suspended sentences were given in 6.5 per cent of cases prior to the legislative reform. All of these were 'non-statutory.' Moreover, suspended sentences were given 'without any conditions attached and without any intention of bringing the offender back if he should fall from grace' (ibid: 25, 24).

This tendency towards leniency by the court, which was already evident at the beginning of the 1960s, greatly increased during the remainder of the decade. Where 91 per cent of cases in Toronto had resulted in a fine during 1960–1, by 1971 fines were imposed in only 19 per cent of cases. This striking decrease was made possible by an increased rate in the use of suspended sentences, which rose from 6 per cent of cases in 1960–1 to 73 per cent of cases in 1971. Meanwhile, where the average fine imposed was $17.01 in 1960–1, by 1971, it was lower, at $14.46. Further, where 2.1 per cent of cases had led to a direct sentence of imprisonment in 1960–1, by 1971 the percentage had decreased to 1.5 per cent. Finally, where the average length of sentence imposed had been 10.64 days in 1960–1, by 1971 the average stood at 7.05 days (Oki et al 1976: 22).

In sum, fine-default admissions to prison for intoxication decreased during the postwar period as a result of changing practices by the police and courts, as supported by legislation. Specifically, modification of police procedures in handling charges, a decrease in pretrial detention, and subsequently high rates of failure to appear, all contributed to the decreasing likelihood of drunkenness offenders being sentenced for all the offences for which they were initially apprehended. For those who did appear in court, modifications in sentencing practices reduced the severity of the penalties applied. The use of fines decreased, and that of suspended sentences increased. The amounts of fines imposed were reduced (even without taking inflation into account). As the numbers of those subject to fines, and their apprehension declined, and as jail terms ensuing from default similarly declined, default admissions to prison decreased accordingly. Overall, where those sentenced for drunkenness in Toronto accounted for 121,095 days spent in prison in 1960–1, those sentenced in 1971 accounted for only 13,380 days of incarceration.

The Lack of Net-widening in the Decarceration of Drunkenness Offenders

> As a result of current release procedures, a large number of public drunkenness arrests in Toronto could be considered to be 'diverted' from the traditional sequel stages of trial and custody, though not formally diverted to anything. (Oki et al 1976: 54)

Clearly, Ontario decarceration and the lack of net-widening – in the sense of more people coming into the correctional system – are primarily accounted for by the deinstitutionalization of drunkenness offenders. There was a huge reduction in the use of imprisonment for this group of minor offenders. They were not transferred to that major correctional disposition of probation.

Despite, and because of, this lack of correctional net-widening, it is important to question whether a form of transinstitutionalization or 'transcarceration' (see Lowman, Menzies and Palys 1987; Warren 1981) might have occurred. That is: Were drunkenness offenders merely transferred to another, and potentially more oppressive, institutional location? If such a process occurred, it could then be argued that net-widening had taken place, albeit in the form of social, rather than penal control.

The most likely place for drunkenness offenders to have been relocated is within Ontario's network of detoxication centres. As clarified earlier, the dominant discourse was as much, and more, concerned with moving drunkenness offenders into the ambit of the health-care field, as it was with moving them away from the sphere of penal control. The repeated proposals for the maintenance of public intoxication as an offence, coupled with advocacy of a system of detoxication centres to which police could bring offenders, are indications of this. It was also hoped that 'with their active system of referral to social welfare and health care agencies, detoxication centres would be successful in gradually reducing the number of drunkenness arrests' (Annis and Smart 1975: 21).

The information that is available strongly suggests that drunkenness offenders were not simply transferred to detoxication centres. Moreover, while detoxication centres were central in proposals for changing procedures dealing with drunkenness offenders, in practice the advent of these centres appears to have had little to do with the decarceration of drunkenness offenders. Penal agents' more general moderation of their procedures seems to have been far more important.

This moderation of penal practices, which resulted in the decarceration of drunkenness offenders, appears to have been well under way *prior* to the establishment of detoxication centres. This is evident, for example, in a study by Margaret Benson (1971) of admissions to a women's correctional centre in Toronto during the 1960s.

Benson documents that, in 1966, of a sample of 525 admissions to the centre, 41 per cent were associated with defaulting on a fine. Further, of these fine-default admissions,' 77 per cent were for 'liquor offences,' with 69 per cent for the specific offence of 'intoxication.' Overall, liquor offences accounted for 181, or 34 per cent, of admissions to the centre (ibid: 62–4, 27).

By contrast, in the 1969 admissions sample analysed by Benson, only 16 offenders, or 6 per cent of 271 admissions, were accounted for by liquor offenders. In turn, only 6 of this 16 were for 'intoxication.' Where, in 1966, the specific offence of intoxication had accounted for 28 per cent of admissions, by 1969 it accounted for only 2 per cent.

TABLE 8.2
Admissions to the Correctional Centre for Women in Ontario, 1961–1970
year ending 31 March

	1970	1969	1968	1967	1966	1965	1964	1963	1962	1961
Number of admissions	287	289	413	450	610	576	559	655	650	670
Liquor offences excluded	271	253	329	310	321	347	355	402	401	408
Types of offences										
Against the person	19	15	26	20	14	21	21	20	23	16
Property	169	153	186	171	146	159	154	153	116	117
Against public morals and decency	32	31	55	79	101	121	135	187	175	188
Against public order and peace	38	20	25	19	32	23	35	39	19	21
Under the Narcotic Control Act	11	28	26	13	21	20	8	–	66	64
Liquor	16	36	84	140	289	229	204	253	240	262
Traffic and other	2	6	11	8	7	3	2	3	2	2

Source: Benson (1971), Table 35

Additional data (see table 8.2) presented by Benson reveal that this decline in female admissions for intoxication and other liquor offences was part of a longer-term trend. While total admissions to the centre declined from 670 in 1961 to 287 in 1970 (a 57 per cent decrease), admissions for liquor offences experienced a proportionately greater decrease: the drop from 262 liquor-related admissions in 1961 to 16 in 1970 represented a decline of 94 per cent. This decline in liquor-offence admissions exceeded that in any other category, although substantial decreases in admissions for 'offences against public morals and decency' are also of note.

Benson's analysis (ibid: 86) also reaffirms that a substantial decrease in the incarceration of women for liquor offences had taken place before the development of a detoxication centre for women.

In June, 1968 a detoxication centre was opened for women in Metropolitan Toronto as a pilot project. Police took women who would formerly

TABLE 8.3
Disposition of male drunkenness arrests of one central Toronto police division, 1973 and 1974

Year	Taken to detox		Refused at detox or detox full		Held for various reasons	
	N	%	N	%	N	%
1973	876	10.4	5,815	68.7	1,771	20.9
1974	627	8.3	6,072	80.9	811	10.8

Source: Annis and Smart (1975), p. 22

have been arrested for intoxication in a public place to the centre and as long as they voluntarily remained there for a minimum of 8 hours, no charges were laid. The opening of this centre would seem to have had the most relevance to the decrease in Toronto's admissions to the provincial correctional centre. However, admissions to the provincial correctional centre for liquor offences had already decreased by two-thirds during the 2 year period prior to the opening of the detoxication centre. Thus the existence of the facility was not in itself the explanation for the decrease.

Meanwhile, other sources reveal that not only did changes in the processing of drunkenness offenders precede the development of detoxication centres, but, once they were established, the use of detoxication centres for offenders was quite limited. For example, in the case of one Toronto Skid Row area documented by Annis and Smart, the authors report that 'admission to a detox centre was a relatively rare event for arrestees: only 10.4% were taken to a detox in 1973 and 8.3% in 1974' (see table 8.3). The authors also report that 'early indications suggest that a similar situation holds, on a reduced scale, in many other designated regions throughout the province' (1975: 22, 23).

Detoxication centres received only a small percentage of drunkenness offenders for a variety of reasons. An inadequate number of centres were planned and developed, which resulted in an insufficient supply of bed-space. Moreover, planners had 'assumed that the great majority of inebriates would be detoxified in less than 24 hours,' but in the mid-1970s the centres had 'mean duration of stay of 3.9 days' (Annis and Smart 1975: 22, 23). This created additional demand on the already inadequate bed-space. Requirements as to 'voluntariness' on the part of the inebriate, and police dissatisfaction with the lack of custodial emphasis in detoxication centres, also appear to have limited their use for drunkenness offenders (see Drigo 1984; Torrie 1987).

Perhaps more important, however, is the fact that, although the original development of detoxication centres was primarily a response to the perceived problems of chronic drunkenness offenders, and although, during the pilot-project stage, they were used exclusively for police referrals, once detoxication centres were formally implemented their client group rapidly changed. By the mid-1970s, it was reported that 'only one-third of the beds have been allocated to police admissions with the remaining beds being assigned to self and hospital referrals' (Annis and Smart 1975: 23; see Drigo 1984: 50). As Bottomley, Giesbrecht, and Giffen (1976: 68) summed up the situation: the detoxication system 'is not serving the clientel [sic] that it was designed to handle.' As a result, both of the inadequate availability of the detoxication centres and of the use of existing centres by a client group who tend to have a relatively higher social status, relatively few drunkenness offenders have been catered to by the centres.[5]

In short, despite the quasi-medical reform discourse on matters of public drunkenness, the changes that actually took place rarely resulted in offenders being shifted to the therapeutic environment of detoxication centres, halfway houses, and the like. Rather, the ensuing situation closely accords with Scull's early portrayal of decarceration as primarily resulting in neglect. Following attempts at reform, the deinstitutionalized are most likely to be found in the streets, in Salvation Army hostels, and in other 'traditional resorts of the down and out' (Scull 1977: 153). Moreover, where Scull, as we have seen, later revised this interpretation in the case of correctional decarceration, and rather emphasized the conventional wisdom of net-widening and penal expansion, in practice, his initial interpretation is most apt in relation to the situation of drunkenness offenders in Ontario.

The lack of net-widening in the decarceration of drunkenness offenders raises important issues for wider analysis of penal and social control. As documented earlier, reforms directed at probationers have generally involved an *intensification* of penal control. By contrast, reforms directed at drunkenness offenders have generally involved some *moderation* of penal control. It is important, therefore, to recognize not only that contemporary trends in one jurisdiction may be very different to those elsewhere, but that trends for different groups of offenders within a particular jurisdiction may differ considerably.

Caution also needs to be exercised in unreflexively accepting the value-judgments and boundaries that sometimes characterize basic concepts. For example, net-widening and transcarceration are often seen as, by definition, undesirable consequences. In the case of drunkenness offenders, however, given the wider context of homelessness, some forms of transinstitutionalization might actually have been desirable, since, following reform and decarceration, the health of chronic drunkenness offenders apparently declined (Bottomley, Giesbrecht, and Giffen 1976:69). For all its undesirable features, the rapidly 'revolving' door did at least provide a regular source of accommodation, nourishment, and social contacts.

This is by no means intended to suggest that intense penal processing of drunkenness offenders should be supported. But critics of penal policies and practices must consider other ways of responding to people whose difficulties have typically been met by incarceration or neglect (for one approach of this kind, see Christie 1989). Analytically, the question is: What steps can be taken towards identifying not only the repressive aspects of existing procedures, but also ways that might be preferable from the perspective of people in need? In short, how can critical analysis be more closely integrated with progressive politics?

I will return to issues of critical analysis and preferred sociopolitical strategies in the final chapter. At this point, having sketched the salient features of changes in the processing of drunkenness offenders that took place prior to the mid-1970s, I will examine subsequent, and more explicit, attempts at reducing fine-default admissions to prison.

Developments in Countering Fine-Default Admissions to Prison

> [a] jail term in default of a fine is of course open to the criticism that it is a penalty which applies only to the poor, who cannot afford to pay the fines. (Ontario, Ministry of the Attorney General 1976: 44)

> the persistence of jailing in default of a fine as a Canadian problem is astounding. (Havemann et al 1984: 128)

What has been the situation of fine default and imprisonment in the later postwar period? Although, as we have seen, the rate of imprisonment has decreased substantially since the 1950s, with a decrease in fine-default admissions having played a large part in this, the rate of fine-default admissions continued to be high. As was illustrated in table 7.1, from 1982 to 1985, fine-default admissions still accounted for about a third of 'sentenced' admissions.

Ontario's continued high rate of imprisoning people following from fine-default for liquor and other minor offences is particularly striking in light of the Ministry of the Attorney General's commitment to countering the problem. In the mid-1970s, the ministry acknowledged the injustice of fine-default procedures when experienced by the poor. The ministry also stated that the introduction of the Provincial Offences Act would solve the problem. Specifically, according to the ministry, the act 'is intended to resolve the present anomoly [*sic*] of large numbers of people being jailed for failing to pay fines imposed for minor offences while extremely few persons are being sent to jail as punishment for even the serious provincial offences' (Ontario Ministry of the Attorney General 1978: 14). In particular, provisions of the act that were due to come into force in July 1980 sought to reduce imprisonment as a consequence of default on fines. According to the ministry (ibid: 15–17),

> the basic thrust of the Act is to keep fines from being in default and to end the automatic issuance of a warrant of committal when they are. A justice who imposes a fine may elicit and consider evidence concerning the economic circumstances of the offender. The court may direct questions to the offender to obtain this information, but, of course, the offender need not answer. The principal purpose of this direction is to prevent fines being imposed which simply must go into default because the defendant cannot pay them ... Under the Act, virtually nothing short of willful non-payment will result in incarceration ...

A later guide to the Provincial Offences Act, provided for the public by the ministry, emphasized similar themes. It is again acknowledged that 'previously, large numbers of people went to jail because they failed to pay fines which were imposed for minor offences, outnumbering the few individuals who were sentenced to imprisonment for even the most serious provincial offences.' It is stated that the act 'is intended to keep people from going to jail solely because of a genuine inability to pay a fine.' It is further stated that, following from this reformist legislation, 'imprisonment will be ordered only for the most obstinate and willful defaulter' (Ontario, Ministry of the Attorney General 1987: 15, 16). Clearly, according to the ministry's stated objectives, those who continued to be incarcerated for fine default in the 1980s would not be there because of any injustice on the part of the penal system. Rather, as the ministry had described them, 'these relics of a by-gone age,' that is, the 'debtor's prison and the use of constables to collect money debts' (ibid 1976: 47), were to be dispensed with under the act. Jail in default of a fine would be virtually eliminated (ibid), and the remaining few for whom it would be used were the 'obstinate' and 'willful' defaulters, or the 'scofflaws' of the system (ibid 1978: 15). From the ministry's description it appeared that imprisonment on default of a fine would receive minimal use and would be reserved for those whom penal authorities believed definitely deserved it.'

It is very difficult to trace the precise consequences of the legislation. In the more recent, as in the earlier period, little information is published on processes of fines, fine default, and imprisonment. For example, the amount of fines imposed and collected for criminal offences in Ontario in any given year, never mind longitudinally, remains a mystery. The proportion of fine defaulters incarcerated of the total fine defaulters, and the aggregate social characteristics of those selected, also remain unknown, at least in the public realm.

Nevertheless, despite this dearth of information, and despite the ministry's assurances that imprisonment for non-payment of fines would be all but eliminated, the correctional data on prison admissions in the late 1980s clearly reveal that fine-default admissions continued to be high. Moreover, despite the ministry's assurances that special vigilance should be exercised in the case of poor people charged with minor offences, there are indications that the poor and powerless continued to disproportionately experience imprisonment on fine default during the 1980s. This tendency can be exemplified through an examination of the situation of native fine defaulters in the area of Kenora in Ontario.

Native Fine Defaulters in Kenora

> The exceptional resort to imprisonment, which is the most severe sanction of the criminal justice system, for minor liquor offences such as public intoxication and its almost exclusive impact on the native minority [in the District of Kenora] raise nagging questions about the use of police discretion, the sentencing practices of the Provincial Offences Court and the wisdom of making public intoxication an offence. (Jolly and Seymour 1983: ix–x)

Jolly and Seymour (1983) have presented a detailed and insightful study of the penal processing of provincial offences in the Kenora area. Their study includes an examination of people in the Kenora Jail in 1981 following from such offences. The fact that Jolly and Seymour's report to the Ontario Native Council on Justice is titled *Anicinabe Debtors' Prison* reflects the centrality of imprisonment for fine default as an issue in Kenora.

Where total admissions to Kenora Jail in the 1981–2 fiscal year were concerned, Jolly and Seymour found that, while native people accounted for about 44 per cent of total population in the District of Kenora, they accounted for 78 per cent of total male admissions, and for 97 per cent of female admissions, to the jail. They document how this disproportionate incarceration of natives in Kenora is accomplished primarily through the high rate of fine-default admissions to the jail: 119 people, representing 71 percent of total admissions to the jail, were for fine default. In turn, 71 per cent of these fine-default admissions were for defaulting on fines for provincial liquor offences.

This intersection of intoxication, fine default, and incarceration in Kenora during the early 1980s was in accordance with longer-term penal trends in the area. During the postwar period more generally, natives in Kenora have experienced intense penal processing in connection with intoxication by the police, the courts, and correctional authorities. According to Torrie (1987: chapter 4.1), from about the mid-1940s, 'Indian drunks became defined as the central issue of public order in Kenora.' Following from this, native intoxication offences 'became the central policing focus and practice upon which the modern force evolved.'

From the mid-1950s, the rate of native and 'half-breed' prosecutions for alcohol relative to other prosecutions began to grow. This trend coincided with the relaxing of restrictions that had been suffered by natives prior to 1954. Until that time, native persons had not been allowed to vote, and had been 'given segregated seating arrangements in the Kenora movie theater' (ibid). Nor had they been allowed into beer parlours. With the opening of beer parlours to treaty Indians, a substantial proportion of the municipal police department's resources were devoted to the 'revolving door' of drunks in Kenora. Increases in the rate of prosecutions for alcohol relative to other prosecutions continued until the late 1960s. Moreover, early involvement of the Alcohol and Drug Addiction Foundation in the area apparently did little to affect the high rates of apprehending drunkenness offenders. Indeed, the official opening of the detoxication centre in 1972 in Kenora was marked by a sharp increase in the police arrest rate for liquor offences. As the local police chief stated in his annual report for 1973 (quoted in Torrie 1987):

In 1971 the Liquor Control Act was amended to allow offenders to be taken to the Detoxification Centre rather than being lodged in the cells and appearing in court. As a result of this amendment such a Centre was opened in Kenora in September of 1972 and it was felt that the alcohol problem would diminish. This, however, has not proven to be the case. A most dramatic increase in the incidents of arrest for liquor offences in the history of the Town of Kenora has occurred since the Detox Centre opened its door. During the month of March 821 arrests were made for liquor offences. This was 55 more than for the entire year in 1962 and an increase of 280% for the corresponding month of 1972. During the year 1973, 6,831 persons were arrested for intoxication, an increase of 111% over 1972 ... The Detoxification Centre has become a revolving door syndrome, mainly due to the reluctance in setting up restraints within the system whereby the attendants would have the authority to detain persons for a longer period of time ... With the time consumed in arresting as many as 76 persons in one day for drunkenness very little time is left for other investigative police duties or area patrols in an attempt to prevent crime.

However, despite their dissatisfaction with the detoxication centre, the police continued to cooperate with it until the end of 1978. At that time, a decision was taken 'to by-pass the Detoxification facilities for an indefinite period and have those arrested be processed through the courts' (Annual Report, quoted in Torrie 1987). Following from this, the number of arrests dropped substantially. But, at the same time, the rate of convictions increased, and continued to do so until 1983.

Meanwhile, during the 1980s, those drunkenness offenders who had been held in the Kenora police building following arrest were often subject to deplorable conditions. According to the 1977 Annual Report (quoted in Torrie 1987), a grand-jury panel had visited, and had found that 'lockup cells were considered adequate for the average number of individuals incarcerated in them, however, the [grand jury] panel was advised that as many as sixty individuals have been locked up in twelve cells at one time. Only one bunk and toilet are provided in each cell. The panel was shown several areas such as vents, ceilings, and bunks where the cells have been damaged. No mattresses, toilet paper or blankets were available in cells, because of damage caused by fires or materials stuffed into toilets.'

In the early 1980s, and as the high rate of fine-default admissions to prison indicates, Kenora procedures for dealing with native drunkenness offenders continued to be harsh. This situation was obviously contrary to the stated objectives of the Provincial Offences Act, which was now in operation. But, as Jolly and Seymour (1983) document, rather than the act constraining imprisonment for fine default, police and prosecutorial decisions about how to exercise the discretion available to them under the act itself largely account for the high rate of imprisonment.

First, policing practices in Kenora were such as to yield a proportionately high rate of liquor charges to be dealt with. While, in 1981–2, the Kenora area included only about 0.6 per cent of total Ontario population, it supplied 4.2 per cent of the province's Liquor Licence Act charges. Liquor charges in Kenora, then, were being received at 'seven times the rate which the district's share of total population would seem to warrant' (Jolly and Seymour 1983: 6).

Once these numerous charges had been laid by the police, subsequent practices were severe. This is evident, for example, in the disproportionate use of Part III of the Provincial Offences Act, which had been intended for use only in cases where the 'alleged offence against a provincial law is of a more serious nature' (Ontario, Ministry of the Attorney General 1987b, 1987a). In 1981–2, Kenora police were using this section of the act in 13 per cent of cases, a rate more than double that for the province as a whole (Jolly and Seymour 1983: 9). Moreover, when those charged subsequently appeared in court, the judiciary imposed prison sentences in 30 per cent of cases, a rate three times as high as the provincial average. This judicial severity was also reflected in the fact that, while judges in other parts of the province sometimes imposed probation on liquor offenders, Kenora judges never used this option.

Nevertheless, while these uses of Part III of the act are one indication of penal severity in Kenora, in practice, most liquor-related admissions to prison were deriving from the more 'informal' prosecutorial and fine-default procedures allowed for under Part I of the act. Surprising as it may seem, therefore, most of these prisoners had not appeared in court at all, or been directly sentenced by a judge. Rather, their 'sentences' followed from police and prosecutorial decision making. In light of widespread perceptions that prison terms are served only on the basis of court and judicial activity, this sentencing process carried out without such participation warrants examination.

As Jolly and Seymour (1983) explain, there are several stages in the more informal procedures allowed under Part I of the Provincial Offences Act. First, the police ticket the defendant by serving him or her with an offence notice specifying the amount of the fine being imposed for the violation. Once ticketed, the defendant has fifteen days in which to plead guilty and pay the fine, plead guilty with an explanation that might affect the penalty, or plead not guilty and thereby request a trial. If, when fifteen days have expired, the accused has failed to follow any of these options, and if no request has been received for an extension of the time to pay, a notice of intent to issue a warrant is mailed to the offender. The offender again has fifteen days to respond by payment or by requesting an extension of time to pay. If no response is made, a warrant for committal of the person is issued. Subsequently, through these warrants of committal, the police can jail offenders for non-payment of a fine.

As can be seen, the individual's response to the initial offence notice, or, failing that, to the ensuing note of intent, is crucial in precluding the possibility of imprisonment. In practice, the response typically entails payment of the fine. Notably, in Kenora there have been high rates of failure to respond to offence notices. In 1981–2, the failure rate for liquor charges was fully 98 per cent (Jolly and Seymour 1983: 7).

Yet, although Kenora's rate of failure to respond has been high, subsequently high rates of fine-default admissions to prison are largely explained by the proactive policing to which such failures have been subject by the police and prosecution. Once a fine has not been paid, the decision as to whether or not to follow up the notice of intent to issue a warrant with the actual issuing of a warrant is discretionary. During the period of Jolly and Seymour's study, the 'ratio of notices of intent to issue a warrant to warrants for committal was almost 1:1 in Kenora; whereas the ratio throughout the province was 2:1' (ibid: 8). In short, liquor-offence-fine-defaulters in Kenora were far more likely than were liquor-offence-fine-defaulters elsewhere to be subject to further pursuit by the police and prosecution. Overall, as Jolly and Seymour (ibid) document 'although the Kenora office accounted for 2.2 per cent of all the *Liquor Licence Act* charges which were received throughout the province during the nine month period, it generated 6.1 per cent of all the notices of intent to issue a warrant – 2.8 times the proportion one would expect – and 9.2 per cent of all the warrants for committal – 4.2 times the share one would expect.'

This proactive activity yielded not only 71 per cent of admissions to the jail during the period studied, but also sufficient liquor violators with outstanding warrants to 'fill the Kenora District Jail four times over' (ibid: 9).

Despite this high volume of candidates for imprisonment for fine default in Kenora, the volume of such admissions is still perplexing. As observed earlier, according to the Ministry of the Attorney General's explanation of the Provincial Offences Act, incarceration on default of a fine would be used only sparingly, and only for 'willful' and 'obstinate' defaulters, or the 'scofflaws' of the system. Yet, as Jolly and Seymour (1983) document, imprisoned fine defaulters in Kenora could not be described in this way. Their failure to pay fines is better understood in the context of their socio-economic and cultural situation, which mitigated fulfilment of the financial, formal, and legalistic demands of the criminal-justice bureaucracy.

One of the major difficulties experienced by natives was that of responding to the mailings that are integral to the procedures under Part I of the Provincial Offences Act. As Jolly and Seymour (1983) explain, Kenora natives 'may not pick up their mail regularly' as they 'may change their place of residence frequently as they migrate back and forth between the reserves and the towns in search of social and economic opportunity' (ibid: 71). Moreover, even those who did get their mail could experience difficulty in understanding it, as the sample's average level of formal education was only grade six, and some natives did not have sufficient 'reading skills in English to decipher legal terminology' (ibid: 6, 71).

The economic conditions of natives also mitigated payment. Fully ninety-two, or 76 per cent of the fine defaulters 'reported that they did not have the money and could not have obtained the money to pay their fines this last time' (Jolly and Seymour 1983: 33). Only five of the sample had regular full-time jobs. Not surprisingly then, seventy-two people, or 61 per cent, reported that their average monthly income was $400 or less. With such low incomes they were 'below the 1980 updated poverty lines for a single person established by Statistics Canada (revised), the Canadian Council on Social Development and the Senate Committee on Poverty' (ibid: 27, 69).

In addition to these difficulties in fulfilling fine conditions, the interviews reported by Jolly and Seymour also cast doubt on whether those charged were properly notified by the authorities about their fines and the consequences of default. Only 61 per cent of the fine defaulters could remember receiving a 'notice of the fine.' Where warrants were concerned, only 50 per cent recalled receiving a 'notice of intent to issue a warrant,' while 9 per cent said that they had received some, but not all, of the notices relevant to the issuing of warrants. A further 39 per cent 'insisted' that they had not received the final notice about a warrant. As Jolly and Seymour (1983: 36) observe: 'almost half of this sample of fine defaulters are therefore in effect claiming that they missed their last opportunity to avoid imprisonment.'

Following from the severity of procedures in dealing with natives, and from natives' difficulties in satisfying the system's requirements, fine defaulters for strictly provincial offences averaged sentences of fourteen days for a $75 debt. Most cases involved four days in jail for a fine of $15, but the average was increased by some 'rather extreme situations.' For example, 'one individual had been fined $150 or nine days in jail for one charge of public intoxication. Another had been given a fine of $110 or eight days imprisonment for one offence of public drunkenness' (Jolly and Seymour 1983: 19).

In sum, despite the commitment expressed during the late postwar period to the termination of incarceration on the basis of fine default, supposedly enabling procedures have failed to have this effect. As exemplified in the case of Kenora, low-income groups continue to be disproportionately vulnerable to intensive policing, penal processing, and imprisonment for debt. As this case further exemplifies, the bureaucratic procedures of criminal justice fail to take account of the differing sociocultural circumstances of natives. Ethnic discrimination compounds that of class. As Rusche and Kircheimer (1939: 170) have observed in historical context: 'carefully drawn legislation and administrative practice may reduce the injustices inherent in the operation of the fine system as it affects the lower classes, but this cannot solve the fundamental problem.'[7]

Imprisonment for Fine Default and Corrections

To recapitulate, we have seen that Ontario postwar decarceration is largely explained by a reduction in fine-default admissions to prison. Moreover, this reduction was concentrated in that of drunkenness offenders. At the same time, by the early 1980s, fine-default admissions continued to account for about a third of 'sentenced' admissions to Ontario prisons, with liquor offences in turn accounting for about a third of these. By the early 1990s, fine-default admissions had further declined to about a quarter of 'sentenced' admissions. Legislative and other reforms, therefore, appear to have had some effect, but have far from eliminated the phenomenon of either incarceration following from fines for intoxication or incarceration following from the imposition of fines more generally.

Given my focus on issues of imprisonment and alternatives, one striking feature of these developments concerning the fine has been the rather limited role of correctional authorities themselves in seeking to bring imprisonment for fine default to an end. In the case of drunkenness offenders, for example, from the 1950s quasi-medical agencies – notably the Addiction Research Foundation – were far more prominent than Ontario's Correctional Services in seeking reform. From the 1970s, the Ministry of the Attorney General was also in the forefront in expressing commitment to ending imprisonment for fine default and in developing procedures that were supposed to have this objective.

This quiescence of the Ministry of Correctional Services is particularly striking in light of the agency's growing emphasis on the development of community corrections from the early 1970s. Given that those incarcerated for fine-default are frequently convicted of minor violations rather than serious offences, one would have thought that they would provide an ideal group to be decarcerated and transferred to the less-custodial ambit of community corrections. But it was only in the early 1980s that the annual reports of the Ministry of Correctional Services even began to provide data on fine-default admissions to prison. Even then, there was little discussion of strategies towards countering fine-default admissions. Rather, in their presentation of the data, the ministry has typically emphasized that, while fine defaulters may be numerous as regards admission, because they receive short sentences, their contribution to daily counts is relatively low.

Only three pilot-project fine-option programs had been initiated by the ministry by the early 1990s. In short, the correctional agency's strategies in dealing with fine defaulters appear to have changed little during the postwar period.

Overall, reform movements and changing procedures *beyond* the immediate realm of corrections were of most significance in yielding Ontario postwar decarceration. It is important, therefore, to examine more closely the phenomenon of community corrections in the Ontario context. What factors gave rise to the discourse and practices of community corrections during the 1970s? In discussing alternatives to imprisonment, why have correctional reformers emphasized community corrections rather than other, more effective, strategies? What have been the major accomplishments of community corrections? As the next chapter clarifies, a closer examination of the genesis and purposes of community corrections helps to explain both why they have had little impact in reducing imprisonment and why issues such as fine default have received minimal attention from correctional authorities.

9

The Origins and Accomplishments of Community Corrections in Ontario

The Intentions and Effects of Community Corrections

Decarceration in Ontario derived more from changes in the administration of fines than from the development of new community programs. Questions therefore arise about the intentions of correctional reformers who enthusiastically supported community corrections. Why, from the 1970s, was there an increased emphasis on, and development of, probation, halfway houses, community service orders, victim–offender reconciliation, and other such programs? Further, given that the new community programs typically took the form of adjuncts to the disposition of probation, why was their development associated with discourses of alternatives to prison?

Such questions are important not just in the particular case of Ontario, but also in relation to the development of community corrections in Western jurisdictions more generally. Despite the wealth of publications on community corrections, it is a curious feature of the literature that the voices of relevant agents and agencies have rarely been heard. While decarceration analysts often claim that correctional reformers had a reductionist intent in their support for community corrections, they have rarely interviewed reformers for their own accounts of their objectives. Rather, decarceration analysts' claims that community corrections were originally intended to reduce the use of imprisonment have typically been made by reference to the work of other analysts, or by presenting well-chosen fragments from reformist documentary sources. Analysts then go on to contrast the expansionist consequences of the programs with their supposedly reductionist intent.

This analytical tendency can be seen, for example, in Hylton's critique of community corrections in the Canadian province of Saskatchewan from 1962 to 1979. According to Hylton, 'a number of so-called alternative programs were developed and implemented *in order to reduce reliance on correctional institutions*' (emphasis added). He documents how, despite these objectives, the period was characterized by 'steady increases in the number and rate of admissions to prisons and in the numbers and rate of persons incarcerated on any given day' (Hylton 1982: 345). For Hylton, this case illustrates the more general gap between community correctional rhetoric and reality. But the reader has not been told anything about Saskatchewan officials who introduced alternatives with the purpose of reducing custody.

This tendency is also evident in Pratt's emphasis on the differences between the official intentions, and actual effects, of penal reform in New Zealand. Pratt (1987: 150) quotes a statement that 'prison authorities are puzzled by a 16 per cent increase in New Zealand's jail population in the past year … It was hoped that fewer would go to prison because of the more community-based sentences.' This statement (apparently from a media source) is the major documentation Pratt provides about officials' objectives. Again, in comparison with the substantial research on the dismal consequences of reform, that on the intentions of insider reformers appears rather sparse.

Similar problems are evident in Muncie and Coventry's (1989) predictions about the likelihood of the Australian province of Victoria's new 'alternative' for youth resulting in net-widening and failure to provide an alternative to custody. According to the authors, the relevant policy – which provides for an 'attendance order' involving community work and activities – is 'couched in terms of an ongoing decarceration strategy,' and is in accordance with the government's policy to 'divert young offenders away from custody and institutional detention' (ibid: 181). But the quotes they give from official sources explaining the rationale for the new program do not include any statement about reducing custody. Yet again, the reader is told that the official objective is decarceration – including deinstitutionalization – without this assertion being documented in any great depth.

The lack of consultation with correctional officials, and the rudimentary presentation of their objectives, are problematic. As Cohen (1985: 22) has observed, for many decarceration analysts 'stated intentions are assumed *a priori* to conceal the real interests and motives behind the system.' Some of the most theoretically sophisticated analyses involve such a deconstruction. But if stated intentions have not been documented in much detail, surely the basis of these arguments must be considered shaky. What have been the objectives of insider reformers in supporting community corrections in different jurisdictions? Are prison and correctional systems as impervious to insider reform efforts as many decarceration analysts seem to suggest?

In turn, these empirical issues link with broader analytical ones. The decarceration literature has implied that the mysterious logic of history repeatedly subverts original goals. The expansion of correctional control appears to occur despite – rather than because of – the activities of reformers. It is disturbing that agency – as expressed in political action and policy making – seems irrelevant in face of structure. Functional logic, structuralist explanations, and the view that 'nothing works' hold the day.

In this chapter, I elaborate on the significance of community corrections in Ontario, and, in particular, on the objectives of correctional officials who supported their development. In doing so, I illuminate that Ontario community corrections can be better understood as marking the *culmination* rather than the *initiation* of decarceration. Drawing from interviews with senior correctional officials of the 1970s, I document how their growing emphasis on community corrections was a response to 1 / the emergence of the issue of overcrowding; 2 / a need to enhance the ministry's image; and 3 / the occurrence of fiscal restraint in the province. Officials' adoption of community corrections had the objectives of organizational maintenance, legitimacy, and expansion in face of these problems. From their perspectives, community corrections served their intended purposes quite well. Moreover, these purposes never included a substantial reduction of prison population. In short, the activities of penal agents themselves should be recognized as an important influence on correctional trends.

The Emergence of the Issue of Overcrowding in the Mid-1970s

> In 1975 ... the Ministry was faced with an unexpected explosion in its jail populations ... This change quickly resulted in serious over-crowding at many institutions and the old problems arising from the under-utilization of Ministry resources were replaced by the pressing need to find additional accommodation for the burgeoning inmate population. (Smith 1976: 2)

Identification of the emergence of the issue of overcrowding as an

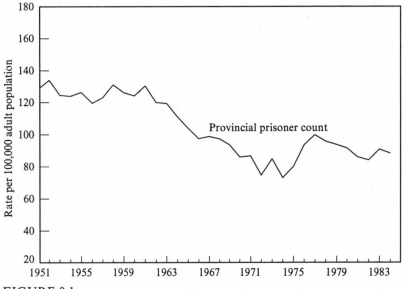

FIGURE 9.1

Ontario: provincial prisoner counts, 1951–1984

Note: 'Provincial prisoner counts' refers to prisoners in provincial institutions, i.e., remand prisoners and those serving sentences of less than two years.

important factor in the genesis of community corrections in Ontario may initially appear puzzling. I have argued that imprisonment decreased in Ontario during the postwar period, with the rate for the 1980s being substantially lower than that for the 1950s (see chapter 5). However, up to this point in the analysis, I have used rates per 100,000 population as the major indicator. By standardizing the data in this way it has been possible to document longitudinal trends in the prison population in proportion to the total population. Such proportional documentation is particularly important in a jurisdiction such as Ontario, which has experienced more than a doubling of population during the period under study. The use of imprisonment rates per 100,000 is also preferable as it facilitates not only longitudinal comparisons, but also those between provinces and internationally.

By contrast, for correctional officials, imprisonment rates per 100,000 population are not of special interest. They are more immediately concerned with the absolute numbers of prisoners under their jurisdiction, and, in particular, with the capacity of existing penal insti-

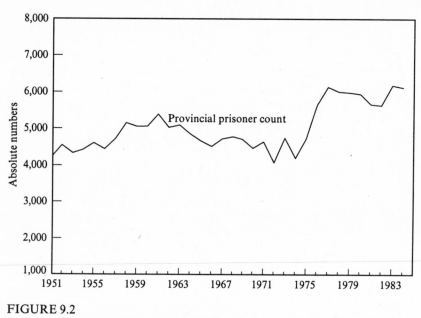

FIGURE 9.2
Ontario: provincial prisoner counts, 1951–1984

tutions to accommodate those numbers. Of key importance for officials, therefore, is the absolute count of prisoners at any given time.

Significantly, when the Ontario longitudinal provincial prisoner count data are re-examined with attention to absolute numbers, it can be seen that the picture is quite different from that which emerged from rates per 100,000 (see figures 9.1 and 9.2). Specifically, although in rates per 100,000, the overall trend is one of decarceration and its levelling off, in absolute numbers, the trend is one of relative stability and then increase – while the prisoner count population from 1951 until 1975 was fairly constant, it then began to rise rapidly. By 1976, the absolute count of prisoners was already higher than at any other time during the post-war period. A year later, in 1977, the population was higher again. While the population then stabilized, from 1976 onwards it continued to be higher than at any other time since 1951. Therefore, although Ontario's imprisonment rate from the mid-1970s was still lower than it had been in the 1950s, it was also true that the ministry experienced a greater 'demand' on its institutional resources than had been the case throughout the postwar period.

The difficulties created for the ministry in accommodating a larger prison population were exacerbated by the policies it was in the process of implementing, following its assumption of responsibility for local jails in 1968. Specifically, the ministry was in the process of replacing thirty-five old jails with fourteen new (and smaller) regional detention centres (see Oliver 1985). This plan was being undertaken, first because of the deplorable physical conditions of some of the jails; second, because of the belief that smaller institutions were more conducive to rehabilitation; and, third, because of the possibility that long-term savings on administrative costs could be made as many institutions were being underutilized during the 1950s and 1960s, and into the early 1970s.

In short, the ministry experienced growing population pressure precisely at a point when its institutional capacity was decreasing. According to ex-ministry official Donald Evans, one of the agency's responses to this situation was that programs such as community resource centres, which had originally been started as a form of graduated release for 'rehabilitative purposes,' now 'changed their focus.' Ministry officials, informed by recent criminological literature, and by study visits and participation in conferences elsewhere, began to more frequently describe pre-existing programs in terms of 'alternatives.' More generally, alternatives 'became touted as the solution to overcrowding' (ibid; see Smith 1976).

Initially then, community corrections in Ontario involved not so much the development of new programs as a discursive shift in describing programs that already existed or were already being developed. By redefining existing community programs as alternatives, the ministry could foster the impression that it was taking steps to deal with overcrowding. As overcrowding continued to be a feature of Ontario's prison system during the 1970s, additional impetus was provided for the further development of community programs. Meanwhile, other factors, both within the ministry and in the broader economic and political climates, also precipitated the development of community corrections.

Officials' Perception of a Need to Enhance the Ministry's Image

Any correctional agency responsible for keeping people locked up is vulnerable to criticism from reformist, civil-libertarian, media, and other sources. In the mid-1970s, the credibility of the Ministry of Correctional Services appeared to be in danger of waning. At that time in Canada, as in many Western countries, growing scepticism about the viability of rehabilitation was being expressed, and its repressive aspects were being identified. Canadian prison systems were also vulnerable to criticism owing to the high rate of imprisonment, the growing problem of overcrowding, and the perceived lack of alternatives to prison.

Ontario ministry officials were sensitive to such criticisms. Moreover, they also saw recent developments within the ministry as threatening to legitimacy. Some senior officials were even concerned about the continued existence of the ministry. In 1976, the correctional agency lost jurisdiction over young offenders under sixteen years of age, responsibility for them being transferred to the Ministry of Community and Social Services. With this major loss of jurisdiction, correctional officials believed that the ministry's position was being weakened, not only in the perception of public-culture commentators, but also within the province's network of justice agencies.

Some of the implications of this transfer of juveniles were elaborated in interview by ex–ministry official Art Daniels. According to Daniels, prior to this transfer, the ministry's innovative accomplishments had been far greater in the case of juveniles than in that of adults. Such innovations in corrections for young offenders had kept the ministry 'vibrant,' and the transfer of juvenile offenders was, therefore, 'a tough loss.' As the ministry now had only one division, and primarily a custodial one, it felt threatened by the possibility of being merged with the Ministry of the Solicitor General.

In order to prevent such a merger, officials felt that the Ministry of Correctional Services needed a second division. According to Daniels, 'obviously community was the next thing to split out.' In 1978, a new community programs division was formed, with Daniels himself as director. In short, as confirmed by several interviewees, the major objectives of the growing emphasis on community corrections included strengthening the ministry's organizational position by enhancing its image. It was thought that community corrections would give the ministry a more prominent and positive profile. Studies of the development of individual community programs reaffirm the importance of this objective. For example, in the case of community service orders, Menzies (1986: 160) reports that ministry officials 'suggested to the Minister that cso's would be both popular and generate favourable publicity.'

There is no inherent reason as to why problems of overcrowding and officials' perception of a need to enhance the agency's image should necessarily have resulted in an increasing emphasis on community corrections. It appears that, while problems of overcrowding and credibility were important in generating official perceptions that *something* needed to be done, economic factors were crucial in directing the ministry's reformist endeavours towards community corrections. Put simply, an emphasis on community corrections provided a convenient means whereby the ministry could try both to increase its legitimacy and to secure new organizational resources during an era of fiscal adversity.

Privatized Community Corrections as a Response to Fiscal Adversity

> Economic constraints throughout the Ontario government have necessitated reductions in operating costs and staff. As a result, increased emphasis is being placed on community-based programs. (Carey 1978: 2)

Similarly to most organizations, Ontario Correctional Services has tended to seek, and welcome, the growth of their resources and activities. Where adults are concerned, the postwar period saw substantial increases in the scope of the agency. As discussed earlier, in the decade prior to the formation of the Community Program Division in 1978, two major forms of expansion occurred. First, with the province's assumption of the full costs of the administration of justice in 1968, county and city jails were 'integrated into the provincial correctional system.' In conjunction with this integration, the department 'was given nine hundred new employees' (Oliver 1985: 187). Oliver reports that this move was 'long favoured' by the Correctional Minister, and that he and his officials 'were delighted' (ibid). As both the physical conditions of many of the jails and the manner in which they were being run were considered to be unsatisfactory, this transfer of responsibility greatly increased the resources and scope of the agency's activity. It also provided a catalyst and locus for insider reform.

A second major expansion occurred in 1972, when the Correctional Services took over responsibility for probation from the Attorney General. With this transition, nearly 400 – and more professional – employees were acquired. This transfer of responsibility greatly increased the agency's immediate and potential involvement in non-incarcerative sanctions.

By contrast, in the mid-1970s the Ministry of Correctional Services' ability to continue expanding its resources and jurisdiction faced several major impediments. As already observed, responsibility for juveniles had been withdrawn. Meanwhile, the provincial government was increasingly emphasizing fiscal restraint. Unless the ministry could find a way of overcoming economic constraints, its tendency to expand its activities would be curtailed.

While 'privatization' as a government strategy in the provision of Canadian correctional strategies (see Ericson, McMahon, and Evans 1987) as well as in the provision of state services more generally (Neilsen 1986) became most obvious in the 1980s, such a tendency was evident far earlier in Ontario. Government concern about provincial economic trends provided an important rationale for initiatives towards privatization. From the early 1960s, a marked growth in public expenditure and activity had been taking place (Davis 1980a: 9). For example, where there were 32,000 public servants in Ontario in 1960, by 1973 there were approximately 66,000. Meanwhile, total population grew, from just over 6 million in 1960, to just under 8 million in 1973. Therefore, an increase of slightly less than a third in population was accompanied by more than a doubling of employees in the public sector. By the early 1970s, although economic growth also continued to be high, inflation and increased provision of services were resulting in government revenue being outpaced by expenditure. Accordingly, the provincial deficit was increasing (ibid).

Prior to the mid-1970s, the provincial government was already expressing concern about these fiscal trends. Proposals had been made towards curbing public expenditure (ibid: 10; Toronto, Committee on Government Productivity 1969; Ontario, Ministry of Treasury, Economics and Intergovernmental Affairs 1972). However, as Davis (ibid) recounts, the Ontario budget of 1975 was 'the first concrete action put forth to curb the growth of government spending, hence to curb the growing fiscal crisis. It included a 2.5% cut in the civil service complement, a requirement that all ministries absorb any in-year cost increases related to inflation within their estimates, a postponement of building projects where feasible, and an extensive assessment of the efficacy, effectiveness, and relevance of major spending programs' (see Ontario, Ministry of Treasury, Economics and Intergovernmental Affairs 1975).

The movement towards fiscal constraint was also advanced by the report of the Special Program Review Committee published in 1975. This report recommended that government policies should remain oriented towards economic growth, and that government expenditures should decline as a percentage of gross provincial product (Davis 1980a: 11; Special Program Review Committee 1975). Strategies advocated towards the accomplishment of these objectives included: investigation into the privatization and reprivatization of service responsibilities; governmental assumption of a regulatory role with respect to the private-sector delivery of services; decentralization of responsibility for service delivery to local agencies; accountability of the private sector to government; reduction of the personnel costs of the civil service; the allocation of unconditional grants in order to facilitate appropriate responses to local priorities;[1] and the shifting of responsibility for expenditure to other levels of government and to the private sector. In sum, the report advocated increased decentralization and privatization of government services. Meanwhile, in the specific case of correctional services, the 1975 report identified the high costs of incarceration, and recommended a shift to the use of alternatives (Davis 1980a 11–13, 16; Special Program Review Committee 1975; see Roe 1980: 4–5).

As the 1970s progressed, the Ontario government moved from a position based primarily on the advocacy of fiscal restraint to that of imposing fiscal constraint. In 1977, government control of numbers of personnel was introduced, and involved rigid ceilings on the level of spending. Where there had been a 24.7 per cent increase in provincial spending in 1974–5, that for 1978–9 was estimated at 6.9 per cent (Davis 1980a: 16). Also in 1977, a report of the Workload Management Committee stated that the Probation and Parole Service should not necessarily undertake the provision of all services for the offenders for which it was statutorily responsible. Rather, it was recommended that the service undertake a more managerial role. These recommendations again affirmed and stimulated corrections' growing involvement in community corrections.

In some ways, the Ministry of Correctional Services initially seemed to be in a 'particularly vulnerable' position in face of the changing fiscal priorities of the provincial government (Roe 1981: 55). Where the institutions were concerned, at the beginning of the 1970s, the ministry was in the process of implementing its policy of replacing old jails with new regional detention and correctional centres. The recommended postponement of building projects would hamper this process. It would also inhibit the building of extra institutions to absorb increases in the institutional population. Meanwhile, where probation services were concerned, the ministry was experiencing a rapid increase in the number of probationers in an era unfavourable to the employment of additional probation officers. Overall, about 90 per cent of the ministry's budget was being used for salaries and operating costs (ibid), both of which were being increasingly subject to constraint.

Given this economic context whereby greater fiscal resources were available for private-, than for public-sector initiatives, community corrections – with an emphasis on private-sector involvement – represented the most viable policy through which the ministry could realize its expansionist interests. As Art Daniels summed up the situation in interview: community corrections in Ontario constituted a situation where 'a tremendous idea comes from necessity.' Or, as Don Evans more bluntly expressed it: 'the alternatives came about as a response to fiscal crisis.' Taken together with the ministry's image and overcrowding problems, the theme of 'alternatives' provided an ideal focus for the agency in selling its policies. As we have seen, the ministry's emphasis on alternatives was, first, a discursive one. As reaffirmed by Don Evans: 'really what happened is programs we already had became alternatives. They weren't alternatives before.' And, as Evans went on to specify, it was 'in the restraint period [that] they became alternatives.'

The content of the discursive transition was clearest in the case of pre-existing community resource centres. The centres had been 'started for rehabilitative purposes,' and, in the first evaluation of them, the researcher 'was not asked to evaluate the program from a cost-effectiveness standpoint' (Smith 1976: 1). With the dual emergence of overcrowding and fiscal restraint, however, questions of whether they could provide 'additional low-cost accommodation' in lieu of the 'more expensive alternative of providing additional institutional bed-space' (ibid: 2) became crucial. In the mid–1970s, rather than trying to justify further development of community resource centres on the basis of their rehabilitative potential and accomplishments, it was argued that 'the program can more or less be justified on the basis of cost factors alone' (ibid: 3).

Over time, Ontario community corrections have involved far more than the reformulation, and accelerated expansion, of programs with a 'community' component. For example, the introduction of fee-for-service contracting has been an important development in the exercise of penal control. Contracting began in 1975, when the ministry entered arrangements with four branches of the John Howard Society to carry out probation supervision (Davis 1980a: 42). During that year contracts totaled $116,460 (ibid). By 1981, the value of contracts had increased enormously, not only in probation supervision, but also in the wider range of community programs fostered by the ministry. As a part of these developments, and in keeping with government priorities, the Probation and Parole Service itself had undergone a 'radical transformation': 'where once the province was divided into four regions there are now nine, and these are further sub-divided into some 40 areas, each with an area manager responsible not only for supervising his/her staff but for contracting with the local community for a wide range of services' (Roe 1981: 56).

In summary, a full understanding of the origins of community correctional strategies requires attention not only to the changing climate of criminological and correctional ideas as outlined in chapter 2. No doubt the movement towards community corrections was affected by the reformist and 'community' orientations of influential senior correctional civil servants during the 1970s. But it was the distinctive economic context within which they were working that directed them towards privatized forms of community corrections in responding to critiques of imprisonment and overcrowding, and in crystallizing their reformist ideas and aspirations.

One important point arising from this analysis is that the development of community corrections in Ontario – both in intention and as implemented – had little to do with the reduction of the pre-existent prison population. At best, it was hoped that the development of 'alternatives' would curtail the need for the provision of additional institutional bed-space. In light of this observation a question arises: If community corrections in Ontario have not accomplished their objectives of being 'alternatives' as defined by outsider critics, what *have* been the major accomplishments of related programs in the province?

The Uses and Accomplishments of Community Corrections

In light, first, of the fiscal and ideological climate within which community corrections were developed from the early 1970s, and, second, of the manner in which they have been implemented, how are the consequences of Ontario community corrections best described? Most generally, community corrections have greatly furthered the interests of the Ontario Ministry of Correctional Services. On the one hand, through the growth of community programs, the agency's organization, budget, and personnel have expanded. On the other hand, and less immediately apparent, community corrections have also been used in reinforcing the historical locus of power within the ministry: community corrections have been accepted and supported insofar as they contribute to the interests of prisons themselves. Therefore, although public-culture discourse about community corrections, and about privatization more generally, typically emphasize the objectives of reducing the state's size, budget, and involvement in public life, the opposite consequences have ensued in the case of corrections.

Where the organization, budget, and personnel of the ministry are concerned, while the 'blurring' of boundaries characteristic of community corrections sometimes impedes precision, a general trend of expansion is clearly identifiable. Organizationally, the ministry has expanded its operations through its fostering of numerous community-service-order, victim–offender reconciliation, alcohol-awareness, residential, driving-while-impaired, and other community programs. Moreover, and as has been documented, for the most part these programs have not been developed as substitutes for the use of imprisonment. Rather, they have taken the form of add-ons to probation, or as additional programs to be participated in by those who are incarcerated.

Along with this organizational and operational expansion, the ministry's overall budget has grown substantially. This growth has been possible partly as a result of the ministry's strategy of privatization in the development of community corrections. As one ex–ministry official expressed it in interview, senior officials of the 1970s were able to sell community corrections to ministers on the basis of their 'investment' potential: given the lack of state finance available for prison construction and other expenditures within government, and given the resources available for securing private-sector involvement, community corrections with participation by non-state organizations represented an ideal means of enlarging the ministry's operations. Circumstances of fiscal adversity, therefore, were transformed into a means of fiscal and organizational gain. More generally, as Davis (1980b: 34) observes,

> budgetary expenditure by the Ministry of Correctional Services did not consistently reflect the constraints program of the government. Budgetary expenditure in 1974–75 was $101 million. Given the 10.6% rate of inflation expenditure for 1975–76 should not have exceeded $110.5 million, yet it was $121 million – $10.5 million above the allowed expenditure according to the 1975 Budget. In 1976–77, the $146 million expenditure exceeded the 6.2% rate of inflation by $5.5 million. In 1977–78, the expenditure was $154 million exceeding the 7.5% inflation rate by $10.5 million.

An important component of the ministry's growing organization and resources has been the increase in the number of personnel involved in the agency. This increase took place partly through the growing number of volunteers associated with the ministry. By 1983, there were approximately 4,200 volunteers working, with 2,500 of these involved in institutional programs, and 1,600 in probation services (Leluk 1983: iii).

It has also taken place through the involvement of non-state groups who, through privatization, deliver services and exercise penal control on behalf of the ministry. Many of these contracts for service go to groups such as the John Howard Society and the Salvation Army, which have a long-standing involvement – and historically received little funding from government sources – in the field of corrections. Overall, however, a diverse range of organizations, many with little or no prior correctional involvement, have become involved in contracting with the Ministry of Correctional Services.

While this increase in the involvement of non-state organizations resulted in a vastly increased personnel at the disposal of the Ministry of Correctional Services, it has also had important consequences for penal reform more generally, and particularly with respect to the role of non-state groups. Put simply, community corrections in Ontario have had effects for private-sector agencies themselves. Davis (1980b) has aptly described these effects in terms of 'the seduction' of the private sector. Traditionally, some of the leading non-state correctional agencies have primarily had an advocacy and/or non-state-funded role of service provision. With community corrections, however, they – along with other groups that have got involved – have the major function of fulfilling the ministry's requirements and participating in the exercise of penal power. With this change in the role of non-state agencies, their oppositional role vis-à-vis penal authorities and the extension of penal power has diminished. In particular, the involvement of non-state agencies in fee-for-service contracts appears to have had this effect.

This diminishing advocacy on the part of non-state agencies was discussed by several ex–ministry officials in interview. They claimed that, during the mid-1970s, they had envisaged that their community correctional relationship with John Howard and Elizabeth Fry Societies, and other organizations, would be one of 'partnership.' But, in practice, it has evolved into one of 'accountability, a contractual relationship ... partnership is not there.' The major reason was that, as non-state agencies became increasingly dependent on government funding, their reformist activities became circumscribed. As one interviewee observed: 'the John Howard Society, like most other voluntary societies, were sold out a long time ago ... You don't bite the hand that feeds you. It's just that simple' (for a detailed account of changes in the role and autonomy of the private sector following privatization, see Scott [1990]).

While community corrections have greatly extended the Ministry of

Correctional Services' activities beyond the prison, they have not done much to disturb the power of the institutional sector within the ministry itself. Even with the substantial growth in community programming, the major portion of the ministry's budget is spent in the institutional sector. In general, the development of community corrections has been supported insofar as they extend the ministry's ambit. In cases where community-correctional programs might actually have the consequences of reducing pre-existing levels of imprisonment, support within the ministry is lacking. In describing these tendencies, ex–ministry officials made unsolicited and repeated reference to the 'dominance' of the institutions. This institutional dominance helps to explain why Ontario community-correctional developments have been concentrated in the realm of probation, that is, in the context of a long-established-community program to which offenders are assigned by courts.

Institutional dominance also helps to explain the limits of the ministry's enthusiasm for residential community programs to which they could transfer prisoners. Here, a ministry evaluation of community resources centres, conducted in the mid-1970s, is instructive. As noted earlier, ministry researcher Robert Smith (1976: 3) identified the value of such centres during that period of overcrowding and fiscal constraint when he said that 'the program can be justified on the basis of cost factors alone.' In general, and as reaffirmed in Smith's (ibid: 3–14) following comments, the value of community resource centres was considered to lie primarily in their potential for alleviating the need to provide additional bed-space during overcrowding, rather than in serving as an alternative to the pre-existing prison population.

> It is important to note, however, that in the event of a sudden decrease in jail population and a return to the conditions that existed in 1974 the real saving attached to the operation of the c.r.c. programs could not be justified on the basis of costs alone ...
>
> One obvious response to the argument that real savings would disappear if there was a reduction in jail populations would be the suggestion that since c.r.c.s are less expensive to operate than large institutions, it would seem reasonable to close several large institutions and retain the c.r.c.s. As a long-term alternative this might be feasible, but as a short-term solution it is not particularly feasible. Large institutions cannot be phased out overnight and many jails, etc. must be maintained for geographical reasons. In addition, in the event of any large scale reduction in inmate populations, it is likely that a large

proportion of the remaining population would consist of hard-core offenders who require the greater security of the institution and could not be housed in c.r.c.s regardless of any cost-saving factors.

As Smith's commentary suggests, for correctional authorities, 'alternatives' such as community resource centres to which prisoners can be transferred are most likely to be considered favorably when the prisons themselves are full. The possibility that, at some time in the future, when overcrowding did not exist, the centres could be used in lieu of existing bed-space is not viewed with much enthusiasm. Rather, the perspective is taken that, once overcrowding no longer exists, economic justification for their use would also be lacking. Moreover, this economic argument is made despite the fact that the *per diem* costs per inmate in community resource centres have generally been about half of those in the prisons.

As well as pointing to the lack of economic justification for the use of community resource centres as a more general substitute for imprisonment, Smith also draws on a frequent theme of prison-oriented correctional officials in highlighting the 'hard-core' nature of offenders who would remain and their need for 'security.' The implication is that the remaining offenders would be dangerous ones. But the ministry's jurisdiction over sentenced prisoners only extends to those serving under two years, and thereby involves less serious offenders. Moreover, the vast majority of these offenders are imprisoned only for short periods. For example, in 1984, of 47,662 sentenced admissions for under two years, fully 41,883, or 88 per cent, were for less than six months. Certainly, then, in terms of admissions, nearly total provincial decarceration would have to take place before that of more serious offenders would be an issue. Further, the Correctional Service of Canada, which deals with federal prisoners serving sentences of two years and over, has been able to transfer some of these prisoners to residential community programs. Therefore, even with longer-term prisoners, the issue of security does not always impede release to community settings. The organizational interests of prisons, rather than the unsuitable characteristics of the prisoners they contain, seem to mitigate the transfer of inmates to residential programs such as community resource centres.

Ironically, while the purported need of some prisoners for security can inhibit their transfer to halfway houses, those who are clearly not dangerous, and who appear to be particularly good candidates for community residency, also face obstacles. From the perspective of prison authorities, the labour of 'low-risk' inmates is a valuable resource in the everyday running of the institutions. We have already seen this in the particular case of drunkenness offenders in Toronto's Don Jail during the 1960s. In the 1980s, McKessock (1984) argued that those inmates who were most suitable for rehabilitative programs were most useful to authorities in carrying out institutional chores. That 'low-risk' inmates do more generally perform useful tasks, and that these provide a deterrent to decarceration for ministry officials, is evident in Madden and Hermann's (1983: 37) remarks following their analysis of community resource centres:

> There also exists a situation where programmes and institutional activities are in effect competing for the same group of low-risk inmates. This, in itself, does not diminish the potential value of any specific programme but should be kept in mind when considering expansion. Its all very well, for example, to point out that the need for kitchen staff is a poor justification for keeping an inmate in an unnecessarily secure institution. However, if Superintendents are to be encouraged to place these inmates into CRCs [community resource centres], some alternative means of putting the meals on the table will have to be devised. Similarly, a coordinated approach is required in areas where CRCs, community work projects, and parole all find themselves vying for the same inmates.

It seems, therefore, that the Ministry of Correctional Services has tended to support community correctional policies and programs insofar as they have reinforced or extended its organizational ambit and insofar as they have not disturbed the functioning of institutions. Where initiatives might served to restrict the ministry's scope, and particularly where they might serve to reduce prison population, support within the agency has seemed to diminish.[2] These observations help to explain the ministry's support for probation-related community programs as against its lack of initiative in finding alternatives for fine defaulters. Programs taking the form of conditions-of-probation orders provide opportunities for the ministry to expand its activities with probationers coming under its jurisdiction. They do not involve the ministry transferring individuals from custodial to community settings. By contrast, successful non-incarcerative alternatives for fine-defaulters would result in a transfer of these offenders from the prisons to the non-institutional sector, and possibly beyond the realm of corrections altogether. Such reform would tend to reduce the ministry's ambit and has therefore not been an attractive focus for their insider reform activity.

Analysing Community Corrections

This investigation obviously reaffirms some of the conclusions of decarceration analysts: since the 1970s community corrections have been associated with penal expansion. Yet these – and longer-term – developments in Ontario also provide some insights that suggest that the conventional wisdom on the origins of decarceration may need to be modified.

In particular, there is a need for greater attention to the *intentionality* of penal expansion. Ontario correctional officials supported community corrections as a response to overcrowding, legitimacy, and fiscal pressure. Their response was very effective in dealing with these problems, and in enabling the expansion of correctional activities. Therefore, where the tendency of penal expansion is often seen as indicative of the 'failure' of penal reform, in the case of Ontario it seems more indicative of the 'success' for insider reformers.

Arguably, this difference in terms of success/failure is more than a semantic one. For, in turn, decarceration analysts view the expansionist effects of community corrections as evidence of the immutability of the correctional system to reform. By contrast, if it is accepted that community corrections in Ontario were effective in securing the objectives of administrators, then the possibility is again opened that the correctional system may also be amenable to more progressive forms of change. The view that 'nothing works' obscures the connections that can exist between proposals, policies, and practices. This is not to deny the complexity of penal politics, or the intransigence of institutions. But there is a need to recognize that, sometimes, policy objectives might actually be accomplished.

Yet, while this analysis illuminates that penal agents within the correctional system have influenced both imprisonment and community corrections, it also highlights some of the broader stimuli and constraints to which they are subject. In particular, the provincial economic climate had a major impact in shaping community-correctional developments. More generally, correctional trends are also shaped to a large extent by penal agents outside of the correctional system itself: public, police, prosecutorial, and judicial decision making all affect the correctional population with which the Ministry of Correctional Services eventually deals. In order to more completely elaborate the picture of Ontario correctional trends, therefore, it is necessary to address the broader context of penal trends in the province.

10

Penal Trends in Ontario

One of the criticisms I have made of previous analyses of decarceration is that their focus has frequently been too narrow. Trends in imprisonment and community corrections are presented in tandem. Subsequent explanations of these trends, while replete with reference to economic and other structural moving forces of history, rarely examine the actions of penal agents beyond the correctional system itself. Little inquiry has been made, for example, into changes in crime rates, or into the changing practices of the public, the police, and the courts, which have an impact on the size and content of the correctional population.

In this study of decarceration in Ontario, therefore, I have sought to identify relevant factors not only within the correctional system of imprisonment and community corrections, but also beyond it. This sensitivity directed the analysis towards some important insights. For, while the growing use of the community program of probation contributed to decarceration, other factors have been of far greater significance. In particular, changes in the use of fines – most notably for offences of public intoxication – have played a major part in Ontario decarceration.

In turn, one of the insights yielded by inquiry into fines and their relationship to imprisonment is that of the important role played by the police in the determination of rates of incarceration. Legislative procedures during the postwar period involved practices whereby offenders could be effectively sentenced to imprisonment without direct judicial intervention. As we have seen, during the past few decades many of those serving prison sentences as a consequence of fine default may not have been to court or appeared before a judge at all. Rather, under the Provincial Offences Act, once an offender has been apprehended by the police for drunkenness and other minor violations, the ensuing process-es of penalization are mediated by documentary forms, and take place at the initiative of police, along with prosecutorial discretion. When these forms – that is, the offence notice and notice of intent to issue a warrant of committal – are not satisfactorily responded to by the offender, the decision to execute a warrant of committal again rests largely with the police. When it is recalled that, during the early 1980s in Kenora, for liquor violations alone, there were sufficient outstanding warrants to 'fill the Kenora jail four times over' (Jolly and Seymour 1983: 9), it becomes clearer that any changes in the exercise of police discretion, even with respect to drunkenness and other minor violations, can have a significant impact on the entire penal system, including prison. Meanwhile, the room of correctional authorities themselves to manoeuvre in changing the size of prison population is limited, as acknowledged by correctional minister Leluk in his statement: 'We have to accept these people who are brought to our jails and detention centres by the police with proper war-rants of committal' (Ontario *Hansard*, 5 June 1984, 2169). Analysis of trends in imprisonment and alternatives, therefore, needs to consider not just the arena within which correctional authorities do have the ability to change the size of their population, but also wider penal trends and prac-tices that help to determine the numbers of people coming into the cor-rectional system in the first place.

What have been the characteristics of broader penal trends in Ontario since the 1950s? How have penal agents other than correction-al ones influenced those trends? Adequately addressing these questions goes far beyond the scope of the present study. Nevertheless, prelimi-nary inquiry into the broader contours of police, judicial, and public activity in socially producing and reacting to crime provides some important clues.

Most generally, it appears that the Ontario postwar correctional trends documented in earlier chapters represent a microcosm of overall penal trends. Similarly to developments in corrections, growth in crim-inal-justice activities during the postwar period has, for the most part, been concentrated at the 'soft' end of the penal spectrum. Despite the public-culture emphasis on more serious forms of crime, when one looks at the system as a whole, one sees that exceptional procedures for dealing with the more serious categories of indictable offences have been increasingly overshadowed by the bureaucratic, routinized, and techni-cist administration of the less serious categories of summary offences and other minor infractions.

In the late twentieth century, the primary activities of penal agents have come to reside in policing the growing field of bureaucratic administrative law (see Law Reform Commission of Canada 1986; Kamenka and Tay 1975), and ensuing potential, and actual, violations.

The Police, Crime, and Sentencing

> Crime in our times may appear a phenomenon of baffling complexity, an intricate and shifting web of social, economic, psychological, biological, political, legal, moral – and even spiritual – factors. But today it is statistics that, rightly or misleadingly, give it social definition and increasingly diagnose, prescribe and predict it. (Hopkins 1973: 124–5)

> The government are very keen on amassing statistics. They collect, raise them to the 4th power, take the cube root and prepare wonderful diagrams. But you must never forget that every one of those figures comes in the first instance from the village watchman, who just puts down what he damn pleases. (Sir Josiah Stamp, cited in Nettler 1974: 45)

In looking more directly at broader penal trends, examination of the phenomenon of crime, and its extent, is a logical point of departure. At the same time, it must be recognized that crime itself is a socially constructed entity rather than an inherent property of particular forms of behaviour. This is not to deny that individually and socially harmful, and reprehensible, forms of behaviour occur. They do. Rather, the point is to acknowledge that the processes whereby some actions and events become a focus of criminal-justice attention, and others do not, are complex ones. Any analysis of criminal activities, therefore, must pay attention to the ways in which certain acts become defined as criminal.

In the social construction of crime rates, the role of the police is of fundamental importance. For, while most potentially criminal acts do not even come to the attention of the public police, and while the police by no means retain a monopoly over the exercise of social control, it is they who initially compile statistics on crime, and thereby shape public-culture conceptions of the nature and extent of crime (Black 1970; McDonald 1976; Manning 1977; Carr-Hill and Stern 1979; Ericson 1981, 1982). As Bottomley and Coleman (1981: 18) emphasize, 'official statistics of "crimes known to the police" and "crimes cleared up" owe their existence to the record keeping activities of the police and any attempt to understand those statistics in a comprehensive way should be based on some knowledge of the record keeping process.' In short, while

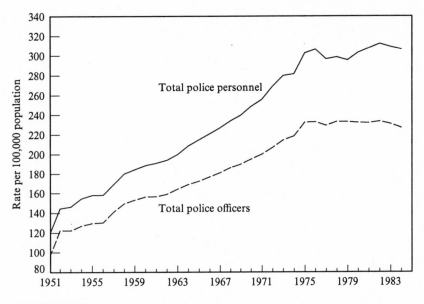

FIGURE 10.1
Ontario: police personnel and officers, 1951–1984

social, economic, political, technological, and other factors also affect crime rates, the rates themselves are, in the first instance, 'indices of organisational processes' (ibid; Ericson and Shearing 1986; Kitsuse and Cicourel 1963: 137).

Given this importance of the police in the broader organization of criminal justice, an examination of statistics on the police themselves, and in conjunction with those on crime, provides a useful perspective on the broader contours of penal trends. How did the size of Ontario police forces change in the postwar period? How did changes in the size of police forces relate to those in statistics on crime and the nature of police activity?

Since 1951, there has been a considerable increase in the number of police officers in Ontario (see figure 10.1).[1] The number of police officers has grown more than twice as fast as that of the general population, from a total of 97 per 100,000 in 1951 to 227 in 1984 (in absolute numbers, 4,483 officers in 1951; 20,275 in 1984).

When police employees other than full-time peace officers are included in the calculation, the growth of Ontario police forces is more pronounced. There was a growth in total police employees from 120 per

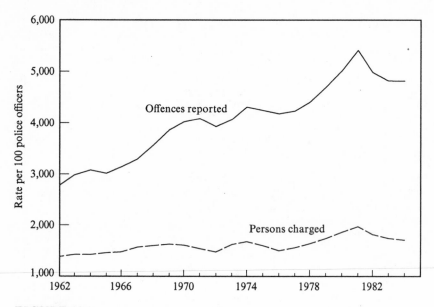

FIGURE 10.2
Ontario: ratio of total offences recorded and persons charged to police
officers, 1962–1984

100,000 of population in 1951 to 306 in 1984 (5,535 full-time personnel
in 1951; 27,375 in 1984). With the growth of total police personnel out-
stripping that of actual police officers, there has been a decline in the
proportion of officers to total personnel. Where in 1951 police officers
constituted 81 per cent of the police employees, by 1984 they constituted 74 per cent.

Given this changing constitution of police forces, one might expect
more intensive apprehension and processing of suspects on the part of
individual officers. Specifically, with non–peace officer police employees
taking on many of the organizational tasks associated with policing
(e.g., answering phones), it would seem that police officers themselves
should have proportionately more time to spend on actual policing,
including the apprehension and processing of suspects. The enhance-
ment of police technology over the period would also support such an
expectation. However, while the average number of offences reported
annually per officer greatly increased over the past few decades, the
number of persons charged per police officer grew at a far lower rate
(see figure 10.2). Increased police resources, therefore, have been asso-

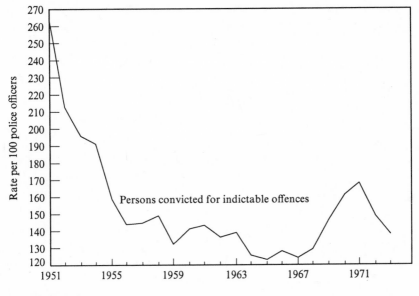

FIGURE 10.3
Ontario: ratio of persons convicted for indictable offences to police officers,
1951–1973

ciated more with the growing identification of crime than with the initiation of criminal procedures against suspects.

Have the police, and the criminal-justice system, become more
effective in proving cases against those suspects who are apprehended,
particularly in cases of more serious offences? One way of exploring this
issue is to examine data on the ratio of persons convicted for indictable
offences to police officers. Unfortunately, the lack of sentencing data
after 1973 impedes inquiry. Nevertheless, the available data for 1951–73
indicate a relatively stable rate in the processing of offenders for
indictable offences, especially since the mid-1950s (see figure 10.3).
Overall the ratio is very low as, from 1953, there were fewer than two
persons convicted of indictable offences annually per individual police
officer. In short, increased numbers of police officers, and the growth in
their civilian personnel, technological, and other resources, has not been
associated with more persons being convicted for indictable offences per
individual officer.

When the population of Ontario, rather than the police, is taken as
a control variable, the increase in recorded offences appears quite dra-

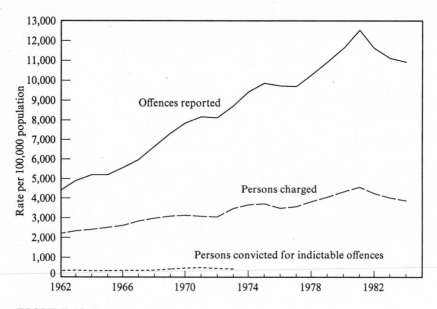

FIGURE 10.4
Ontario: total offences reported, persons charged, and persons convicted of indictable offences, 1962–1984
Note: Data on offences reported and persons charged are per 100,000 total population. Data on persons convicted for indictable offences are per 100,000 adult population.

matic, with 1984 registering a 147 per cent increase over 1962 (see figure 10.4). In the same period, the rates of those charged increased 75 per cent. Therefore, despite the relatively stable rate at which individual officers have laid charges over time, the disproportionate growth of police forces in Ontario is associated with a growth in population being charged. By contrast, until 1973 (the last year for which sentencing data are available), no dramatic growth is evident for those convicted of indictable offences.

An examination of longer time-series data for Canada as a whole reveals that the trend of stability observed in rates of convictions for indictable offences applies nationally and historically (see figure 10.5). By contrast, convictions for summary offences, and especially those related to traffic regulation, have increased phenomenally. As Giffen (1976: 88–90) observes in presenting these data, the rate of adult-court convictions per 100,000 population age sixteen and older 'rose from

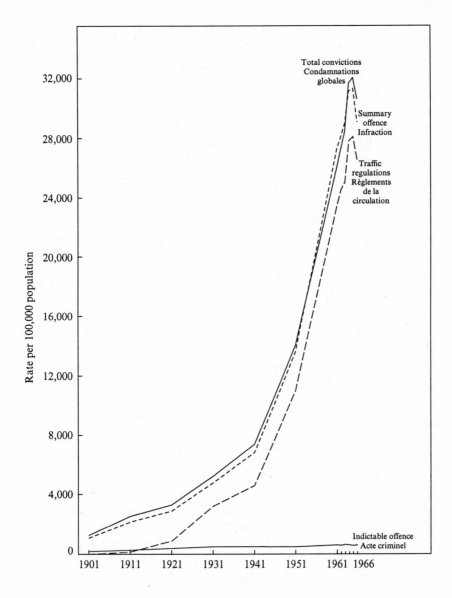

FIGURE 10.5
Canada: rate of convictions per 100,000 population by type of offence,
1901–1966
Reproduced from Ouimet (1969)

1,236 in 1901 to 32,010 in 1965, a twenty-five fold increase ... However ... 98 percent of this increase is accounted for by traffic offences, which in turn are responsible for 90 percent of the increase in summary convictions.' The disproportionate focus on policing traffic may be even more marked in Ontario than in most Canadian provinces. In 1977, Ontario had an enforcement rate of 16,666 per 100,000 population of provincial traffic statutes (excluding 'serious driving offences' and 'impaired driving'). Only Alberta had a higher rate. The average rate for the remaining provinces taken together was far lower, at 6,739 (National Task Force on the Administration of Justice 1979: 21). Clearly, the growth that has occurred in the conviction of offenders is accounted for almost entirely by the pursuit of minor violations, especially those connected with vehicular-traffic regulations.

Observational research confirms that police work more generally is primarily concerned with traffic and other minor violations (see Wilson 1968; Gardiner 1969; Webster 1970; Cumming, Cumming, and Edell 1970; Reiss 1971; Cain 1973; Manning 1977; Cordner 1979; Punch 1979). For example, Ericson (1982: 53), in his study of an Ontario police force, elaborates that the 'vast majority of the patrol officer's time is not spent working on crime-related troubles.' In the course of 348 shifts observed by the team of researchers, it was found that 'citizen contacts' did not occur at all during one-quarter of the shifts, and averaged just over two per shift. Almost one-half of those contacts that did occur were initiated by the police, and primarily involve their stopping vehicles that were considered to have made questionable moves and/or to contain questionable occupants. Overall, police patrol work was made up of 'routine stops and checks of motor vehicles and their occupants where no major investigation and no charges other than traffic summonses arise; dealing with found property; dealing with neighbour complaints of a trivial nature; checking the occupants of parked vehicles; checking hitchhikers or youths in parks; asking "disorderlies" to move on; and responding to a complaint that is immediately judged to be "unfounded"' (ibid: 53). For the average police patrol officer, therefore, 'crime work' occurred very rarely, and, when it did occur, it most often involved officers 'ordering petty disturbances, regulating driving, and sorting out property relations' (ibid: 206).

A focus on the criminal-justice system from the perspective of the courts also confirms that activity is concentrated at the soft, rather than the hard, end of the penal system. The complexities, and limited availability, of court sentencing data in Ontario mitigate concise and com-

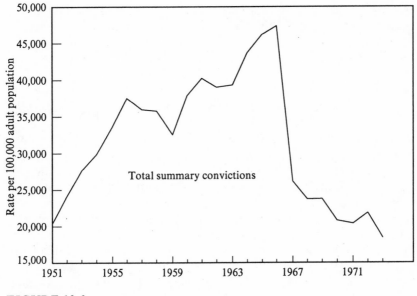

FIGURE 10.6
Ontario: total summary convictions, 1951–1972

prehensive documentation of these tendencies. Nevertheless, some general points can be made.

Most importantly, and as we have already seen, until the mid-1960s in Canada as a whole, the rates of convictions for summary offences vastly exceeded those for more serious indictable offences. This situation also applied in Ontario. Following the mid-1960s however, the picture becomes more complicated as, in 1966-7, there was a decrease of almost 50 per cent in summary convictions. Indeed, while the rate per 100,000 population of summary convictions had greatly increased (i.e., by more than 100 per cent) between 1951 and 1966, it then declined to such an extent that there were 10 per cent fewer summary convictions in 1973 (the final year for which data are available) than in 1951 (see figure 10.6).

Initially, this decrease in summary convictions in Ontario might appear to contradict the more general thesis that criminal-justice activity has been increasingly concentrating on the soft end of the penal spectrum. Closer examination of the trend, however, provides several clear reasons as to why the soft-end thesis is still supported. First, the dramatic decrease in summary convictions in 1966–7 was accomplished by the removal of data on 'prohibited parking' from the statistics. As, for example, in 1966, 'prohibited parking' had accounted for 56 per cent of all summary convictions, a decrease in overall summary convictions by definition followed the removal of this category. At the same time, police and other penal agents continued to pursue, administer, and penalize this minor violation on a massive scale. By removing this category from the data, and thereby recognizing that dealing with parking violations hardly constitutes crime work, the decrease in officially defined summary convictions confirms that the evolution of police work is in increasingly regulatory, and administrative, directions.

Second, the dramatic decrease in summary convictions confirms that criminal-justice activity is concentrated at the soft end of the penal spectrum because it reveals that, even when traffic violations were removed from the data, the aggregate of summary convictions continued to vastly exceed that of more serious indictable offences. Further examination of Ontario summary convictions excluding traffic from 1951–73 reveals that this situation applied throughout the period. For example, in 1951 there were 105,070 summary convictions excluding traffic, representing a total of 3,188 per 100,000 population. Meanwhile, 11,801 persons were convicted of indictable offences, representing a total of 358 per 100,000. In 1973, there were 231,184 summary convictions excluding traffic, representing a total of 4,134 per 100,000 population. The rate of persons convicted of indictable offences continued to be far lower: there were 23,408, representing a total of 419 per 100,000.

The court sentencing data available until 1973 also reveal the growing preoccupation of the penal system with soft-end activities as they document the proportionately declining use of imprisonment. For indictable offences, the imposition of imprisonment on persons convicted decreased from 50 per cent in 1951 to 34 per cent in 1973. In the case of summary convictions, the picture is again more complex. In particular, the high rate of sentences to a fine (i.e., over 90 per cent) tends to obscure the use of, and trends in, other dispositions. The classifying of some sentences under the uninformative category 'other disposition' also impedes analysis. Nevertheless, when the three dispositions of imprisonment, and suspended sentences with and without probation, are taken together, where imprisonment had constituted 35 per cent of such dispositions in 1956, its share had dropped to 21 per cent in 1972. In short, during the postwar period, judicial use of imprisonment proportionately declined, and there were corresponding increases in more administrative and regulatory dispositions, namely, the fine, and suspended sentences with and without probation.

Overall, there are multiple indicators of growing activity by the police, courts, and corrections, in the definition, pursuit, apprehension, administration, and penalizing of less serious offences. These indicators, however, provide little information on trends in potentially criminal behaviour itself. It is important, therefore, to address two questions: What have been the trends in behaviour liable to being defined as criminal? Have putative criminal events such as robbery, assault, and burglary actually increased? While it is impossible to answer definitively such questions, consultation of the findings of victimization surveys both in Canada and elsewhere provide useful insights on people's experiences of, and responses to, victimization. They also further illuminate how crime and crime rates are a socially constructed product largely shaped by police definitions.

Victim and Police Tendencies in Reporting and Recording Crime

The data on police and crime rates presented thus far give rise to more questions than answers about the trends in behaviour dealt with by the criminal-justice system. In particular, there is much ambiguity about trends in more serious forms of illegal activity liable to definition as indictable offences. If persons convicted of indictable offences are taken as the major indicator, the growth that has occurred appears to be as much related to that in police forces as to incidences of such behaviour in the general population. However, if offences reported, or charges laid, were to be taken as the major indicator, given that their increases have outpaced those in the size of police forces, the ensuing impression is that an increase in more serious criminal activity may well have occurred.

Given that many potentially criminal actions are not reported to the police, never mind effectively followed up by them, inquiry into trends in potentially criminal activity needs to go beyond the realm of official police data on crime. As they stand, Ontario official data on crime in the postwar period suggest that what may have occurred is an increase in police proactivity in recording and charging, coupled with a relative stability in the actual occurrence of more serious offences.

Victimization surveys – whereby people are interviewed about their experiences (and lack of experience) of victimization – offer another way of knowing about the extent of particular forms of, and responses to, troublesome behaviour, and about the complex interrelationship of policing and crime (Solicitor General of Canada 1983, 1984a, 1984c; Schneider 1982; Hough and Mayhew 1983; Birbeck 1983). In general, trends in crime rates reported in victimization surveys contrast sharply to those evidenced in official statistics.

Ideally, the official data I have presented should be compared with those of longitudinal victimization surveys carried out in Ontario. However, no longitudinal data are available for the province. Given the dearth of such data, I must draw primarily on the longitudinal u.s. Victimization Survey, which has been described as 'the most extensive survey of its kind in the world' (Doleschal 1979a: 125). I shall also draw on the only longitudinal Canadian data presently available, namely, the Edmonton Victimization Survey (EVS) (Solicitor General of Canada 1986). I shall also draw on the Canadian Urban Victimization Survey (CUVS) (Solicitor General of Canada 1983, 1984a, 1984c), which involved the original Edmonton Survey and surveys of six other major urban centres, including Toronto.

All of these surveys reaffirm that the majority of criminal incidents never come to the attention of the police. In Toronto, for example, it was estimated that, during the 1981[2] calendar year, 58 per cent of incidents involving sexual assault, robbery, assault, break and enter, motor-vehicle theft, household theft, personal theft, and vandalism were not reported to the police (Solicitor General of Canada 1983: 5). It can be seen, therefore, that even if official data on crimes reported had doubled, no increase in crime would necessarily have occurred. Meanwhile, the primary reason for victims not reporting was the common perception that the incident was 'too minor.' For example, 66 per cent of respondents in the 1981 Edmonton Survey gave this as their main reason. The second-most-often cited reason for not reporting was the victims' belief that the 'police couldn't do anything about it anyway,' with over 60 per cent of respondents stating this (Solicitor General of Canada 1984a: 2–3; Solicitor General of Canada 1986: 15).

Where reasons for reporting are concerned, the 1981 Canadian Survey (1984a, 3: 6) suggests that the requirement of insurance companies that auto and other thefts be reported to the police probably provides 'a powerful incentive for reporting such crimes.' This finding is supported by the 1984 Edmonton Survey (1986: 15), in which 50 per cent of those who had reported criminal incidents did so in order to 'file a report to claim insurance or compensation.' These major rationales both for, and for not, reporting crime open to dispute the extent to which victims see the occurrence of some criminal incidents – especially those involving property – as actually constituting serious 'problems,' and as likely to benefit from police and criminal-justice intervention.

TABLE 10.1
u.s. victimization rates per 1,000 persons twelve years and over, 1973–1976 and 1982

	Personal robbery	Robbery resulting in injury	Aggravated assault	Household burglary
1973	6.7	2.3	10.0	91.5
1974	7.1	2.3	10.3	92.6
1975	6.8	2.1	9.6	91.7
1976	6.5	2.1	9.9	88.9
1982	7.1	2.2	9.3	78.2

Sources: 1973–6 figures: Doleschal (1979a), p. 2; 1982 figures: u.s. Department of Justice, *Criminal Victimization in the U.S. 1982*, National Crime Survey Report

Victimization surveys also provide important insights on longer-term trends in the incidence of crime. Here, as noted, the u.s. Victimization Survey has offered the most detailed information. Notably, the survey suggests that, at least in the decade from the early 1970s, there was a pattern of stability and sometimes decline in the actual incidence of what are usually considered to be some of the more serious forms of criminal activity. Yet, during the same period, and as Doleschal (1979a: 1–2) has pointed out, the official u.s. Uniform Crime Reports were suggestive of a 'crime epidemic such as the world has never known.' The suggestion of the u.s. official data that crime was rising at a much faster rate than population growth was not borne out by the Victimization Survey. Focusing on the period 1973–6, Doleschal concludes that 'crime rates while far exceeding the reported level, were remarkably stable.' He further observed that 'the more serious the crime, the more stable the rate' (ibid: 2). An examination of the figures cited by Doleschal, in conjunction with those of the later 1982 u.s. Victimization Survey, indicates that the predominant trend of stability continued, and that, in the case of household burglary, a decline occurred in the rate of victimization (see table 10.1).

The Edmonton Victimization (EVS) Survey covers only two years – 1981 and 1984 – but nevertheless includes useful information about experiences of victimization, and about the anomalous relationship of official crime rates to criminal activity. Overall, the study reports a 15 per cent drop in estimated incidents in 1984 compared to 1981. According to the survey, decrease was also reflected in official statistics (Solicitor General of Canada 1986: 3, 4).[3] However, the survey's reference to official crime rates, along with failure to provide many details of the statistics, complicates analysis. Nevertheless, while the overall trend may have been similar, a focus on the more specific categories of 'violent' crimes, particularly 'sexual assault,' illuminates some of the divergences and discrepancies between the victimization and official data. Most notably, the differing accounts which they provide testify to police proclivity in recording offences.

Where the category of 'total violent' offences is concerned, when the 'victimization' rate (i.e., number of victims per 1,000 of population) is used, the EVS reflects a decline of 11 per cent, from 82 per 1,000 in 1981 to 73 per 1,000 in 1984 (Solicitor General of Canada 1986: Appendix 1, Table A1). The same data represent a decline of over 7 per cent – from 70 per 1,000 in 1981 to 63 per 1,000 in 1984 – when the 'incident' rate is used (i.e., number of incidents per 1,000 population) (EVS: 15–16). Yet, despite these decreases, the report states that 'the rate for all violent crimes remains unchanged' (ibid: 4). Apparently the basis for this statement is the finding that the 11 per cent drop in 'victimization' is 'not statistically significant' (ibid: Appendix 1, Table A1). The report then goes on to make an observation that illuminates some of the discrepancies between the accounts of victims and those of the official statistics. Specifically, according to the report, 'these declines in the crime rate are also evident in the official (U.C.R.) statistics which reflect a very marginal increase (.4%) in the rate of violent crimes' (ibid: 4). Therefore, criminal acts that represent a minimum of 7 per cent *decrease* in the victimization survey appear as a marginal *increase* in the official reports.

This discrepancy is partly explained by the Edmonton Survey's finding a decline in occurrences of sexual assaults (pp. 5–6) in 1984 along with an increase in their rate of being reported (p. 12). However sexual assaults only constituted 2.3 of the total rate of 63 violent incidents per 1,000 population, so it is unlikely that this could account for the increase reflected in the official statistics. Examination of the other two components of 'violent' offences cannot explain the increase in official rates either. Assault, the largest category of offence according to victims' accounts, declined from a rate of 56 per 1,000 in 1981 to 51 in 1984. Coupled with the identical level of reporting by victims, this should have led to a decrease in the official statistics. Robbery remained stable, with an estimated rate of 9 per 1,000 in both 1981 and 1984. Along with a slight decline in the proportion of incidents reported, this should also have led to a decrease in the official statistics.

In the absence of Edmonton's official statistics it is difficult to draw final conclusions as to the exact bases of these discrepancies. Certainly, one cannot expect exact congruence between the definition of categories in victimization surveys and those of the official crime rates. Nevertheless, the content of the 1984 Victimization Survey suggests that there should have been a decline in the rate of violent crime compared to 1981, instead of which a marginal increase occurred. Overall, the inference can be made that official crime rates are affected not only by the level of reporting by victims, but also by police practices in defining and reporting crime. In this instance it seems likely that, in 1984, the Edmonton police had a greater propensity to classify and record acts as criminal than was the case in 1981.'

The importance of police trends in reporting in determining official crime rates is also affirmed by the 1984 Edmonton Victimization Survey's comments on 'property crime rates.' In this case, victim reporting underwent a 'dramatic and significant decline of between 15% and 28% over the three year period.' The official crime rates, meanwhile, reflected 'a decrease of 16% in the property crime rate over the same period' (p. 4). Given that 'household theft' constitutes the most common type of theft, and that its occurrence had decreased by 21 per cent (with the reporting rate dropping by 2 per cent),' it would be expected that the official crime rates would evidence a larger decrease than 16 per cent. Here, as in the case of violent crimes, it appears that the police had an increased propensity to classify and record crimes in 1984, with the result that the official property crime rate did not decrease to the extent indicated by the victimization survey.

In light of these observations, the Edmonton Survey's conclusion that 'the decline in [official] crime rates ... is not an artifact of shifts in reporting patterns, but reflects a decrease in the types of criminal victimizations surveyed in Edmonton' glosses over the disjunctures that exist between the different sources. In so doing, it also fails to explore how changes in reporting patterns, and especially those of the police, did affect the official crime rates.

In addition to illuminating the socially constructed and organized nature of crime statistics, the 1984 survey also illustrates contradictory aspects of public perceptions of crime. As noted earlier, the survey data document a decrease of 15 per cent of the occurrence of criminal incidents in 1984, as compared to 1981. When questioned about the level of crime in their own neighbourhoods, the majority of respondents considered it to be low (60 per cent) and stable (58 per cent). Yet, at the same time, over half of the respondents believed that 'city-wide crime had increased over the past two years' (p.16). It seems, then, that public perceptions of the extent of crime generally may be more influenced by public-culture presentations than immediate experience. This discrepancy, coupled with the finding that in practice most victims considered the crimes they experienced 'too minor' to report to police, highlights the need for gathering data from a number of sources in formulating and in justifying criminal-justice policy.

In sum, owing to the lack of longitudinal victimization data in the Ontario context, it is impossible to specify trends in the occurrence of potentially criminal behaviour during the postwar period. Nevertheless, inquiry into the findings of existing Canadian and American surveys reaffirms the need for caution in interpreting increases in officially recorded criminal offences as reflecting real increases in such offences. 'Crime' is a social product, not only with respect to traffic and other minor violations, but also in relation to more serious offences.

Trends in Penal and Social Control

> ... the predominating tendency in modern social control is, first, away from reliance on secondary social control (through the penal area, for example), and towards control of primary relations; and secondly, within the sphere of secondary control, 'to displace control away from detention (incarceration) towards police measures of various forms of social surveillance.' (Bottoms 1983: 191, citing Melossi 1979: 96)

Taken together, data on crime, policing, sentencing, and corrections yield a more complete picture of contemporary penal trends. The extent to which potentially criminal activity has grown – particularly, more serious forms of such activity – remains unknown, and open to question. However, it is clear that definitions of behaviour as criminal, and the processes whereby people become subject to penal orders including incarceration, depends largely on police mobilization and exercise of discretion. During the postwar period the size of police forces in Ontario grew at over twice the rate of that of the general population, and their growth has been associated with growth in the recording and charging of criminal offences per member of the population.

Examination of police and official data on crime has revealed that police mobilization has more usually consisted of proactively pursuing, processing, and penalizing minor violations than in their reactively responding to, and dealing with, more serious criminal offences. Consistently over time, the 'average' police officer in Ontario could expect to make approximately one indictable-offence charge every three weeks, apart from those that were traffic related. The officer could expect to see one charge made leading to conviction for an indictable offence about once every nine months. By contrast, the officer could expect to process a far greater number of people and violations in the context of traffic situations. However, although police officers' activities have been concentrated in the realm of petty traffic and other minor violations, these encounters have provided the opportunity for the police to invoke their substantial powers – including decisions to incarcerate – in situations where those being apprehended have violated previous penal orders. Over time, the growing use of the fine for indictable offences, for summary convictions other than traffic, and for parking infractions has provided a large number of defaulters vulnerable to the threat of further penal intervention.

This analysis of penal trends accords with observations made by Melossi (1979) and Bottoms (1983): the locus of social control within the penal sphere has shifted away from incarceration and towards social surveillance by the police and other penal agents. First, where corrections are concerned, there has been a clear decrease in imprisonment. At the same time, there has been a growing involvement by correctional authorities in the management of non-carceral sanctions. Substantively, community corrections have evolved such that the exercise of penal control includes surveillance not only by penal agents directly employed by the state, but also by those associated with non-state agencies.

Second, where the courts and sentencing are concerned, the use of 'soft end' sanctions has increased at a far greater rate than has the use of imprisonment. Indeed, for indictable convictions, the use of imprisonment declined between the early 1950s and early 1970s, relative to the population as well as to the use of other sanctions. Increasingly, both fines and probation have been used instead of imprisonment. In the case of summary convictions, the use and growth of non-incarcerative dispositions are also striking. Summary convictions are overwhelmingly associated with the use of fines. Moreover, there has been a substantial growth in the use of suspended sentences without probation. Not surprisingly, therefore, the use of imprisonment on summary conviction declined proportionate to that of other offences. However, along with the more general increase in summary convictions excluding traffic, in rates per 100,000 population the use of imprisonment grew. As these findings show, penal trends are by no means unilinear.

Third, the police have constituted the major growth sector of criminal justice during the postwar period. Their numbers have more than doubled in proportion to the population. The police have consistently accounted for the majority of criminal-justice expenditures, and, during the 1970s, the pre-existing gap between spending on the police compared to on the courts and corrections widened further (Solicitor General of Canada 1984b: 1). Given their powers in defining crime rates, apprehending and charging suspects, and enforcing penal orders, police can be considered to be the primary penal agents. However, rather than fighting crime, the police are more engaged in bureaucratic-administrative regulation, and in seeking compliance with norms (Kamenka and Tay 1975; Reiss 1984). Similar to that of community-correctional workers, police power often resides more in the threat of the exercise of penal power than in the process of invoking specific penalties.

Overall, penal control has changed substantially during the postwar period. Penal agents have fostered new areas of intervention, and have adopted new penal strategies, methodologies, and technologies in doing so (see Ericson and Shearing 1986). Individuals who are offenders, or who are considered to be potential offenders, may have the familial, work, recreational, financial, and other aspects of their lives investigated, monitored, managed, and controlled by penal agents, from the police to community-correctional workers. The penal surveillance of whole areas and groups has changed, with an increased emphasis on state-fostered community policing including Neighbourhood Watch, Crime Stoppers, and other such programs (see Bottoms 1983; Mathiesen 1983). Meanwhile, the development of the numerical strength, of the resources, and of the territorial ambit of private security personnel has also fostered new areas of penal regulation (see Shearing and Stenning 1981, 1983b). In sum, penal control in the late twentieth century goes far beyond the ambit of criminal justice as popularly conceived. The primary actions of penal agents and agencies lie in the pursuit and management of actual, and potential, petty violations.

11

Knowledge, Power, and Decarceration

Decarceration in Ontario

Decarceration is possible. In Ontario, prison admissions declined by about 31 per cent and prisoner counts by about 20 per cent, per 100,000 population between the 1950s and the 1980s.

As documented in previous chapters, this decarceration reflected changing perspectives and policies in dealing with offenders. Both criminal justice and social reform played a part. The development and growing use of probation from the 1950s provided an alternative that appears to have been used instead of imprisonment in some cases. Even more importantly, changing perceptions of, and responses to, those charged with public intoxication resulted in their deinstitutionalization. During the 1950s, intoxication offenders had accounted for about 50 per cent of total admissions to Ontario prisons. By the early 1980s, they accounted for only about 14 per cent of sentenced admissions.

The major findings of this study clearly run contrary to the common view that the growth of prison population is inexorable, and largely beyond control. These findings also run contrary to basic premises of the conventional wisdom on decarceration. Where critics have argued that the growth of community corrections is typically accompanied by the maintenance and increase of imprisonment, I have documented that the growth of Ontario's primary community program of probation was accompanied by a decrease in imprisonment. Where critics have argued that the growth of community corrections has been synonymous with net-widening in terms of those coming into the system, I have documented that such net-widening did not occur in Ontario during the postwar period: in 1961, prison plus probation admissions represented a total of 1,622 per 100,000 population; in 1984, the rate stood at 1,402.

These findings are particularly striking in light of the fact that Ontario trends have previously been posited, and have been internationally accepted, as reflecting net-widening, including the maintenance and growth of imprisonment (Chan and Ericson 1981; Austin and Krisberg 1982; Bottoms 1983; Chan and Zdenkowski 1986a; Cohen 1985; Mathiesen 1983, 1986; Scull 1984). The discordant findings documented here affirm that other critical analyses of imprisonment and alternatives might benefit from further re-examination.

Empirically, one area in need of re-examination is the meaning of the word 'alternatives' as used in the literature. Critical analysts of decarceration have usually limited their attention to alternatives that take a community-correctional form. Other sentencing dispositions, and their impact on the use of imprisonment, have been neglected. Yet examination of Ontario developments has illustrated how trends in imprisonment are related to those in alternatives outside of the correctional realm. Most notably, trends in the administration and enforcement of fines have been directly relevant to the decrease in imprisonment: decreases in fine-default admissions to prison for intoxication primarily account for decarceration in Ontario.

As several other authors (Bottoms 1983; Young forthcoming) have emphasized, failure to consider fines has seriously limited analyses of the power to punish. Nor is this omission merely a matter of another empirical detail to be included. As Peter Young (ibid) has suggested: 'the question to ask about the fine is why it is used such a great deal yet hardly registers in our conception of punishment at all.' The empirical omission signifies some deeper analytical issues.

Critical analyses have been circumscribed, not only by their omissions, but also by their interpretations of what has been included. In particular, the concept of net-widening has been associated with empirically problematic statements. As I have documented, net-widening – in terms of correctional counts – is by definition a feature of community alternatives to imprisonment. Especially in a case such as Ontario – where average prison terms are far shorter than average probation terms – any transfer of prisoners to community correctional programs will necessarily result in a growth in the numbers under correctional control on any given day. Here, as in many jurisdictions, a growth in correctional counts *must* occur, even where community corrections begin to be used instead of imprisonment, and with no new people being brought into the system. If the implementation of community alternatives, even in ideal-typical form, must lead to net-widening in terms of counts, how can this occurrence be used as an indicator of the failure of penal reform?

As with the neglect of fines, the conceptual obfuscation associated with net-widening suggests that the problems are not merely ones of mis- or inadequate counting. Rather, there are deeper theoretical and political matters to be considered.

The Contradiction between Theories and Politics

> The economy of decarceration has the same features as the economy of earlier reforms, and penal reforms simply reflect the wider economy of power relations under welfare state capitalism. Except for continued, perpetual tinkering at the organizational level among interested professionals in the crime-control business, we cannot expect much change in this state. After all, it is part of the order of things. (Chan and Ericson 1981: 68)

> Where should reform efforts be directed when all paths seem corrupted and no enlightening solutions are apparent? (Cullen and Gilbert 1982: 245–6)

> Suppose one *had* an alternative: should one keep quiet about it? (Downes 1980: 82)

In pointing to deeper problems characteristic of the conventional wisdom, I initially highlighted analysts' lack of attention to the position of critical criminology within the wider network of knowledge-power relations. Critical criminologists have incisively deconstructed the assumptions, latent agenda, and ominous consequences of correctionalist, official, and reform discourses. By contrast, they have been far less reflexive about the parameters and uses of critical discourses themselves. Yet – and as the use of net-widening argument by Ontario officials illustrates – critical discourses also become a part of the penal complex. Therefore, adequate study of penality must involve scrutiny of the contours of critical analysis. This need for reflexivity is reaffirmed by critical awareness, first, that the social formation of knowledge, and the exercise of power, intersect with and mutually reinforce one another; second, that knowledge is fundamentally ideological (Smith 1974, 1984); and third, that one's frame of reference both defines and limits the story that can be told.

One way of identifying and addressing the deeper problems characteristic of the conventional wisdom is in terms of a divergence, or contradiction, that has come to exist between critical theories and politics. Put simply, the conclusions of critical analyses and the political objectives of analysts have often seemed to be in conflict with one another. At an extreme, one might say that many critical theories have seemed to deny the very possibility of a progressive penal politics.

This conflict between critical theories and politics can be illustrated through retracing important landmarks in the evolution of critical criminology. As elaborated in chapter 3, early critical criminology had as a major objective the development of a progressive penal politics. Where positivist and correctionalist criminology was seen as having primarily served the interests of officials engaged in the exercise of penal control, critical criminology aspired to serve those people subject to this control. In keeping with this objective, criminology was 'reconceived as politics' (Garland and Young 1983: 6; Cohen 1979a). Theoretically, the agenda was broadened, with attention being paid to political, economic, and ideological issues (Sim, Scraton, and Gordon 1987: 5). Politically, commitment was made to intervention, with critical criminologists' participation in prisoners' movements of the 1970s being one important reflection of this (ibid: 10 et seq).

Over time, the outlook of critical criminology has become decidedly gloomy. The themes associated with the net-widening argument are key signifiers of this trend: it has been claimed that prison populations have been maintained and increased, while community corrections proliferated; it has been asserted that more people are coming into the correctional system; and then it has been concluded that 'alternatives' are better understood as 'add-ons.' As encapsulated by Downes (1988: 60): 'we end up with the worst of both worlds: an unreconstructed *ancien regime penal* and a new-style carceral society.' Within corrections, as in penal and social systems more generally, the overarching historical and contemporary tendency is seen as being one towards 'more social control' (Cohen, 1989). With reform merely serving the interests of control, the prospects for progressive intervention seem bleak. It is hardly surprising that aspiring activists acquainted with the literature utter heartfelt cries about what should be done.

How did this gloomy perspective evolve? Ironically – and as I have documented – despite critical criminologists' desire to supersede the logic and constraints of their correctionalist predecessors, their reasoning and conclusions often bear a strong similarity. Specifically, the conclusion of many positivists that 'nothing works' in rehabilitating the recalcitrant offender appears to have been transmuted by critical criminologists: 'nothing works' in reforming the recalcitrant criminal-justice system. The decline of optimism in mainstream criminology, therefore, has its parallel within critical criminology.

Nevertheless, while the notion that 'nothing works' is important, Foucault's work has been more, and more explicitly, pertinent in the genesis of gloomy critical perspectives, particularly where corrections have been concerned. This influence can be seen in relation to both theoretical and political matters.

Theoretically, Foucault's *Discipline and Punish* was an important landmark for critical criminology. Critiques of imprisonment – informed by destructuring movements such as anti-psychiatry, and by the attacks made on rehabilitation – were already well developed. But, as David Garland has observed (1990: 867), *Discipline and Punish* 'was able effectively to reinvent the field of penology. It provided a conceptual and historical basis for subsequent research and gave to penal studies a specific direction and a critical ambition.' Critical analyses of punishment began more clearly to move beyond technicist criminological concerns, and to address wider issues of power. Within the growing literature, themes derived from Foucault were affirmed and reaffirmed: power can be analysed as a 'thing' with even apparently trivial or benign developments facilitating its refinement and extension; the development of the human sciences has been associated with the emergence of new, and ever more ominous, disciplinary mechanisms of power; the endless process of penal reform facilitates the growing subtlety, complexity, and pervasiveness of control.

Politically, similarly distinctive, and gloomy, interpretations have often been derived from Foucault. Where struggle is concerned, Foucault has sometimes been interpreted as implying that 'every gesture of resistance turns out to be an extension and refinement of power, that resistance is ultimately collaboration, and that no effective politics is possible' (Gandal 1986: 121). Following from this, for critical criminologists – as for many other critical theorists – the major political option often read into Foucault has been that of 'an ethic of non-participation' (ibid: 22).[1] When critical criminologists have drawn on Foucault in arguing that not only does 'nothing work,' but that this failure facilitates the refinement of control, political participation has appeared redundant. At best, critical politics becomes that of protesting current conditions and tendencies in prisons and other parts of the criminal-justice system. At worst, it results in the abstentionist stance of doing nothing.

In short, critical criminology arrived at an internally contradictory position. The more sophisticated the sociology of penal control has become – particularly in documenting the expansion of penal control in ever more subtle, complex, and effective forms – the less prospect there seems to have been for developing the progressive penal politics claimed to be aspired to by critical criminology. The end result is that, as expressed by Garland and Young (1983: 7), 'the findings and politics of radical criminology seem to evaporate before the reality of that which it says is central and abiding; the politics of control.'

No doubt, critical criminologists have found their own ways of resolving this 'tension between our macro-theory and analysis which often ends up in a pessimistic, nihilistic, demystificatory frame of reference ... and our sense as political animals that we can still do something about the world' (Cohen, in interview with McMahon and Kellough 1987: 140). Many critical criminologists *do* actively engage penal politics in various shapes and forms. But the decarceration literature gives little indication of this. In particular, there is a dearth of analysis of struggles around, and attempts to develop, progressive alternatives to imprisonment and critical criminologists' participation in this (for some notable exceptions, see Brown and Hogg 1985; Brown 1987; Mathiesen 1974, 1990; Miller 1991; Morris 1989). Even left realists – that sector of critical criminology that has most resolutely addressed the need to engage penal politics – have tended to focus far more on issues of victimization and policing than on punishment. And, when they have focused on the latter, while their tendency has been 'to suggest that we are currently overusing imprisonment, and this is a flaw in need of immediate rectification' (Schwartz and DeKeseredy 1991: 67), there has not been much elaboration of how this might be accomplished (for the most detailed statement, see Matthews 1989).

Perhaps the contradiction between theory and politics is one that individuals should simply acknowledge and live with. Such individually schizoid solutions, however, do little to ameliorate the wider abstentionist message deriving from critical criminology. The question remains: What, if anything, can be done?

When this question has been raised and addressed in the critical literature, ensuing discussion has primarily focused on the realm of political activities and strategies: admiration is expressed for the odd process that seems not quite to fit with the sad general story (e.g., deinstitutionalization of juveniles in Massachusetts in the early 1970s); attention is called to some apparently progressive developments (e.g., rape crisis centres); speculation is engaged in about how various interest groups might more effectively coordinate and cooperate in challenging current penal developments.

Stimulating as such discussions are, they seem strangely separate from the broader theoretical analysis. For example, where deinstitutionalization in Massachusetts is concerned, despite the laudatory tone of much of the literature, subsequent developments in the state have also been subject to a conventional-wisdom reading: by the end of the 1970s, it had been alleged that the budget of the Youth Department had risen substantially; that the number of youngsters coming under its jurisdiction had grown; that hundreds of new community residences had been developed;that the recidivism rate was higher than under the old training-school system; and that the number of youngsters being sent to secure custody was gradually increasing. The treatment of young people in some of the new residential facilities had also given rise to scandal (Greenberg 1975; see generally *Corrections Magazine* 1975). In short, it is probably not difficult to develop an argument that the ensuing system widened the net and was more expensive, less effective, and just as inhumane as the old system. Meanwhile, where rape crisis centres are concerned, beneficial as they certainly are to many victims, from the conventional-wisdom perspective it could easily be argued that they also facilitate expansion of the criminal-justice system and its ultimately oppressive activities.[2]

All too often, therefore, it seems that one has had to leave behind one's critical theoretical insights in order to discuss the prospects of meaningful political engagement. This separation between what might crudely be described as theoretical pessimism and political optimism has also been alluded to by Cohen (in interview with McMahon and Kellough 1987: 144, 143) in discussing the last chapter of his *Visions of Social Control*:

> I wrote that chapter – 'What is to be Done?' – and I was uncomfortable about it all the time. I often thought of not doing it altogether. I just thought I had to. Many people have criticized me for doing it, saying 'That's spoilt the book – it's great up to there.' It *is* unsatisfactory because it leaves so many questions unanswered ... It obviously doesn't all fit together. It intrudes a note of optimism in what seems to be a rather nihilistic position ... I think it's fair to say that much of where I went (despite adding on that last chapter) shows an irresolvable gap between the kind of analysis I present up to there and my attempt afterwards to find cracks.

In this study, I have sought to demonstrate that the question 'What can be done?' needs to be addressed not just in the political, but also in the theoretical context. The quest is that of accomplishing a more harmonious relationship between critical analyses and politics. At issue are: Can critical analytical frameworks be modified such that they better accord with our preferred political stance? What are the theoretical constraints that currently inhibit the development of a progressive penal politics?

Constraining Conceptions of Power

The first step towards dealing with current constraints is to acknowledge that, in critical criminology, as in criminology more generally, '"politics" enters into "discourse" *at the level of discourse*: in the texts and theoretical statements themselves, and not just in their context or deployment' (Garland 1985a: 4; emphasis in original). The problem in critical criminology is that the politics that has been most effectively entered into theoretical discourse is a nihilistic or pessimistic one. By contrast, few theoretical concepts reflecting a more liberative, or transformational, politics have been developed. Put crudely, decarceration analysts, and other critical criminologists, have been far more adept at analysing the ominous, as opposed to the admirable, aspects of any given phenomenon.

A range of core critical concepts effectively inhibit recognition, articulation, and affirmation of potentially liberative penal politics. The net-widening argument is a good example of this. The concept of 'wider,' along with 'stronger' and 'different,' nets is effective in directing attention *towards* trends in the expansion and extension of penal control. These concepts also serve to direct attention *away* from any moderation of penal control that might have taken place, and from the superseding of some previous forms of control by preferable ones. Ability to recognize any reductions of penal control is limited. Any diminution can analytically be quickly overshadowed by the discovery of other, new forms of control considered of more significance in their sinister potential. Within this perspective – as I have sought to document – assumptions and conclusions are easily confused. With the very notion of 'different' becoming synonymous with 'sinister,' it is difficult to see how any innovation could be recognized as even potentially progressive.

Critical concepts such as 'net-widening,' 'discipline,' and 'control' are pseudonyms for the exercise of power. As Young (forthcoming) has expressed it, the sociology of punishment can be interpreted as that of power. It is in a similarly one-dimensional conception of power that the crux of the contradiction between critical theory and politics may rest.

The work of critical theorists reflects a distinct stance towards the phenomenon of power: 'the fundamental position of many of those who work within the modern sociology of punishment can be summarized thus – beware of power, distrust those who hold it, resist its exercise, attack its institutions' (Young forthcoming). Therefore, although power – following Foucault – is usually depicted as a creative or productive force, critical assessments of the exercise of power, and of its effects, are overwhelmingly negative (see Garland 1990: 173).

This overwhelmingly negative stance towards power has had problematic reverberations throughout the literature. For example, with the penal realm being recognized as an important site for the exercise of power, there has been a tendency to take a unitary view of state, as well as of other agents and agencies involved in criminal justice. The activities of politicians, policy makers, administrators, officials, the judiciary, state researchers and non-state agencies and reformers who participate in criminal-justice activities and politics have been eyed with suspicion. With such a unitary view of those involved in the penal realm, its internal contradictions and complexities are easily obscured. The experiences of those who have struggled for progressive changes within the penal realm have all too often been omitted from the critical criminological story.

In face of the overwhelmingly critical view, it is difficult to distinguish what forms of the exercise of penal power, and by whom, might be preferable to others. For example, where policing is concerned, the arbitrary exercise of power by the public police has been well documented, with even community forms of policing being located on the carceral continuum, and serving to reinforce discipline (e.g., Ericson 1981, 1982; Gordon 1987). Attempts at controlling the police through internal or external agencies have generally been seen as ineffective, co-opted, and/or 'cooling out' mechanisms that serve to reinforce, rather than modify, police power (e.g., McMahon 1988a; McMahon and Ericson 1984). Meanwhile, with various forms of 'community' involvement in policing, the story is also grim: Crime Stoppers turns out to be not of the grass roots, and to primarily serve in the interests of 'elite players in private corporations, the police and the mass media' (Carriere and Ericson 1989: 105); Neighbourhood Watch, while it might actually benefit some (middle-class) sectors of the community, also yields the threat that it 'simply widens the nets of surveillance and increases the amount of intelligence-gathering, with all the threats to civil liberties such activities pose' (Brogden, Jefferson, and Walklate 1988: 180). The situation of policing activities farther removed from the purview of the state is, if anything, even more worrying: private security personnel have greatly increased and are even less accountable to their subjects than the public police; their activities represent the dispersal of discipline par excellence; one of their likely consequences is 'a widening and deepening of the social control net' (Reichman 1987: 249; see generally Shearing and Stenning 1981, 1983b, 1984, 1987).

A similar story of the exercise of power, and its apparent immutability, has been told about courts and the legal process. For the most part, justice is summary. Even when it is brought into play, 'due process' turns out to be 'for crime control' (McBarnet 1981). Accordingly, 'defendants' turn out to be 'dependants,' with even the work of the defence lawyers contributing to this view (Ericson and Baranek 1982). Meanwhile, where new and alternative kinds of informal justice are concerned, as Cain (1985) has observed, much of the critical literature again ends up in a gloomy school of thought: informalism is 'sinister' and 'a disguised form of state expansion' is 'a failure in its own terms,' and/or is 'impossible.'

A summary as brief as this one necessarily overrides the sophistication and insights of these literatures. What is important for the present purposes, however, is their general thrust. As is the case in the literature on decarceration, the general conclusion arrived at is that penal control is ominous, impervious to modification, and expanding, and that the most recent proposals and innovations should be considered the most suspect.

One of the dilemmas that arise from this perspective is that critical criminologists sometimes find themselves implying that earlier ways of exercising penal power, which they have already rejected, might be preferable, or at least less objectionable. This situation can be seen, for example, in relation to recent developments concerning probation in England and Wales. There, the general tendency is towards the managerial situation that already applies in some Canadian jurisdictions: the probation officer's role should more explicitly become one of control, and the private sector should be more involved in the delivery of services to probationers. In short, the traditional role of advising, assisting, befriending, and attempting to respond to the 'needs' of offenders would no longer be the important component it has been of the probation officer's mandate (see Ward 1989; Ryan and Ward 1991).

Critical commentators have vigorously protested these proposals, and their potential for strengthening the controls involved in a probation disposition. But, at the same time, there is an 'understandable ambivalence' about 'supporting a position which remains close to the discredited tradition of individualized casework' (Ward 1989: 19). Once again, the initiative in setting the reform agenda is left to more conservative forces. Critics appear to be 'incapable of doing more than criticizing, that is incapable of being more than negative' (Greenberg 1983: 325). The current tendencies are opposed; previous approaches cannot be defended; alternative proposals about what should be done with those likely to be subject to control are not forthcoming.

The repudiation of power also helps to explain why critical analysts have often been 'paralysed by a lack of any alternative basis upon which to think forms of penal regulation' (Garland and Young 1983: 34). The very notion of regulation implies that of power. Accordingly, thinking of alternative bases of regulation implies thinking about ways of exercising power. But, with even apparently benign and trivial forms of power having been analysed as suspect, thinking about alternative ways in which penal power might be exercised becomes difficult. Ensuing analyses might be read as strategies towards the taking of power. With the exercise of penal power generally being opposed, such analyses become unthinkable. Political activity is stymied.

Changing Conceptions of Power

> I will ... not deny the validity of the perspective Foucault sets out, but will challenge its capacity to stand on its own as an explanatory framework for the analysis of punishment and penal change ... a wider more pluralistic vision is necessary. (Garland 1990: 157)

Just as constraining conceptions of power – along with allied ones such as net-widening, the dispersal of discipline, and the expansion of penal control – have been becoming dominant, a growing number of authors have begun expressing a variety of concerns about their implications for critical analyses (e.g., Cain 1985; Chunn and Gavigan 1988; Cohen 1988b; Garland 1986, 1990; Nelken 1989; Rodger 1988; Ryan and Ward 1989: ch. 5). More broadly, feminist and sociolegal scholars – often drawing from postmodern perspectives – have been focusing attention on the potential and possibilities of, as well as limitations on, progressive developments (e.g., Cain 1991; Chesney-Lind 1991; Dobash and Dobash 1991; Lacombe 1991; Snider 1991b). Within the decarceration literature, related expressions of concern about dominant concepts – including more or less explicit autocritiques – have also been developing (e.g., Bottoms 1983; Cohen 1988a; Ericson and McMahon 1987; Matthews 1987, 1989; Vass and Weston 1990). In light, first, of the theoretical constraints that exist and concerns being expressed about them; second, of the fact that some of the troubles and problems currently dealt with by the criminal-justice system do, and will continue to, merit some form of response and thereby exercise of penal power; and third, of the peculiarity of critical abhorrence of power in the penal realm as against a willingness to engage other power relations,[3] a modified perspective on power appears necessary for the advancement of critical criminology.

Advocating that critical perspectives on power be modified is by no means suggesting that a naïve optimism should be substituted for radical pessimism. But a modest proposal can be made. Rather than seeing the exercise of penal power as always, and everywhere, involving only more social control, repression, domination, and subjection, the possibility should be raised. What are the situations – be they occasional, and historically, culturally, and geographically specific – where there have been components of the exercise of penal power that have accorded with progressively preferred values? Where, how, and when – whether accidentally or even purposefully – have penal developments reflected elements of the 'paradox of a liberative penalty' (Garland and Young 1983: 33)?

I have sought to document the rather different story that such a modified perspective can provide in the particular case of postwar penal trends in Ontario. By simply bearing in mind that the consequence of penal and social reform might not always be only expansionist, a more complete story – pointing to the complexities and contradictions of penal trends, including their reductionist aspects – could begin to be told.

Arguably, this more open stance also provides better prospects for those who wish to struggle for reductionism to participate in penal politics. Rather than being limited to dismissing all innovations as inherently expansionist, more informed speculation about the likely consequences of different strategies becomes possible. In the particular case of Ontario, and Canada more generally, reductionist reformers would vigorously argue against the newer community programs that have been developed as *adjuncts* of probation. Yet, at the same time, there are strong grounds for supporting the disposition of probation per se.

More specific to imprisonment, Ontario, and Canada's continuing high rate of imprisonment should be challenged: in 1988, Canada's national prisoner count stood at about 109 per 100,000 population.

This rate was higher than the equivalent rates provided by the Council of Europe (1988) for more than twenty member states as of 1 February 1988,[4] with the average rate being about 65 per 100,000. In particular, the continuing Canadian phenomenon of imprisoning people for defaulting on fines warrants the attention of serious advocates of decarceration, and especially in cases where economic and ethnic characteristics have impeded payment. In conjunction, the more general tendency of imprisoning large numbers of people for short periods should also be addressed:[5] in the 1990 fiscal year, 44 per cent of all sentenced admissions in Ontario were for under thirty days, and fully 78 per cent were for less than four months. The high rate of people remanded in custody should also be a major concern.

A more open perspective on penal power that acknowledges its potential to develop in more progressive as well as repressive directions might also yield historically different stories about other strategies and policies. For example, where rehabilitation is concerned, the key themes of the critical story have converged on the charge that 'treatment is punishment.' But, here again, important subplots of the story have been forgotten or overlooked. For example, little attention has been given to the period prior the 1970s when the ideology of rehabilitation 'served as the reference point for critics of the penal system' (Bayer 1981: 186) and to such gains as were made through this point of reference.

For example, in the case of Ontario, we have seen that the ideology of rehabilitation provided justification within the prison system for small – but arguably important – reforms in prisoners' living conditions and autonomy (Oliver 1985). Moreover, the wider possibilities afforded under the ethos of rehabilitation in terms of how it facilitated liberative transformations of regimes for groups of prisoners, and even the accomplishment of decarceration, have largely been overlooked. Here, the work of David Downes is a notable exception. First, where individual institutions are concerned, Downes (1980: 78–9) has reminded critics of penal reform about how the rehabilitation ethos facilitated the development of a comparatively liberal regime for some long-term prisoners through the development of a special unit at Barlinnie Prison in Scotland:

> the development of the special unit at Barlinnie Prison, arguably the most promising innovation post-war, comes at a time when 'treatment' and 'rehabilitation' are being written off as useful goals for the penal system. Yet the prisoners selected for Barlinnie were among the most

violent in Scottish jails: the concept of a 'therapeutic community' was at the core of the thinking that made the creation of the special unit possible; and the initiative for its establishment came from within the Scottish prison service (see Johnston and MacLeod 1975). Eloquent testimony to the flexibility and willingness to experiment with democratic procedures within the unit has been provided by Jimmy Boyle (1977), himself sentenced to life imprisonment for murder, and scarred by having spent four of his six years in prison in solitary confinement ... The experience of growing trust between inmates and staff, the gradual extensions of freedom within the unit, led Boyle (1977) to describe it as a 'rebirth': 'This is the only place I know of that is offering any realistic hope for guys serving long sentences, or short ones for that matter' (pp. 247, 253).

As Downes (ibid: 79) goes on to emphasize: 'No professional psychiatrist or psychological expertise was involved in this transformation, but the "treatment" umbrella still provided the broad justification for the experiment.'

Second, Downes (1988) has pointed to the importance of the rehabilitation ethos in facilitating the striking decarceration that did take place in The Netherlands during the postwar period. Having scrutinized the relevant data, including the professional socialization and perspectives of prosecutors and the judiciary, Downes (1988: 101) concludes that 'what is incontestable ... is that rehabilitative policies, in the Dutch context, were clearly compatible, if not causally connected, with the striking reduction in the prison population.'

Given that decarceration in Ontario coincided with the rise of the 'medical model' and rehabilitation, and that the United States also experienced decarceration during the postwar period prior to the mid-1970s, the proposition arises that, rather than accomplishing only expansion and intensification of punishment, it is possible that the ideology of rehabilitation also facilitated some reductionist tendencies. Overall, rather than merely equating rehabilitation with punishment, a more complete approach to telling the historical story would ask: 'What range of meanings and implications have been signified under the sign of "rehabilitation"?' (Garland and Young 1983: 17). What spaces for the amelioration of the pains of imprisonment did rehabilitation provide?

Again, the objective of such an analysis is not just to substitute a naïve and unreflexive affirmation of rehabilitation for the previous pessimistic critique. There is no doubt that the ideology of rehabilitation and its use *did* have punitive consequences (as, for example, in cases of inmates being pressured and coerced into treatment programs, in the incarceration of children labelled 'pre-delinquent,' and in the extended length of sentences imposed on some prisoners). But it also needs to be recognized that ideologies of rehabilitation did sometimes facilitate moderation in authoritarian and punitive prison regimes, and – in some places – appear to have been linked with reductionist penal strategies.

In modifying perspectives on power, and so moving critical analyses beyond the dark side of penal reform, another issue that needs to be addressed is that of the experiences of those subject to control. Despite the wealth of literature on community corrections, there has been a dearth of critical inquiry into the perspectives and opinions of offenders given these dispositions. As Downes (1988: 64) has put it, 'what one wants to know is whether the pedlars of "social control talk" so tellingly catalogued by Cohen (1985: ch. 5 and app.) make the same sort of impact on people's lives as the "cruelty man" (officers of the National Society of the Prevention of Cruelty to Children) in late Victorian and Edwardian England.' Given the dominant emphasis on the expansion of control and its sinister aspects, such inquiry has become redundant: if some offenders expressed appreciation of community programs, and/or perceived them as alternatives to imprisonment, they have to be charged with some variant of false consciousness (see, for example, Stoops 1983). We need to explore the situation of those subject to various forms of community sanctions, and to investigate not only their penalizing aspects but also any 'social and personal benefits that accrue to participants' (Vass and Weston 1990: 191).

There is also a need to investigate more closely the views and experiences of those administering different kinds of programs. With control agents being seen as uniformly suspect, the internal contradictions and complexities of control agencies have often been overlooked. But, in Ontario, prison officers have strongly criticized the conditions to which they and inmates are subject. As well as advocating improvements within the prisons, they have also called for the development of alternative community programs (OPSEU 1983). And, where community-correctional workers are concerned, as has been demonstrated in the case of the English probation service, the 'so-called "coercive social worker"' may 'become their own policy-makers in miniature. They invent new, informal means of control. These may expand the informal networks of social control, but may also help to protect and modify and negotiate disciplinarian regimes' (ibid: 190). As Ward (1989) has documented, sectors of the English and Welsh probation service more generally have resisted, and sometimes have refused to implement, a series of government strategies aimed at strengthening the controls involved in probation. Contrary to the impression one might get from the critical literature on decarceration, many probation officers, and other community-correctional workers, are opposed to being 'screws on wheels' (ibid: 8). Indeed, this opposition to exerting undue control partly explains the government's more recent support for turning to agencies other than probation in developing tougher non-custodial sanctions and 'punishment in the community' (ibid; see HMSO 1988; Rumgay 1989; Ryan and Ward 1991).

Undoubtedly, a critical objection to analysing anything other than the dark side of penal reform – be it in relation to decarceration, community corrections, rehabilitation, or future policies – will be that such an approach is vulnerable to the bogeyman of co-optation: to acknowledge that even select aspects of penal reform could be perceived as admirable merely provides the authorities with discourses, and practices, that can be used in refining and expanding penal control. This possibility is real. But other factors and perspectives must also be considered.

In the first place – and as we have already seen in the particular case of Ontario – critical analysis is already not only vulnerable to co-optation, but has been coopted in such a way as to facilitate the intensification of penal control. The argument of net-widening was used by correctional officials in attempting to terminate a potentially reductionist bail program. Ironically, the finances so released were then to be used in furthering community-service-order programs whose net-strengthening effects (given their status as conditions of probation) were clear. Moreover, critical analysis has been such that not only was it vulnerable to this form of co-optation, but it could not oppose it. For, according to the net-widening argument, all community programs tend to be seen as inherently expansionist. Therefore, no political argument could be advanced in illustrating how it would have been preferable, from a reductionist point of view, to retain these finances for the bail program.

By contrast, the modified analysis suggested here – which more carefully specifies the differing consequences of a range of programs – would at least provide a basis for challenging such clearly expansionist forms of co-optation.

More generally, in conjunction with modifying critical perspectives on power, a re-examination of those on co-optation itself may also be required. Typically, because co-optation is primarily defined as assimilation or usurpation by the powers that be, it is seen as reprehensible. Critical criminologists see it as somehow purer to remain clearly outside of the system. Discourses that emerge as clearly powerful within the system are seen as suspect.

Yet, as with power, co-optation can take a variety of shapes and forms, and can be perceived in different ways. Here, some of Foucault's observations on matters of political strategy offer an alternative interpretation of issues of co-optation (Foucault 1985, 2; quoted in Gandal 1986: 131):

> some political groups have long felt this fear of being co-opted. Won't everything be inscribed in the very mechanisms that we are trying to denounce? Well, I think that it is absolutely necessary that it should happen this way: if the discourse can be co-opted, it is not because it is vitiated by nature, but because it is inscribed in a process of struggle. Indeed, the adversary pushing, so to speak, on the hold you have over him in order to turn it around, this constitutes the best valorization of the stakes and typifies the whole strategy of struggles. As in judo, the best answer to the opponent's maneuver never is to step back, but to re-use it to your own advantage as a base for the next phase.

Viewed this way, co-optation does not only mean absorption and manipulation by the authorities. Rather, and as Gandal (ibid: 131) surmises, it can mean that, in the process of assimilating challenges and resistance, 'the terms of power have been changed.'

David Downes (1988: 75) has provided a tantalizing glimpse of such a process in relation to abolitionists' participation in Dutch penal politics, and their contribution to the reductionist orientation of penal policy making:

> The various pressure groups lock into the politics of penal reform, and even advocates of extreme positions, such as abolitionism, take the business of participation seriously, avoiding the polarization so evident in Britain. Criminologists like Bianchi and Hulsman, whose views on criminal justice would tend to exclude them from advisory roles in Britain or the United States, have served on commissions of inquiry, are quoted by quite orthodox members of the judiciary as holding views that deserve to be taken seriously, produce 'green' papers as alternative policy proposals that are published along with official policy statements by the government, in short, operate perhaps to shift the axis of debate to more radical positions of compromise than would otherwise occur. Informed

criticism by the Coornhert-Liga (the radical Dutch penal reform group)
since the early 1970s almost certainly stiffened resistance to the swing
away from reductionist policies.

These observations also point to an interesting feature of critical
criminology more generally: those perceived as its most radical elements, namely, Scandinavian, Dutch, and other European and North
American abolitionists, have often been most willing to dialogue with
criminal-justice policy makers, practitioners, and reformers, as well as
with those being dealt with by the system. This situation is reflected not
only in the participation referred to by Downes, but also in the making
of proposals that would facilitate the demise of imprisonment (e.g.,
Mathiesen 1974, 1986, 1990), in documenting experiences in the creation of communes for those vulnerable to various forms of institutionalization (Christie 1989), and in the organizing of conferences that
promote the sharing of knowledge and ideas among a wide range of
interested people (Bianchi and van Swaaningen 1986; van Swaaningen,
de Jonge, and McMahon 1989). Overall – similar to critical criminology more generally – abolitionism has been guided 'by an overwhelming
concern with criticism' of the existing system (Brants and Silvis 1987:
145). But abolitionism also has 'one great advantage' over other forms
of critical criminology: 'it has consistently refused to allow the limits of
the debate to be set by the other side' (ibid: 146). While abolitionists
have contributed greatly to critical understanding of the social reproduction of power relations through criminal-justice discourses and practices, they have also sought to identify, appreciate, and facilitate such
visionary spaces and struggles as do exist (e.g., Blad, van Mastrigt, and
Uildriks 1987a, 1987b; Christie 1977, 1982, 1986b; de Haan 1990; Hulsman 1986; Pepinsky 1988; Scheerer 1986; Steinert 1986).

Conclusion

The conventional wisdom on decarceration has reflected, and reinforced, problems in critical criminology more generally. Despite the
progressive political aspirations of many critical criminologists, their
theoretical frameworks have contributed to an activist impasse. With
penal power being perceived as reprehensible, and with penal reform
being depicted as contributing to the refinement and extension of penal
control, recognition of any amelioration that may have taken place, and
participation in criminal-justice politics, are impeded.

The first step towards addressing this contradiction between theory and politics may lie in a re-examination of critical conceptions of power. Sophisticated conceptual means have been developed for identifying resilient, changing, and expanding mechanisms of penal power: the themes of wider, stronger, and different nets, as well as that of the dispersal of discipline, are important exemplars of this. But the conceptual ability to recognize resistance to such trends, and movements towards the realization of progressive values, have been sorely lacking. A more open perspective on power, and one that acknowledges the potential for it to be exercised in admirable, as well as ominous ways, might help to transcend this partial perspective.

Developing critical ability to recognize the accomplishment of progressive values requires greater attention to identifying what those values might be. Critical criminology has been far more adept at elucidating what it is *against* than what it is *for*. As David Garland (1990: 174) has expressed it, 'the ultimate questions which need to be faced, whether in penal policy or in social policy are not about power or no-power but rather about the ways in which power should be exercised, the values which should inform it, and the objectives which it should pursue.'

Addressing these questions requires moving more deeply into areas of social and moral philosophy than criminologists have been prone to do (Bottoms 1987: 261). While critical discourse has a distinctive moral and ideological tenor, the underlying values have rarely been directly confronted. With being against power as the primary value, the primary critical vision is that of (more) social control. Acknowledgement of other values might allow more creative, imaginative, and liberative perspectives to be developed.

To date, the various strands of critical criminology's radical edge of abolitionism have been most promising in these respects. Some would charge that abolitionist approaches are naïve, romantic, unrealistic, and unsociological. But abolitionists have most satisfactorily addressed issues of values, have repeatedly reminded us of the pain that comes with present penal strategies, and have pointed to the possibility of doing things otherwise. Maybe such confrontation with basic issues of values, and of the directions in which they might lead, is possible only when the ideological boundaries of sociology itself are broken.

Neglect of values yields a progressive political void rather than a vision. It ensures that the terms of penal discourses, and the development of practices, remain the preserve of more conservative forces.

Perhaps more directly confronting values will be at the price of developing ever more sophisticated, and transnational, sociological analyses. But such modification of critical knowledge, and thereby power, might better facilitate decarceration and other liberative strategies. If so, such modifications will be worthwhile, at least for those most vulnerable to, and affected by, the exercise of penal control.

Notes

CHAPTER THREE

1 Volumes can be, and have been, written on the perambulations and conurbations of what can generally be described as 'critical criminology.' Here, rather than providing numerous details about its various 'schools,' I am more interested in illustrating the general spirit, and project, of critical criminology during the 1970s and into the 1980s, especially with respect to issues of imprisonment. Put crudely, my aim is to identify key *ideas*, not to provide a detailed taxonomy of *isms*.

   The story of critical criminology's frequently competing 'isms' is both fascinating and frustrating. As Thomas and O'Maolchatha (1989: 145) illustrate in their review of critical criminology, it has by no means been immune to the process whereby 'historically, leftists have been their own worst enemies finding creative new ways to fragment and destroy themselves. Demands for ideological purity and correct political thought accelerate this tendency, preventing alignments with potential allies who may differ, but who nonetheless voice similar concerns and who march at least part of the way in the same direction.' For excellent accounts of critical criminology's internal dilemmas, difficulties, and disputes during its first few decades, see Stanley Cohen's collection of articles in *Against Criminology* (1988). Readers with a particular interest in the development of critical criminology in Canada should consult the *Journal of Human Justice* (and see also Snider 1991a).

2 Scull's thesis also applied to mental health populations, where it has been comparatively better received and substantiated (see Scull 1984: 161–75).

CHAPTER FOUR

1 Between 1951 and 1984, the Canadian population grew from 14 million to 25 million, and the population of Ontario grew from 4.6 million to 8.9 million.

2 Similar to Hylton, Chan and Ericson's (1981) Ontario prison-count data include only provincial inmates, and not federal inmates in the province. In 1972, there were 29.3 inmates per 100,000 population in Ontario federal institutions; in 1978 the figure was lower, at 25.5.

3 For arguments that problems of crowding in Kansas prisons would have been worse but for community corrections, see Jones (1990a, 1990b).

CHAPTER FIVE

1 For a discussion of a similar military orientation in Ontario police forces following the Second World War, see Kashmeri (1991).

2 Guelph reformatory was a large institution (with population counts in the 1950s sometimes reaching 900 and more) for young adult offenders with less serious offences.

3 The population capacities of jails varied enormously. For example, the annual report of the Department of Reform Institutions for 1951 indicates that capacities ranged from a high of 360 in Toronto's Don Jail to a low of 12 in Goderich. The actual population pressures on the jails also varied greatly. The Don Jail had an average daily population of 475 prisoners, while Goderich had 5. The report also indicates that more than a third of the jails had an average daily population of fewer than 15 prisoners, and that several jails occasionally contained no prisoners at all.

4 Oliver (1985: 175) quotes Colonel John Foote – a former military chaplain who was minister of the Department of Reform Institutions between 1951 and 1957 – as saying: 'I don't think there was one person within Cabinet who was enthusiastic about the Department. They had no use for people who were committed to prison and they didn't think society owed them a great deal. They liked to see people reformed and changed and so on but they weren't very hopeful about it and they didn't want to spend much money on it. We were short of money and the Cabinet just felt that the less they heard of prisons the better.'

Oliver (ibid) also reports that provincial premier Leslie Frost 'firmly believed that criminals were less likely to return to a life of crime if they found their incarceration thoroughly unpleasant. As well, since the province was responsible only for offenders sentenced to less than two years, there seemed little need to deploy substantial resources for treatment and care.'

During the entire period with which I am primarily concerned, that is, from 1951 to 1984, the Progressive Conservative party held power in the province of Ontario. In 1985, they were defeated by the Liberal party; in 1990, the New Democratic Party took power.

5 In the late 1980s and early 1990s many former residents of the training schools came forward with allegations of sexual abuse. By the summer of

1992, more than 100 charges had been laid against former staff, and other investigations were continuing.
6 From 1951 to 1981, figures on sentences and the length of sentences include only those committed and sentenced during the given year. From 1982 to 1985, however, figures also include those convicted in the previous year and sentenced in the given year. While the figures for 1982 are more accurate, they are also inflated compared to those for 1951–81, which, while they may represent slight underestimates, are consistent.

CHAPTER SIX

1 The following data on admissions to probation, 1961–84, have been derived from A.R. Stannah, 'Probation and Parole Services Comparative Statistical Report. Report on the work of provincial probation officers for the years 1962–1973,' unpublished manuscript, Ministry of Correctional Services. Other sources include annual reports of the Ministry of Correctional Services (1972–84); *Justice Statistics Ontario*, 1978, 1980, 1982, 1984, Ontario Provincial Secretariat for Justice; Statistics Canada, Canadian Centre for Justice Statistics.
2 As noted, data on probation prior to 1961 are not systematically available. However, Whittingham (1984: App. IV) does provide a figure of 1,981 probation admissions in 1951. This represents a rate of 60 per 100,000 adult population. Combined with the rate of 1,422 total prison admissions, this yields a total of 1,482 prison plus probation admissions for 1951. This total is also marginally higher than the rate of 1,402 prison plus probation admissions in 1984. In short, when 1951 rather than 1961 is taken as the base year, quantitative net-widening is still not evidenced.

CHAPTER SEVEN

1 The figures in this and the following paragraph are derived from the court sentencing data for summary conviction and indictable offences in *Statistics of Criminal and Other Offences* Cat. 85–201, Dominion Bureau of Statistics/Statistics Canada. Given that these court data use 'sentences' as the unit of count for the summary statistics, and 'persons' as the unit of count for the indictable statistics, the totals derived from summing these two categories are estimates.
2 'Admissions' or 'committals' in the following paragraphs refer to *total* (i.e., sentenced plus non-sentenced) admissions to prison. It would be preferable here to analyse *sentenced* admissions only, because 1 / correctional sources categorize fine-default admissions as 'sentenced' admissions in compiling aggregate data on sentencing; and 2 / this is where the discrepancy between court and correctional data sources arises.

Unfortunately, the annual reports of the Department of Reform Institutions do not provide data on sentenced admissions by specific offence categories. However, they do provide this information for total committals, and these data are drawn upon here.

3 Data on fines for drunkenness are derived from Dominion Bureau of Statistics, *Statistics of Criminal and Other Offences, 1951–1960*. Data on sentences to imprisonment are derived from the Department of Reform Institutions' annual reports, 1951–60.

4 The fact that the discrepancies here are somewhat larger than the totals of fine-default admissions for liquor offences as estimated in table 7.4 may follow from non-sentenced admissions (i.e., primarily remand) also being involved in this calculation. While most of those on remand for liquor offences would have been detained in police lock-ups, the jails were also sometimes used for this purpose (as, for example, when the lock-ups were full). The discrepancy may also arise from the conservative nature of the estimate of fine defaulting in table 7.4.

5 Again, it is unsatisfactory to compare data on 'committals' for 1951 with those for 'sentenced admissions' in 1984. However, the break-down by offence category is only available for total committals in 1951 (i.e., not for sentences), and the reverse situation exists in 1984 where a breakdown is available for sentences (and not for committals) (Department of Reform Institutions, *Annual Report*, 1951; Ministry of Correctional Service, *Annual Report*, 1984).

Nevertheless, the magnitude of the decrease is such that a comparison is viable in this instance. Moreover, as liquor-offence admissions tend to be under-represented in total committals relative to sentence admissions in the 1950s (owing to the probability of remand in a police lock-up), the decrease that has occurred is even greater than suggested here.

CHAPTER EIGHT

1 The relative stability of public-order-offence arrests overall, coupled with the increase in those for drunkenness, is explained by decreasing police attention to the enforcement of city by-laws, arrests for which stood at 1,547 per 100,000 population in 1920, rose to 4,518 in 1928, and then fell to only 561 in 1955. Notable decreases in arrests for prostitution also incurred during the period (Boritch 1985: 262).

2 The detoxication centres established in Ontario reflect this quasi-medical perspective. As Bottomley, Giesbrecht, and Giffen (1976: 49) explain: 'the Ontario detoxication system has become known as the "non-medical detox model" – that is, no physicians are employed on the centres' staffs. Rather non-professionals who are trained to detect serious health problems care for the clients and refer them to the emergency departments of affiliated hospitals if need be. These nearby hospitals serve as sponsors of the

detoxication units – they hire the detoxication centre's staff as hospital employees and assume legal responsibility for that unit.'

3 The ease of release was further facilitated by the Toronto police department's resort to 'provisions contained in the Provincial Summary Convictions Act which allows the police to issue a "ticket" to the accused which is equivalent to a "notice to appear" for trial' (Oki et al 1976: 15). Under the Bail Reform Act, the procedure followed in Toronto was that the officer in charge would release the accused on his or her notice to appear.

As we shall see, many of these people 'failed to appear.' Oki and colleagues explain that the 'result was an expensive and unnecessary (but legally required) amount of paper work since the law required that warrants for arrest be issued for those who failed to appear for trial.' By contrast, the 'advantage' of the 'ticket' system to the police was that 'failure of the accused to appear results in an ex parte trial with a conviction' (Oki et al 1976: 15). I shall later discuss some of the implications of the procedure of 'routine conviction.'

4 Although fine default was cited as a reason in 216 of admissions, 18 of these 'ran concurrent to another sentence' (Benson 1971: 62). Benson separated women in this category for subsequent calculations regarding fine default because, given that the women were also serving another sentence, even if they had paid the fine or a portion of it on admission to the provincial correction centre, the length of their sentences to be served would not have been reduced.

5 Explaining the reasons for this shifting clientele is unfortunately beyond the scope of this analysis. However, there are striking parallels with the deinstitutionalization of the mentally ill, as summarized by Minto (1983: 168–9, quoted in Scull 1984: 188): 'The mental hospital scene has been one of steady and increasing resistance to the provision of psychiatric treatment and long-term support to a group of sick people who do not respond to current treatment ... It is almost as though the patient's inability to be cured has become a personal insult to his treaters, who respond to his continuing disability as if it were a specific act of non-cooperation in the treatment process rather than a distressingly constant malady over which the patient has little control ... [We are witnessing, then] the disowning of the chronic schizophrenic patient by the psychiatric services ... more and more psychiatric resources have been applied to patient groups least needing medical care, whilst the serious neglect, of an overtly ill group of patients continues to exist.'

Caution should be exercised, however, in pushing this comparison too far. In assessing the limited impact of detoxication centres on the behavior of public inebriates, both the 'diagnosis' and the proposed 'cure' are even more problematic than is often the case with mental illness: a quasi-medical solution has been used in responding to the needs of people, many of whose difficulties, as we have seen, derive as much, if not more, from social, legal, political, and economic injustice and deprivation as from alcoholism.

6 In recognizing 'exceptional circumstances' where 'no purpose would be served' if jail was used, the act also gave sentencing justices the power not to allow imprisonment, even in default of payment in certain circumstances. According to the ministry, 'this power will also be useful if the justice is confronted by an offender who wishes to become a martyr by being incarcerated.' Thus it was anticipated that the ability of 'scofflaws' to abuse the justice system would be limited both by the carrying out, and the failure to carry out, the process of imprisonment.

7 During the remainder of the 1980s, and into the early 1990s, the Kenora Jail continued to have a high rate of admissions for fine default. In late 1991 – following legal challenges and other pressures towards reform – a fine-option program was established in the area. Initially, however, it was not being used to any great extent.

From my observations – in Ontario and other provinces – of the situation of fine-default admissions to prison for minor offences such as public intoxication, I would argue that, rather than establishing programs to address the problem, the possibility of imprisonment for fine default should simply be removed from relevant legislation.

CHAPTER NINE

1 In the case of corrections, with privatization, and with the shift towards local delivery of services, the prior unconditional grants to some private-sector agencies were replaced by the development of fee-for-service contracts.

2 The tendency for the Ministry of Correctional Services to support programs that maintain and extend its ambit, and to oppose those that might reduce its area of jurisdiction, is also evident in its response to proposals under the Canadian Young Offenders Act. If the proposals had been implemented, the effect would have been to transfer some offenders to the less institutionally oriented Ministry of Community and Social Services. Menzies and Vass (1989: 209) report that 'as the April 1 1985 deadline for implementing the Young Offenders Act approached, a behind the scenes struggle occurred between the Ministry of Community and Social Services and the MCS [Ministry of Correctional Services] who were then responsible for the 16 and 17 year olds, formally defined as adult offenders [and now to be redesignated as young offenders]. Each wanted responsibility for the twelve up to and including 17 year old offenders and to receive funding to expand into the other's old area. The "solution" was for each group to retain its old responsibilities – Community and Social Services looking after 12–15 year olds, and the MCS looking after 16 and 17 year olds. Organisational convenience won out over the principles of the Young Offenders Act (Reid and Reitsma-Street 1984).'

CHAPTER TEN

1 Police *officers* include all peace officers employed full-time for the preserva-
tion and maintenance of the public peace. Police *personnel* includes cadets
and other full-time employees in addition to police officers.
2 Respondents in the seven cities included in the Canadian survey were
interviewed in 1982, and interviews for the second Edmonton Survey were
carried out in 1985. However, as the content of the surveys relates to each
of the previous calendar years, in this narrative I use the years 1981 and
1984, that is, the years about which data were gathered, rather than the
years in which the data were gathered.
3 The Edmonton Victimization Survey (1985) does not tabulate official crime
statistics for Edmonton during the periods under consideration, although
passing reference is made to official crime rates in the narrative. As a result,
it is more difficult to compare and contrast official and victims' reports.
4 Most discussions of increasing crime rates in the context of the findings of
victimization surveys focus on the increased propensity of the populace to
report crimes. Increases in the crime rate are portrayed in terms of
increased public reporting of crime. As careful examination of the Edmonton data reveals, the same observation also applies to the police. Moreover,
the Edmonton longitudinal survey data reveals that reporting of crime by
the public is subject to decrease as well as increase, with, for example, the
reporting of motor-vehicle thefts dropping from 77 to 68 per cent, and that
of vandalism from 39 to 33 per cent. While victimization surveys clearly
indicate that 'crime' generally is underreported, the level of underreporting
varies within as well as across categories of offences.
5 The reporting rate of 'break and enter' remained stable, while that of
'personal theft' dropped by 2 per cent (Solicitor General of Canada 1986:
12). Therefore, the level at which victims reported property crimes had
decreased slightly overall, and could not account for the less marked
decrease evident in the official statistics.

CHAPTER ELEVEN

1 It is important to note that here I am primarily concerned with the *interpretations*, or *readings*, that have been made of Foucault, and not whether
these nihilistic interpretations are warranted. My major point is that
interpretations of Foucault's work – particularly *Discipline and Punish* –
help to account for the theoretically and politically pessimistic stance that
has often been evidenced in critical criminology, and that is exemplified by
the critical literature on decarceration.
   It is interesting, however, that Foucault's work has been charged with
reflecting a theoretical and political contradiction paralleling that which I
am arguing is characteristic of much critical criminology. For example, in

light of Foucault's own engagement in a militant politics, he has been accused of 'oscillating "between a theoretical skepticism and a practical utopianism"' (Gandal 1986: 122–3, quoting Comay 1986: 11).

In face of this criticism, Gandal (ibid) has made a persuasive argument that, in fact, there was no contradiction between Foucault's politics and his theoretical work. According to Gandal, Foucault's politics were those of a 'radical reformism.' Various interviews with Foucault (e.g., Bess 1988) as well as other sources (e.g. Eribon 1989) also do much to dissolve this apparent contradiction. To focus primarily on *Discipline and Punish*, as was the critical-criminological tendency during the 1980s, fails to do justice to the broader context, and diversity, of Foucault's work and struggles.

At the same time, it must be said that Foucault's comments on the specific issue of alternatives to imprisonment *do* lend themselves to a very pessimistic reading. This is all the more important as Foucault observed that, although the prison has experienced 'extreme solidity' and 'resistance to transformation,' this 'does not mean that it cannot be altered, nor that it is once and for all indispensable to our kind of society' (1977: 305). Indeed, in face of other developments in penal control, Foucault suggested that the 'specificity of the prison and its role as a link are losing something of their purpose' (ibid: 306).

Nevertheless, for Foucault, the rise of alternatives – even given a demise of imprisonment – did not signal a preferable form of penality. Rather, in a public lecture sponsored by the University of Montreal in 1976, Foucault offered the opinion that, essentially, alternatives to prison simply transfer the traditional functions of the prison to new institutions. They exercise on the delinquent, as he put it, a more diffuse and extended power. For Foucault, these new techniques of community control were but a more effective way of reproducing older carceral functions: they constitute a true penal or carceral *sur-pouvoir*, which is in the process of developing step by step with the diminution of imprisonment itself. As Foucault put it, the castle may be falling, but other mechanisms are found which fulfil the social, surveillance, control, and other functions associated with the prison.

While Foucault goes on to raise the crucial question as to whether it is possible to have a society where 'power' has no need to create illegalisms, he offers no hope for intervening in a way that might help to move things in that direction. In light of this, his support for political movements that oppose the prison per se seems like advocacy of a futile exercise, given that the same negatively evaluated mechanisms are just going to reproduce themselves anyway.

Within the decarceration literature, early analyses gave some credence to the possibility that the use of imprisonment was declining (e.g., Cohen 1977; Scull 1977). Such considerations, however, were later displaced in favour of an emphasis on the maintenance and growth of imprisonment, along with the broader trends of net-widening and penal expansion associated with alternatives. With the accompanying loss of faith that alternatives could ever be used as real alternatives to prison, the ensuing futuristic view has become even more gloomy than that offered by Foucault.

2 This potential blending of the work of rape crisis centres with movements towards intensified pursuit and punishment of rapists and other sex offenders accords with a growing trend towards calls for 'criminalization' by critical criminologists. Although early critical criminology raised basic theoretical questions about the concept of crime and advocated decriminalization, there has subsequently been a 'virtual disappearance of decriminalization from the agenda, and along with it any attempt to take a critical stance toward the concept of crime' (Cohen 1988a: 244).

The clearest revelation of this tendency towards criminalization is in left realism. In this case, acceptance of mainstream definitions of 'crime' and emphasis on victimization as a problem for the working class has yielded proposals of criminalization and penal processing as the solution. The irony that arises is that the depiction of the working class as disproportionately victimized gives rise to calls for more intensified policing of them: 'protection' of deprived groups, and increased criminalization of their troublesome members, become synonymous (see McMahon 1988a; Steinert 1985).

This tendency is exacerbated when left realists attempt to deal with feminist issues. For example, in analysing prostitution, Roger Matthews (1986) emphasizes the 'victim' status of prostitutes themselves, rejects the possibility of decriminalization (which is the strategy generally favoured by prostitutes' organizations), and calls for a 'radical regulationism' that would involve greater policing, criminalization, and penalizing, not only of prostitutes, but also of their clients. Thus, even what was previously seen as a 'victimless' crime is reformulated so as to socially construct new victims and offenders.

While many critical criminologists have been vociferous (and sometimes vitriolic) in rejecting the left-realist approach, they also evidence tendencies towards criminalization. Such tendencies are most evident in discussion of violence against women, as well as that of state, corporate, and environmental crime. Again, critical criminology appears to have absorbed, rather than transcended, correctionalist definitions and tenets.

3 I am thinking, for example, of the micro-politics of everyday life – personal and professional, as well as more explicitly political – and their connections to local, and international, power relations. Even a trip to the local store (already a political decision – small-scale business vs. large supermarket), and decisions about what products to buy, and not buy, engage us in power relations, from South African to environmental politics. Awareness that these consumer decisions take place within the exploitative structure of

capitalism itself does not preclude many of us from taking advantage of such progressive opportunities as do afford themselves on that terrain.

4 The one exception to this is the jurisdiction of Northern Ireland, where the rate stood at 125 prisoners per 100,000 population on 1 February 1988.

The following prisoner counts per 100,000 population, as of 1 February 1988, are from the Council of Europe, *Prison Information Bulletin*, no. 11 (June 1988). The Canadian figure is for the 1988 fiscal year: Canada, 109.0; Scotland, 106.2; Luxembourg, 103.4; United Kingdom, 98.2; England & Wales, 96.6; Austria, 96.0; France, 92.0; Turkey, 90.2; F.R. Germany, 86.7; Portugal, 84.0; Switzerland, 77.6; Belgium, 70.5; Spain, 69.2; Denmark, 69.0; Italy, 62.0; Sweden, 61.0; Ireland, 56.0; Norway, 47.0; Greece, 42.9; Cyprus, 42.0; Iceland, 41.3; Netherlands, 36.0; and Malta, 19.7.

5 Compared to European jurisdictions, Ontario's rate of committals to prison seems to be extraordinarily high. For example, in 1984, Ontario had an admissions rate of 983.7 per 100,000 adult population. The comparable data for those European jurisdictions for which data for 1984 are available are: Denmark, 676.2; United Kingdom, 344.7; Turkey, 312.9; Belgium, 214.9; Luxembourg, 210.8; Italy, 182.9; Ireland, 178.9; Netherlands, 175.9; F.R. Germany, 174.8; Spain, 168.0; France, 162.3; Iceland, 127.6; Portugal, 109.8; Cyprus, 106.2; and Malta, 70.2 (Council of Europe, *Prison Information Bulletin*, no. 6, December 1986).

Caution should be exercised in using these data as there can be major discrepancies in the way in which different countries record committals. In particular, where the Ontario data are based on the number of *committals* (i.e., if an individual is committed several times he or she will be recorded several times), the data from some other jurisdiction may be based on *persons committed* (i.e., even if an individual is committed several times, he or she will only be recorded once).

Bibliography

Abt Associates. 1980. *American Prisons and Jails*, vol. 2. Washington, D.C.: Government Printing Office

AFSC (American Friends Service Committee). 1971. *Struggle for Justice: A Report on Crime and Punishment in America*. New York: Hill and Wang

Allen, R. 1991. 'Out of Jail: The Reduction in the Use of Penal Custody for Male Juveniles in 1981–88,' *The Howard Journal of Criminal Justice* 30: 30–52

Annis, H.M., and R.G. Smart. 1975. 'The Ontario Detoxication System: Influence on Drunkenness Arrests in Toronto,' *Ontario Psychologists* 7/4: 19–24

Archambault. 1938. See Canada

Austin, J., and B. Krisberg. 1981. 'Wider, Stronger and Different Nets: The Dialectics of Criminal Justice Reform,' *Journal of Research in Crime and Delinquency* 18: 132–96

– 1982. 'The Unmet Promise of Alternatives to Incarceration,' *Crime and Delinquency* 28: 374–409

Axon, L. 1983. 'Community Service in Canada.' Unpublished manuscript. Toronto: Ministry of Correctional Services

Badillo, H., and M. Haynes. 1972. *A Bill of No Rights: Attica and the American Prison System*. New York: Outerbridge and Lazard

Bailey, W. 1966. 'Correctional Outcome – An Evaluation of 100 Reports,' *Journal of Criminal Law* 57/2: 153–60

Barry, N. 1986. 'Deterrence Research as a Basis for Deterrence Policies,' *The Howard Journal* 18: 135–49

Bayer, R. 1981. 'Crime, Punishment and the Decline of Liberal Optimism,' *Crime and Delinquency* 27/2: 169–90

Becker, H.S. 1963. *Outsiders*. New York: Free Press

– 1970. *Sociological Work*. Chicago: Aldine

Becker, H.S., and I.L. Horowitz. 1972. 'Radical Politics and Sociological

Research: Observations on Methodology and Ideology,' *American Journal of Sociology* 78: 48–66

Benson, M. 1971. *Admissions to the Provincial Correctional Centre for Women in Ontario*. Toronto: Elizabeth Fry Society

Berk, R.A., D. Rauma, and S.L. Messinger. 1982. 'A Further Test of the Stability of Punishment Hypothesis,' in J. Hagan, ed., *Quantitative Criminology: Innovations and Applications*. Beverly Hills: Sage

Berk, R.A., D. Rauma, S.L. Messinger, and T.F. Codey. 1981. 'A Test of the Stability of Punishment Hypothesis: The Case of California, 1851–1970,' *American Sociological Review* 46: 805–29

Bess, M. 1988. 'Power, Moral Values and the Intellectual: An Interview with Michel Foucault,' *History of the Present* 4: 1–15

Bianchi, H., M. Simondi, and I. Taylor, eds. 1975. *Deviance and Control in Europe: Papers from the European Group for the Study of Deviance and Social Control*. London: John Wiley and Sons

Bianchi, H., and R. van Swaaningen. 1986. *Abolitionism: Towards a Non-repressive Approach to Crime*. Amsterdam: Free University Press

Biles, D. 1979. 'Crime and the Use of Prisons,' *Federal Probation*, June: 39–43

– 1982. 'Crime and Imprisonment: An Australian Time Series Analysis,' *Australian and New Zealand Journal of Criminology* 15: 133–53

– 1983. 'Crime and Imprisonment: A Two-Decade Comparison between England and Wales and Australia,' *British Journal of Criminology* 23: 166–72

Biles, D., and G. Mulligan. 1973. 'Mad or Bad? The Enduring Dilemma,' *British Journal of Criminology* 13: 275–9

Birbeck, C.H. 1983. 'Victimization Surveys in Latin America: Some First Experiences,' *Victimology* 8: 7–22

Birkenmayer, A.C., and S. Jolly. 1981. *The Native Inmate in Ontario*. Toronto: Ministry of Correctional Services

Bittner, E. 1967. 'Police Discretion in Emergency Apprehension of Mentally Ill Persons,' *Social Problems* 14: 278–92

– 1970. *The Functions of the Police in Modern Society*. Rockville M.D.: NIMH

Black, D.J. 1970. 'Production of Crime Rates,' *American Sociological Review* 35: 733–48

– 1976. *The Behavior of Law*. New York: Academic Press

– 1980. *The Manners and Customs of the Police*. New York: Academic Press

Blackburn, R., 1969. 'A Brief Guide to Bourgeois Ideology.' In A. Cockburn and R. Blackburn, eds., *Student Power: Problems, Diagnosis, Action*. Harmondsworth: Penguin

– 1973. *Ideology in Social Science: Readings in Critical Social Theory*. New York: Pantheon

Blad, J.R., H. van Mastrigt, and N.A. Uildriks. 1987a. *The Criminal Justice System as a Social Problem: An Abolitionist Perspective* [Liber Amicorum Louk Hulsman]. Rotterdam: Juridisch Instituut, Erasmus Universiteit

– 1987b. *Social Problems and Criminal Justice* [Liber Amicorum Louk Hulsman]. Rotterdam: Juridisch Instituut, Erasmus Universiteit

Blomberg, T. 1977. 'Diversion and Accelerated Social Control,' *Journal of Criminal Law and Criminology* 68: 274–82

– 1980. 'Widening the Net: An Anomaly in the Evaluation of Diversion Programs.' In M. Klein and K. Teilmann, eds., *Handbook of Criminal Justice Evaluation*. Beverly Hills: Sage

– 1987. 'Criminal Justice Reform and Social Control: Are We Becoming a Minimum Security Society?' In R. Lowman et al, eds., *Transcarceration: Essays in the Sociology of Social Control*. Aldershot: Gower

Blumstein, A., J. Cohen, and W. Gooding. 1983. 'The Influence of Capacity on Prison Population: A Critical Review of Some Recent Evidence,' *Crime and Delinquency* 29: 1–51

Blumstein, A., and J. Cohen. 1973. 'A Theory of the Stability of Punishment,' *Journal of Criminal Law and Criminology* 64: 198–207

Blumstein, A., J. Cohen, and D. Nagin. 1976. 'The Dynamics of Homeostatic · Punishment Process,' *Journal of Criminal Law and Criminology* 67: 317–34

Blumstein, A. and S. Moitra. 1979. 'An Analysis of the Time Series of the Imprisonment Rate in the States of the United States: A Further Test of the Stability of Punishment Hypothesis,' *Journal of Criminal Law and Criminology* 70: 376–90

Bohnstedt, M. 1978. 'Answers to Three Questions about Juvenile Diversion,' *Journal of Research in Crime and Delinquency* 15: 109–23

Boritch, H. 1985. 'The Making of Toronto the Good: The Organization of Policing and the Production of Arrests, 1859 to 1955.' Doctoral thesis, Department of Sociology, University of Toronto

Bottomley, K., and C. Coleman. 1981. *Understanding Crime Rates: Police and Public Roles in the Production of Official Statistics*. Farnborough: Gower

Bottomley, K., N. Giesbrecht, and P.J. Giffen. 1976. *A History of Recent Changes in the Social Control of Public Inebriates, with Special Reference to Ontario and Toronto* [ARF Substudy no. 813]. Toronto: Addiction Research Foundation

Bottomley, K., and K. Pease. 1986. *Crime and Punishment: Interpreting the Data*. Milton Keynes: Open University Press

Bottoms, A.E. 1981. 'The Suspended Sentence in England, 1967–1978,' *British Journal of Criminology* 21: 1–26

– 1983. 'Neglected Features of Contemporary Penal Systems.' In D. Garland and P. Young, eds., *The Power to Punish*. London: Heinemann

– 1986. 'Limiting Prison Use: Experience in England and Wales.' In J. van Dijke, C. Haffmans, F. Ruter, J. Schutte, and S. Stolwijk, eds., *Criminal Law in Action: An Overview of Current Issues in Western Societies*. Antwerp: Kluwer [Reprinted in *The Howard Journal of Criminal Justice* (1987) 26: 177–202]

– 1987. 'Reflections on the Criminological Enterprise,' *The Cambridge Law Journal* 46: 240–63

Bowker, L.H. 1981. 'Crime and the Use of Prisons in the United States: A Time Series Analysis,' *Crime and Delinquency* 27: 206–12

Box, S. 1987. *Recession, Crime and Punishment*. Basingstoke: Macmillan Education

Box, S., and C. Hale. 1982. 'Economic Crisis and the Rising Prisoner Population in England,' *Crime and Social Justice* 17: 20–2

– 1986. 'Unemployment, Crime and Imprisonment, and the Enduring Problem of Prison Overcrowding.' In R. Matthews and J. Young, eds., *Confronting Crime*. London: Sage

Boyd, N. 1978. 'An Examination of Probation,' *Criminal Law Quarterly* 20: 355–82

Boyle, J. 1977. *A Sense of Freedom*. London: Pan

Brants, C., and J. Silvis. 1987. 'Dutch Criminal Justice and a Challenge to Abolitionism.' In J.R. Blad, H. van Mastrigt, and N.A. Uildriks, eds., *The Criminal Justice System as a Social Problem: An Abolitionist Perspective*, vol. 1. Rotterdam: Juridisch Instituut, Erasmus Universiteit

Brodeur, J. P. 1984. 'Policing: Beyond 1984,' *Canadian Journal of Sociology* 9: 195–207

Brogden, M., T. Jefferson, and S. Walklate. 1988. *Introducing Policework*. London: Unwin Hyman

Brown, D. 1987. 'The Politics of Reform.' In G. Zdenkowski, C. Ronalds, and M. Richardson, eds., *The Criminal Injustice System*, vol. 2. Sydney: Pluto Press

Brown, D., and R. Hogg. 1985. 'Abolition Reconsidered: Issues and Problems,' *Australian Journal of Law and Society* 2: 56–75

Brownell, E., and G. Scott. 1950. *The Report of the Inquiry into Some Aspects of Juvenile Delinquency*. Toronto: Department of Education

Burton, F., and P. Carlen. 1979. *Official Discourse: On Discourse Analysis, Government Publications, Ideology and the State*. London: Routledge and Kegan Paul

Calahan, M. 1979. 'Trends in Incarceration in the United States since 1880,' *Crime and Delinquency* 25: 9–41

Cain, M. 1973. *Society and the Policeman's Role*. London: Routledge and Kegan Paul

– 1985, 'Beyond Informal Justice,' *Contemporary Crises* 9: 335–73 [Reprinted in R. Matthews, ed., *Informal Justice*. London: Sage 1988]

– 1991. 'Fractured Identities, Standpoints and Social Control: (Yet) Another Essay in Realist Philosophy.' Presentation to the International Conference on Women, Law and Social Control, Mont-Gabriel, Quebec, 18–21 July

Canada. 1938. *Report of the Royal Commission to Investigate the Penal System of Canada* [Archambault Commission]. Ottawa: The King's Printer

- 1973. *Report of the Task Force on Release of Inmates*. Ottawa: Information Canada

Canadian Centre for Justice Statistics. 1983. *Adult Correctional Services in Canada, 1981–1982*. Ottawa: Ministry of Supply and Services

- 1984. *Adult Correctional Services in Canada, 1982–1983*. Ottawa: Ministry of Supply and Services

- 1986. *Custodial Remand in Canada: A National Survey*. Ottawa: Canadian Centre for Justice Statistics

Canadian Committee on Corrections. 1969. See Ouimet

Canadian Criminology and Corrections Association. 1970. 'Drain the Drunk Tank.' An Official Statement of Policy of the Canadian Criminology and Corrections Association. Ottawa

Canadian Sentencing Commission. 1987. *Sentencing Reform: A Canadian Approach*. Report of the Canadian Sentencing Commission [Chaired by J.R. Omer Archambault]. Ottawa: Minister of Supply and Services

Carey, C. 1978. *Inventory of Probation and Parole Programmes in Ontario*. Toronto: Ontario Ministry of Correctional Services, Planning and Research Branch

Carlen, P. 1983. *Women's Imprisonment: A Study in Social Control*. London: Routlege and Kegan Paul

Carlen, P., and D. Cook, eds. 1989. *Paying for Crime*. Milton Keynes: Open University Press

Caron, R. 1985. *Go Boy! A Lifetime behind Bars*. Toronto: McGraw-Hill Ryerson

Carr-Hill, R.A., and N.H. Stern. 1979. *Crime, the Police and Criminal Statistics*. London: Academic Press

Carriere, K.D., and R.V. Ericson. 1989. *Crime Stoppers: A Study in the Organization of Community Policing*. Toronto: Centre of Criminology, University of Toronto

Carson, J. and F. Porporino. 1986. 'Redirecting Corrections,' *Policy Options Politiques* 7/2: 3–5

Chan, J., and R.V. Ericson. 1981. *Decarceration and the Economy of Penal Reform*. Toronto: Centre of Criminology, University of Toronto

Chan, J., and G. Zdenkowski. 1986a. 'Just Alternatives – Part I: Trends and Issues in the Deinstitutionalization of Punishment,' *Australian and New Zealand Journal of Criminology* 19/2: 67–90

- 1986b. 'Just Alternatives – Part II,' *Australian and New Zealand Journal of Criminology* 19/3: 131–54

Chapman, D. 1987. 'The Ballad of Reading Gaol.' In J.R. Blad, H. van Mastrigt, and N.A. Uildriks, eds., *The Criminal Justice System as a Social Problem: An Abolitionist Perspective* [Liber Amicorum Louk Hulsman]. Rotterdam: Juridisch Instituut, Erasmus Universiteit

Chesney-Lind, M. 1991. 'Patriarchy and Prisons: A Critical Look at Trends in Women's Incarceration.' Presentation to the International Conference on Women, Law and Social Control, Mont-Gabriel, Quebec, 18–21 July

Christie, N. 1977. 'Conflicts as Property,' *British Journal of Criminology* 17: 1–14

- 1982. *Limits to Pain*. Oxford: Martin Robertson
- 1986a. 'The Ideal Victim.' In E.A. Fattah, ed., *From Crime Policy to Victim Policy: Reorienting the Justice System*. Basingstoke: Macmillan
- 1986b. 'Suitable Enemies.' In H. Bianchi and R. van Swaaningen, eds., *Abolitionism*. Amsterdam: Free University Press
- 1989. *Beyond Loneliness and Institutions: Communes for Extraordinary People*. Oslo: Norwegian University Press
- forthcoming. *Crime Control as Industry*

Chunn, D.E., and S.A.M. Gavigan. 1988. 'Social Control: Analytical Tool or Analytical Quagmire?' *Contemporary Crises* 12: 107–24

Cicourel, A.V. 1968. *The Social Organization of Juvenile Justice*. New York: John Wiley and Sons

Clemmer, D. 1938. 'Leadership Phenomena in a Prison Community,' *Journal of Criminal Law and Criminology* 28/6: 851–72

- 1958. *The Prison Community*. New York: Holt, Rinehart and Wilson

Cohen, S. 1974. 'Criminology and Sociology of Deviance in Britain: A Recent History and a Current Report.' In P. Rock and M. McIntosh, eds., *Deviance and Social Control*. London: Tavistock
- 1975. 'It's All Right for You to Talk: Political and Sociological Manifestos for Social Work Action.' In R. Bailey and M. Brake, eds., *Radical Social Work*. London: Edward Arnold
- 1977. 'Prisons and the Future of Control Systems: From Concentration to Dispersal.' In M. Fitzgerald et al, eds., *Welfare in Action*. London: Routledge and Kegan Paul [in association with the Open University Press].
- 1979a. 'The Punitive City: Notes on the Dispersal of Social Control,' *Contemporary Crises* 3: 339–63
- 1979b. 'Some Modest and Unrealistic Proposals,' *New Society* 47/860: 731–3
- 1981. 'Footprints in the Sand: A Further Report on Criminology and the Sociology of Deviance in Britain.' In M. Fitzgerald et al, eds., *Crime and Society: Readings in History and Theory*. London: Routledge
- 1983. 'Social Control Talk: Telling Stories About Correctional Change.' In D. Garland and P. Young, eds., *The Power to Punish*. London: Heinemann
- 1984. 'The Deeper Structures of Law or "Beware the Rules Bearing Justice": A Review Essay,' *Contemporary Crises* 8: 83–93
- 1985. *Visions of Social Control: Crime, Punishment and Classification*. Cambridge: Polity
- 1987. 'Taking Decentralization Seriously: Values, Visions and Policies.' In J. Lowman et al, eds., *Transcarceration: Essays in the Sociology of Social Control*. Aldershot: Gower

- 1988a. *Against Criminology*. New Brunswick, N.J.: Transaction
- 1988b. 'Against Criminology.' In S. Cohen, *Against Criminology*, New Brunswick, N.J.: Transaction
- 1989. 'The Critical Discourse on "Social Control": Notes on the Concept as Hammer,' *International Journal of the Sociology of Law* 17: 347–57
- 1990. *Intellectual Scepticism and Political Commitment: The Case of Radical Criminology*. Stichting W. A. Bonger-lezingen. Monograph. University of Amsterdam: Bonger Institute of Criminology.

Cohen, S., ed. 1971. *Images of Deviance*. Harmondsworth: Penguin

Cohen, S., and A. Scull, eds. 1983. *Social Control and the State: Historical and Comparative Essays*. Oxford: Martin Robertson.

Cohen, S., and L. Taylor. 1972. *Psychological Survival: The Experience of Long-Term Imprisonment*. Harmondsworth: Penguin

- 1977. 'Talking about Prison Blues.' In C. Bell and H. Newby, eds., *Doing Sociological Research*. London: Allen and Unwin

Comay, R. 1986. 'Excavating the Repressive Hypothesis,' *Telos* 69: 111–19

Committee on Government Productivity. 1969. *The Ontario Report on Government Productivity*. Toronto

Conly, Dennis. 1986. *Research and Analysis Activities of the Canadian Centre for Justice Statistics*. A report prepared for the Advisory Committee on Research and Analysis, Statistics Canada. Ottawa: Canadian Centre for Justice Statistics, Statistics Canada

Conrad, J.P. 1973. 'Corrections and Simple Justice,' *Journal of Criminal Law and Criminology* 64: 208–17

Cordner, G. 1979. 'Police Patrol Work Load Studies: A Review and Critique.' Unpublished paper, Michigan State University

Correctional Service of Canada. n.d. Institutional Information Brochures. Ontario Region. Prepared by Planning and Coordination

Cottle, T.J. 1979. 'Children in Jail,' *Crime and Delinquency* 25: 318–34

Coughlan, D. 1963. 'The History and Function of Probation,' *Canadian Bar Journal* 6: 198

Council of Europe. 1988. *Prison Information Bulletin*, No. 11. Strasbourg: Council of Europe

Cressey, D.R. 1982. 'Foreword.' In F.T. Cullen and K.E. Gilbert, *Reaffirming Rehabilitation*. Cincinnati: Anderson

Crispino, L., N. Mulvihill, and S. Rogers. 1977. *The Concerns and Attitudes of Probation Officers*. Toronto: Ministry of Community Services

Cullen, F. T., and K. Gilbert. 1982. *Reaffirming Rehabilitation*. Cincinnati: Anderson

Cumming, E., I. Cumming, and L. Edell. 1970. 'Policeman as Philosopher, Guide and Friend.' In A. Niederhoffer and A. Blumberg, eds., *The Ambivalent Force*. Waltham, MA: Ginn

Daniels, A.F. 1980. 'Privatization – An Outline of Progress, Results and Goals.' Unpublished report. Ontario: Ministry of Correctional Services

Davies, M. 1985. 'Determinate Sentencing Reform in California and Its Impact on the Penal System,' *British Journal of Criminology* 25/1: 1–30

Davis, S.L. 1980a. 'Privatization in Ontario Corrections: A Second Opinion.' Unpublished paper, delivered at an Ontario Ministry of Correctional Services Symposium 'Privatization in Corrections: More Economical and Humane' [December]

– 1980b. 'The Seduction of the Private Sector: Privatization in Ontario Corrections.' M.A. dissertation, Carleton University, Ottawa

de Haan, W. 1986. 'Fuzzy Morals and Flakey Politics: The Coming Out of Critical Criminology.' *Journal of Law and Society* 14/3: 321

– 1990. *The Politics of Redress: Crime, Punishment and Penal Abolition.* London: Unwin Hyman

de Jonge, G. 1985. 'Community Service in Holland: A Penal Sham Success.' Unpublished paper presented at the second International Conference on Prison Abolition [ICOPA], Amsterdam, The Netherlands, June

Deichsel, W. 1988. 'Divert Young People from the Criminal Justice System, But Don't Divert Attention from Its Implications, Risks and Dangers! Reflections on the Occasion of the Hamburg Model of Diversion!' Paper presented at the 10th International Congress in Criminology, Hamburg

Demers, D. 1980. *Federal Government Expenditure for Criminal Justice: An Examination of Recent Trends.* Ottawa: Ministry of the Solicitor General

Dijk, J. van, C. Haffmans, F. Ruter, J. Schutte, and S. Stolwijk. 1986. *Criminal Law in Action: An Overview of Current Issues in Western Societies.* Antwerp: Kluwer

Dittenhoffer, T., and R.V. Ericson. 1983. 'The Victim/Offender Reconciliation Program: A Message to Correctional Reformers,' *University of Toronto Law Journal* 33: 314–47

Dobash, R.P., and R.E. Dobash. 1991. 'Social Movements and Social Justice: The Battered Women's Movement in Britain and the United States.' Presentation to the International Conference on Women, Law and Social Control, Mont-Gabriel, Quebec, 18–21 July

Dodge, C.R. 1979. *A World without Prisons: Alternatives to Incarceration throughout the World.* Lexington, MA: Lexington

Doleschal, E. 1979a. 'Crime – Some Popular Beliefs,' *Crime and Delinquency* 25: 1–8

– 1979b. 'Sources of Basic Criminal Justice Statistics: A Brief Annotated Guide with Commentaries,' *Criminal Justice Abstracts* 11: 122–47

Doob, A.N. 1988. 'Community Sanctions as "Real" Alternatives to Prison Rather than as Supplements to it: A Case History of Hoping for a Miracle but Not Bothering Even to Pray for it.' Unpublished paper prepared for the Interregional Meeting of Experts for the Eighth United Nations Congress on the Prevention of Crime and the Treatment of Offenders, 30 May–3 June, Vienna, Austria

Doob, A.N., and A. Cavoukian. 1976. 'The Effect of the Revoking of Bail: R. v. Demeter,' *Criminal Law Quarterly* 19: 196–202

Douglas, J. 1967. *The Social Meaning of Suicide*. Princeton, N.J.: Princeton University Press

Downes, D.M. 1966. *The Delinquent Solution*. London: Routledge and Kegan Paul

– 1980. 'Abolition: Possibilities and Pitfalls.' In A.E. Bottoms and R.H. Preston, eds., *The Coming Penal Crisis*. Edinburgh: Scottish Academic Press

– 1982. 'The Origins and Consequences of Dutch Penal Policy since 1945,' *British Journal of Criminology* 22: 325–62

– 1988. *Contrasts in Tolerance: Post-war Penal Policy in the Netherlands and England and Wales*. Oxford: Clarendon Press

Drigo, J.D. 1984. 'Outsiders Looking In, Insiders Looking Out: A study of the Conflicting Perceptions of Skid Row Inebriates and Their Caretakers.' M.A. dissertation, Centre of Criminology, University of Toronto

Dusen, K.T. van 1981. 'Net Widening and Relabeling: Some Consequences of Deinstitutionalization,' *American Behavioral Scientist* 24: 801–10

Edelman, M. 1977. *Political Language: Words that Succeed and Policies that Fail*. New York: Academic Press

Edwards, J.Ll.J. 1960. 'Canadian Teaching and Research in Criminology,' *University of Toronto Law Journal* 13/2: 1–28

– 1964. 'A Report on Canadian Research and Teaching in Criminology.' Paper delivered at the National Conference on Research and Teaching in Criminology, University of Cambridge, Institute of Criminology. 8–10 July

– 1984. 'Directing the Development of a University Centre of Criminology.' In A.N. Doob and E.L. Greenspan, eds., *Perspectives in Criminal Law*. Aurora, ON: Canada Law Book

Ekstedt, J.W., and C.T. Griffiths. 1984. *Corrections in Canada: Policy and Practice*. Toronto: Butterworths

Ellis, D. 1982. *Disturbances in Canadian Penitentiaries during the Years 1971–1980*, Report no. 4. Toronto: LaMarsh Research Programme on Violence and Conflict Resolution, York University

Emerson, R. 1969. *Judging Delinquents*. Chicago: Aldine

Eribon, D. 1989. *Michel Foucault*. France: Flammarion

Ericson, R.V. 1974. 'Turning the Inside Out: On Limiting the Use of Imprisonment' John Howard Society of Ontario, *Community Education Series* 3:1

– 1975a. *Criminal Reactions: The Labelling Perspective*. Farnborough, Hants: Saxon House

– 1975b. 'Responsibility, Moral Relativity, and Response Ability: Some Implications of Deviance Theory for Criminal Justice,' *University of Toronto Law Journal* 25: 23–41

– 1975c. *Young Offenders and Their Social Work*. Farnborough, Hants: Saxon House

- 1981. *Making Crime: A Study of Detective Work*. Toronto: Butterworths
- 1982. *Reproducing Order: A Study of Police Patrol Work*. Toronto: University of Toronto Press
- 1983. *The Constitution of Legal Inequality*. Ottawa: Carleton University Information Services
- 1987. 'The State and Criminal Justice Reform.' In R.S. Ratner and J.L. McMullan, eds., *State Control: Criminal Justice Politics in Canada*. Vancouver: University of British Columbia Press

Ericson, R.V., and P.M. Baranek. 1982. *The Ordering of Justice: A Study of Accused Persons as Dependants in the Criminal Process*. Toronto: University of Toronto Press
- 1984. 'Criminal Law Reform and Two Realities of the Criminal Process.' In A.N. Doob and E.L. Greenspan, eds., *Perspectives in Criminal Law*. Aurora, ON: Canada Law Book

Ericson, R.V., P. Baranek, and J. Chan. 1987. *Visualizing Deviance: A Study of News Organization*. Toronto: University of Toronto Press

Ericson, R. V., and M.W. McMahon. 1987. *Re-thinking Decarceration: Sentencing Trends in Ontario, 1951–1984*. Report to the Ontario Ministry of Correctional Services. Toronto: Centre of Criminology, University of Toronto

Ericson, R.V., M.W. McMahon, and D. Evans. 1987. 'Punishing for Profit: Reflections on the Revival of Privatization in Corrections,' *Canadian Journal of Criminology* 29/4: 355–87
- 1988. 'Reply to the Critique of "Punishing for Profit,"' *Canadian Journal of Criminology* 30/3: 318–24

Ericson, R.V., and C.D. Shearing. 1986. 'The Scientification of Police Work,' In G. Bohme and N. Stehr, eds., *The Knowledge Society*. Dordrecht: Reidel

Erikson, K. 1966. *Wayward Puritans: A Study in the Sociology of Deviance*. New York: Wiley

Fauteaux, G. [Chairman]. 1956. *Report of a Committee Appointed to Inquire into the Principles and Procedures Followed in the Remission Service of the Department of Justice of Canada*. Ottawa: The Queen's Printer

Feest, J. 1988. 'Reducing the Prison Population: Lessons from the West German Experience?' Paper presented at the Annual Meeting of NACRO [National Association for the Care and Resettlement of the Offender], U.K.

Fitzgerald, M., and J. Sim. 1982. *British Prisons*, 2d ed. Oxford: Basil Blackwell

Fogel, D. 1975. *We Are the Living Proof ...: The Justice Model for Corrections*. Cincinnati: W.H. Anderson

Foucault, M. 1976. 'Alternatives à la Prison.' Unpublished lecture at the University of Montreal
- 1977. *Discipline and Punish: The Birth of the Prison*. New York: Pantheon
- 1980. *Power/Knowledge: Selected Interviews and Other Writings, 1972–1977*, ed. C. Gordon. New York: Pantheon

– 1985. 'Interview with Michel Foucault,' *History of the Present*. Translation of an article from *Les Nouvelles Litteraires*, 17 March 1975

Frankel, M.L. 1972. *Criminal Sentences: Law without Order*. New York: Hill and Wang

Galster, G.C., and L.A. Scaturo. 1985. 'The U.S. Criminal Justice System: Unemployment and the Severity of Punishment,' *Journal of Research in Crime and Delinquency* 22: 163–89

Galvin, J. 1983. 'Introduction, Special Issue: Prisons and Sentencing Reform. Prison Policy Reform Ten Years Later,' *Crime and Delinquency* 29: 495–50

Galvin, J., and K. Polk. 1982. 'Any Truth You Want: The Use and Abuse of Crime and Criminal Justice Statistics,' *Journal of Research in Crime and Delinquency* 19: 135–65

Gamberg, H., and A. Thompson. 1984. *The Illusion of Prison Reform: Corrections in Canada*. New York: Peter Lang

Gandal, K. 1986. 'Michel Foucault: Intellectual Work and Politics,' *Telos* 67: 121–34

Gardiner, J. 1969. *Traffic and the Police: Variations in Law Enforcement Policy*. Cambridge, MA: Harvard University Press

Garfinkel, H. 1956. 'Some Sociological Concepts and Methods for Psychiatrists,' *Psychiatric Research Reports* 6: 181–95

Garland, D. 1981. 'The Birth of the Welfare Sanction,' *British Journal of Law and Society* 8: 29–45

– 1985a. 'Politics and Policy in Criminological Discourse: A Study of Tendentious Reasoning and Logic,' *International Journal of the Sociology of Law* 13: 1–33

– 1985b. *Punishment and Welfare: A History of Penal Strategies*. Aldershot: Gower

– 1986. 'Foucault's Discipline and Punish: An Exposition and Critique,' *American Bar Foundation* 4 (Fall): 847–82

– 1987. 'The Sociology of Punishment.' Unpublished paper presented at the Centre of Criminology, University of Toronto

– 1990. *Punishment and Modern Society: A Study in Social Theory*. Chicago: University of Chicago Press

Garland, D., and P. Young, eds. 1983a. *The Power to Punish: Contemporary Penality and Social Analysis*. London: Heinemann

– 1983b. 'Towards a Social Analysis of Penality.' In D. Garland and P. Young, eds., *The Power to Punish*. London: Heinemann

Gaylin, W. 1974. *Partial Justice: A Study of Bias in Sentencing*. New York: Vintage

– 1976. *Caring*. New York: Alfred A. Knopf

Gaylin, W., I. Glasser, S. Marcus, and D. Rothman. 1978. *Doing Good: The Limits of Benevolence*. New York: Pantheon

Geller, W. 1972. 'The Problem of Prisons – A Way Out?' *The Humanist*, May/June: 24–6

Giffen, P.J. 1966. 'The Revolving Door: A Functional Interpretation,' *Canadian Review of Sociology and Anthropology* 3/3: 154–66

– 1976. 'Official Rates of Crime and Delinquency.' In W.T. McGrath, ed., *Crime and Its Treatment in Canada*. Toronto: Macmillan

Giffen, P.J., S. Lambert, G. Oki, and S. Sidlofsky. 1966. 'The Jail.' In *The Chronic Drunkenness Offender*. Toronto: Addiction Research Foundation

Giffen, P.J., and K. Wangenheim (with collaborators J. McNulty and B. Schloss). 1966. 'The Courts.' In *The Chronic Drunkenness Offender*. Toronto: Addiction Research Foundation

Glaser, B.G., and A.L. Strauss. 1967. *The Discovery of Grounded Theory: Strategies for Qualitative Research*. New York: Aldine

Glaser, D. 1964. *The Effectiveness of a Prison and Parole System*. New York: Bobbs-Merrill.

– 1978. 'The Counterproductivity of Conservative Thinking about Crime,' *Criminology* 16: 209–24

Glasser, I. 1978. 'Prisoners of Benevolence: Power versus Liberty in the Welfare State.' In W. Gaylin et al, eds., *Doing Good: The Limits of Benevolence*. New York: Pantheon

Goffman, E. 1961. *Asylums*. Garden City, NY: Doubleday

Goldring, C.C. (Chairman). 1950. *Report of the Mayor's Conference re Juvenile Delinquency and Associated Problems*. Toronto: Toronto City Council

Gordon, P. 1987. 'Community Policing: Towards the Local Police State?' In P. Scraton, ed., *Law, Order and the Authoritarian State*. Milton Keynes: Open University Press

Goring, C. 1913. *The English Convict: A Statistical Study*. London: HMSO

Gouldner, A. 1970. *The Coming Crisis in Western Sociology*. London: Heinemann

Grabosky, P.N. 1980. 'Rates of Imprisonment and Psychiatric Hospitalization in the United States,' *Social Indicators Research* 7: 63–70

Graham, J. 1990. 'Decarceration in the Federal Republic of Germany: How Practitioners Are Succeeding Where Policy-Makers Have Failed,' *British Journal of Criminology* 30: 150–70

Greenberg, D.F. 1970. *The Problem of Prisons*. Philadelphia: National Peace Literature Service

– 1972. 'Rehabilitation is Still Punishment,' *The Humanist*, May–June: 28–33

– 1975. 'Problems in Community Corrections,' *Issues in Criminology* 10: 1–33

– 1977. 'The Dynamics of Oscillatory Punishment Processes,' *Journal of Criminal Law and Criminology* 68: 643–51

– 1980. 'Penal Sanctions in Poland: A Test of Alternative Models,' *Social Problems* 28: 194–204

– 1983. 'Reflections on the Justice Model Debate,' *Contemporary Crises* 7: 313–27

Greenberg, D.F., and D. Humphries. 1980. 'The Cooptation of Fixed Sentencing Reform,' *Crime and Delinquency* 26/2: 206–25

Greenwood, P.W., J.M. Chaiken, and J. Petersilia. 1975. *The Criminal Investigation Process, vol. 3: Observations and Analysis*. Santa Monica: Rand Corporation

Gusfield, J. 1981. *The Culture of Public Problems: Drinking-Driving and the Symbolic Order*. Chicago: University of Chicago Press

Hagan, J., and J. Leon. 1980. 'The Rehabilitation of Law: A Social-Historical Comparison of Probation in Canada and the United States,' *Canadian Journal of Sociology* 5: 235–51

Hall, S., and P. Scraton. 1981. 'Law, Class and Control.' In M. Fitzgerald, G. McLennan, and J. Pawson, eds., *Crime and Society: Readings in History and Theory*. London: Routledge and Kegan Paul

Hann, R.G., S. Moyer, B. Billingsley, and C. Canfield. 1983. *Sentencing Practices and Trends in Canada: A Summary of Statistical Information*. Ottawa: Department of Justice

Hargreaves, D. 1967. *Social Relations in a Secondary School*. London: Routledge

Hatt, K. 1985. 'Probation and Community Corrections in a Neo-Correctional Era,' *Canadian Journal of Criminology* 27/3: 299–316

Havemann, P., L. Foster, K. Couse, and R. Matonovich. 1984. *Law and Order for Canada's Indigenous People*. Ottawa: Programs Branch, Ministry of the Solicitor General

Hayner, N.S., and E. Ash. 1939. 'The Prisoner Community as a Social Group,' *American Sociological Review* 4: 362–9

Haynes, F.E. 1948. 'The Sociological Study of the Prison Community,' *Journal of Criminal Law and Criminology* 39: 432–40

Healy, Mike. 1981. 'Humanizing Probation: The Concerns of a Probation Officer about the Team Concept,' *Correctional Options* 1/1: 31

HMSO. 1983. *Prison Statistics, England and Wales 1983*. London

– 1988. *Punishment, Custody and the Community*. London

Hogarth, J. 1971. *Sentencing as a Human Process*. Toronto: University of Toronto Press

Hooper, H. M. 1964. 'The Modernization of Canada's Jails,' *Canadian Journal of Corrections* 6: 453–62

Hooton, E.A. 1939. *The American Criminal: An Anthropological Study*. Cambridge, MA: Harvard University Press

Hopkins, H. 1973. *The Numbers Game: The Bland Totalitarianism*. London: Secker and Warburg

Hough, M., and P. Mayhew. 1983. *The British Crime Survey*. First report. Home Office Research Study no. 76. London: HMSO

Hudson, Barbara. 1984. 'The Rising Use of Imprisonment: The Impact of "Decarceration" Policies,' *Critical Social Policy* 11: 46–59

Hugessen, J. 1973. *Report of the Task Force on the Release of Inmates*. Ottawa: Information Canada

Hulsman, L. 1986. 'Critical Criminology and the Concept of Crime,' *Contemporary Crises* 10: 63–80

Hylton, J.H. 1981a. 'Community Corrections and Social Control: The Case of Saskatchewan, Canada,' *Contemporary Crises* 5: 193–215

– 1981b. *Reintegrating the Offender: Assessing the Impact of Community Corrections*. Washington, DC: University Press of America

– 1982. 'Rhetoric and Reality: A Critical Appraisal of Community Corrections,' *Crime and Delinquency* 28: 341–73

Ignatieff, M. 1978. *A Just Measure of Pain: The Penitentiary in the Industrial Revolution 1750–1850*. London: Macmillan

Irwin, J. 1985. *The Jail*. Berkeley: University of California Press

Jackson, M.A. 1982. *Judicial Attitudes towards Community Sentencing Options*. Toronto: Ministry of Correctional Services

Jackson, M.A., C.D. Webster, and J.L. Hagan. 1982. 'Probation Outcome: Is it Necessary to Fulfill the Conditions?' *Canadian Journal of Criminology* 24: 267–77

Jankovic, I. 1977. 'Labour Market and Imprisonment,' *Crime and Social Justice* 8: 17–31

Johnston, J., and C. MacLeod. 1975. 'Barlinnie's Approach,' *New Society* 34: 482–3

Jolly, S. 1982. 'Natives in Conflict with the Law,' *Correctional Options* 21/1: 83–97

Jolly, S., and J.P. Seymour. 1983. *Anicinabe Debtors' Prison: Final Report to the Ontario Native Council on Justice on a Survey of Fine Defaulters and Sentenced Offenders Incarcerated in the Kenora District Jail for Provincial Offences*. Toronto: Ontario Native Council on Justice

Jones, P.R. 1990a. 'Community Corrections in Kansas: Extending Community-Based Corrections or Widening the Net?' *Journal of Research in Crime and Delinquency* 27: 79–101

– 1990b. 'Expanding the Use of Non-Custodial Sentencing Options: An Evaluation of the Kansas Community Corrections Act,' *The Howard Journal of Criminal Justice* 29: 114–29

Kamenka, E., and A.E. Tay. 1975. 'Beyond Bourgeois Individualism – The Contemporary Crisis in Law and Legal Ideology.' In E. Kamenka and R.S. Neale, eds. *Feudalism, Capitalism and Beyond*. Canberra: Australian National University Press

Kashmeri, Z. 1991. 'Metro Police Quickstep to Old Military Traditions,' *NOW* magazine, Toronto, 25–31 July, 13

Kidman, J. 1947. *The Canadian Prison Tragedy*. Toronto: Ryerson

Kirkpatrick, A.M. 1970. 'Report of the Canadian Committee on Corrections (Ouimet Report),' *Chitty's Law Journal* 18/2: 37–53

Kitsuse, J. 1962. 'Societal Reactions to Deviant Behavior,' *Social Problems* 9: 246–56

Kitsuse, J., and A. Cicourel. 1963. 'A Note on the Uses of Official Statistics,' *Social Problems* 11: 131–9

Kittrie, N.N. 1971. *The Right to Be Different: Deviance and Enforced Therapy.* Baltimore: Johns Hopkins University Press

Klein, M. W. 1979. 'Deinstitutionalization and the Diversion of Juvenile Offenders: A Litany of Impediments.' In N. Morris and M. Tonry, eds., *Crime and Justice: An Annual Review of Research*, vol. 1, Chicago: University of Chicago Press

Koza, P., and A.N. Doob . 1975. 'The Relationship of Pre-Trial Custody to the Outcome of a Trial,' *Criminal Law Quarterly* 17/4: 391-400

Kretschmer, E. 1921. *Koerperbau und Charakter.* Berlin: Springe Verlag [Translated by W.J.H. Sprott as *Physique and Character.* London: Kegan Paul, Trends, Trubner 1925]

Krisberg, B., and I. Schwartz. 1983. 'Rethinking Juvenile Justice,' *Crime and Delinquency* 29/3: 333–64

Lacombe, D. 1991. 'Power/Knowledge and Law: The Politics of Pornography Law Reform in Canada.' Doctoral thesis, Department of Sociology, University of Toronto

Larsson, P. 1990. 'Norwegian Penal Policy in the 80s.' Presentation at the Institute of Law, University of Warsaw

Laub, J.H., ed. 1983. *Criminology in the Making: An Oral History.* Boston: Northeastern University Press

Law Reform Commission of Canada. 1974. *The Principles of Sentencing and Dispositions.* Ottawa: Information Canada

– 1975. *Imprisonment and Release.* Ottawa: Information Canada

– 1977. *Administrative Law: Commissions of Inquiry.* Working Paper 17. Ottawa: Ministry of Supply and Services

– 1986. *Policy Implementation, Compliance and Administrative Law.* Ottawa: Law Reform Commission of Canada

Leander, K. 1990. 'Introduction to the European Group for the Study of Deviance and Social Control.' Organizational pamphlet, unpublished

Leluk, N.G. 1983. 'Correctional Volunteers,' *Correctional Options* 3: iii

Lemert, E. 1951. *Social Pathology.* New York: McGraw-Hill

– 1967. *Human Deviance, Social Problems and Social Control.* Englewood Cliffs, NJ: Prentice-Hall

– 1971. *Instead of Court: Diversion in Juvenile Justice.* Chevy Chase, MD: Center for Studies of Crime and Delinquency

Lerman, P. 1975. *Community Treatment and Social Control.* Chicago: University of Chicago Press

Lombroso, C. 1876. *L'Uomo Delinquente*. Milan: Hoepli

Lowman, J., R.J. Menzies, and T.S. Palys, eds. 1987. *Transcarceration: Essays in the Sociology of Social Control*. Aldershot: Gower

Lynd, H., and R.S. Lynd. 1929. *Middletown*. New York: Harcourt, Brace

McBarnet, D. 1981. *Conviction: Law, the State and the Construction of Justice*. London: Macmillan

MacBride, S. 1980. *Report of the Commission of Inquiry into the Irish Penal System*. Ireland: The Commission

McCullagh, C. 1988. 'A Crisis in the Penal System? The Case of the Republic of Ireland.' In M. Tomlinson, T. Varley, and C. McCullagh, eds., *Whose Law and Order? Aspects of Crime and Social Control in Irish Society*. Belfast: Queen's University Bookshop [distributors]

MacDonald, D., ed. 1980. *The Government and Politics of Ontario*. Toronto: Van Nostrand Reinhold

MacDonald, D., and J. Sim. 1978. *Scottish Prisons and the Special Unit*. n.p.: Scottish Council for Civil Liberties

McDonald, L. 1976. *The Sociology of Law and Order*. London: Faber

McFarlane, G.G. 1966. *The Development of Probation Services in Ontario*. Toronto: Department of the Attorney General, Probation Services Branch

– 1979. 'Ontario's Temporary Absence Programs: "Phantom" or "Phoenix"-Like Phenomena?' *Canadian Journal of Criminology* 21/3: 310–29

MacGuigan, M. 1977. *Report to Parliament by the Sub-Committee on the Penitentiary System in Canada*. Ottawa: Minister of Supply and Services

McKelvey, B. 1977. *American Prisons: A History of Good Intentions*. Montclair, N.J.: Patterson Smith

McKessock, B. 1984. *Behind Prison Walls: Justice for All?* Report of the Liberal Task Force on Criminal Justice and Correctional Institutions. Toronto

McMahon, M.W. 1987. 'Review of Stanley Cohen's *Visions of Social Control: Crime, Punishment and Classification*,' *Canadian Journal of Sociology* 12/1–2: 175–8

– 1988a. 'Confronting Crime: A Review Essay,' *Critical Sociology* (formerly *The Insurgent Sociologist*) 5/1: 111–22

– 1988b. 'Police Accountability: The Situation of Complaints in Toronto,' *Contemporary Crises* 12: 301–27

McMahon, M.W., and R.V. Ericson. 1984. *Policing Reform: A Study of the Reform Process and Police Institution in Toronto*. Toronto: Centre of Criminology, University of Toronto

McMahon, M.W., and G. Kellough. 1987. 'An Interview with Stanley Cohen,' *Canadian Criminology Forum* 8/2: 132–49

McNaughton-Smith, P. 1976. *Permission to Be Slightly Free: A Study of the Granting, Refusing and Withdrawing of Parole in Canadian Penitentiaries*. Ottawa: Law Reform Commission of Canada

Madden, P.G. 1978. *A Description of Ontario's Jail Population.* Toronto: Ministry of Correctional Services

Madden, P.G., C.A. Carey, and D.K. Ardron. 1980. *Pre-Trial Services in Ontario: The First Year.* Toronto: Ministry of Correctional Services

Madden, P.G., and S. Hermann. 1983. *The Utilization of Community Resource Centres.* Toronto: Ministry of Correctional Services

Mahaffy, C. 1980. 'The Development of Bail Verification and Supervision Programmes in Ontario,' *Pretrial Services Annual Journal* 3: 116–31

Mandel, M. 1975. 'Rethinking Parole,' *Osgoode Hall Law Journal* 13/2: 501–46

– 1986a. 'Democracy, Class and the National Parole Board.' In N. Boyd, ed., *The Social Dimensions of Law.* Scarborough, ON: Prentice–Hall

– 1986b. 'Marxism and the Rule of Law,' *University of New Brunswick Law Journal* 35: 7–33

– 1991. 'The Great Repression: Criminal Punishment in the Nineteen-Eighties,' in L. Samuelson and B. Schissel, eds., *Criminal Justice: Sentencing Issues and Reform.* Toronto: Garamond

Mann, W.E. 1967. *Society behind Bars – A Sociological Scrutiny of Guelph Reformatory.* Toronto: Social Science Publishers

Mannheim, H. 1960. *Pioneers in Criminology.* London: Stevens and Sons

Manning, P. 1972. 'Observing the Police: Deviants, Respectables and the Law.' In J. Douglas, ed., *Research in Deviance.* New York: Random House

– 1977. *Police Work: The Social Organization of Policing.* Cambridge, MA: MIT Press

Marks, U.M., and R.S. Teau. 1969. 'Bill C-150: The New Probation Clause,' *Criminal Law Quarterly* 11/3: 275–81

Martinson, R. 1974. 'What Works? Questions and Answers about Prison Reform,' *The Public Interest* 35: 22–54

– 1976. 'California Research at the Crossroads,' *Crime and Delinquency* 22: 180–91

– 1979. 'New Findings, New Views: A Note of Caution Regarding Sentencing Reform,' *Hofstra Law Review* 7/2: 243–58

Martinson, R. Willes, and J.D. Lipton. 1975. *The Effectiveness of Correctional Treatment: A Survey of Treatment Evaluation Studies.* New York: Praeger

Mathiesen, T. 1974. *The Politics of Abolition: Essays in Political Action Theory.* London: Martin Robertson

– 1983. 'The Future of Control Systems – The Case of Norway,' In D. Garland and P. Young, eds., *The Power to Punish.* London: Heinemann

– 1986. 'The Politics of Abolition,' *Contemporary Crises* 10: 81–94

– 1990a. 'KROM – Norwegian Association for Penal Reform.' Unpublished presentation prepared for the 18th Annual Conference of the European Group for the Study of Deviance and Social Control, Haarlem, the Netherlands

– 1990b. *Prison on Trial.* London: Sage

Matthews, R. 1979. 'Decarceration and the Fiscal Crisis.' In B. Fine et al, ed., *Capitalism and the Rule of Law*. London: Hutchinson
– 1986. 'Beyond Wolfenden? Prostitution, Politics and the Law.' In R. Matthews and J. Young, eds., *Confronting Crime*. London: Sage
– 1987. 'Decarceration and Social Control: Fantasies and Realities.' In J. Lowman et al, eds., *Transcarceration: Essays in the Sociology of Social Control*. Aldershot: Gower
– 1989. 'Alternatives to and in Prisons: A Realist Approach.' In P. Carlen and D. Cook, eds., *Paying for Crime*. Milton Keynes: Open University Press
Matthews, R., and J. Young, eds. 1986. *Confronting Crime*. London: Sage
Matza, D. 1964. *Delinquency and Drift*. New York: John Wiley
– 1969. *Becoming Deviant*. Englewood Cliffs, NJ: Prentice-Hall
Melossi, D. 1979. 'Institutions of Social Control and the Capitalist Organization of Work.' In B. Fine et al, eds., *Capitalism and the Rule of Law*. London: Hutchinson
– 1985. 'Punishment and Social action: Changing Vocabularies of Punitive Motive within a Political Business Cycle,' *Current Perspectives in Social Theory* 6: 169–97
– 1987. 'The Law and the State as Practical Rhetorics of Motives: The Case of "Decarceration."' In J. Lowman et al, eds., *Transcarceration: Essays in the Sociology of Social Control*. Aldershot: Gower
Menzies, K. 1986. 'The Rapid Spread of Community Service Orders in Ontario,' *The Canadian Journal of Criminology* 28: 157–69
Menzies, K., and A. Vass. 1989. 'The Impact of Historical, Legal and Administrative Differences on a Sanction: Community Service Orders in England and Ontario.' *The Howard Journal of Criminal Justice* 28: 204–17
Menzies, R. 1985. 'Doing Violence: Psychiatric Discretion and the Prediction of Dangerousness.' PhD thesis, Department of Sociology, University of Toronto
– 1989. *Survival of the Sanest: Order and Disorder in a Pre-trial Psychiatric Clinic*. Toronto: University of Toronto Press
Michalowski, R.J., and M.A. Pearson. 1987. 'Crime, Fiscal Crisis and Decarceration: Financing Corrections at the State Level.' In J. Lowman et al, eds., *Transcarceration: Essays in the Sociology of Social Control*. Aldershot: Gower
Miller, J.G. 1991. *Last One Over the Wall: The Massachusetts Experiment in Closing Reform Schools*. Columbus, OH: Ohio State University Press
Mills, C. Wright. 1959. *The Sociological Imagination*. New York: Oxford University Press
Minto, A. 1983. 'Changing Clinical Practice, 1950–1980.' in P. Bean, ed., *Mental Illness: Changes and Trends*. Chicester: John Wiley
Mitford, J. 1973. *Kind and Usual Punishment: The Prison Business*. New York: Alfred A. Knopf

Morris, N. 1974. *The Future of Imprisonment*. Chicago: University of Chicago Press

Morris, N., and C. Howard. 1965. *Studies in Criminal Law*. Oxford: Clarendon Press

Morris, R. 1989. *Crumbling Walls: Why Prisons Fail*. Oakville, ON: Mosaic Press

Morris, T.P. 1968. 'The Sociology of the Prison.' In T. Grygier, H. Jones, and J.C. Spencer, eds., *Criminology in Transition*. London: Tavistock

Muncie, J., and G. Coventry. 1989. 'Punishment in the Community and the Victorian Youth Attendance Order: A Look into the Future,' *Australian and New Zealand Journal of Criminology* 22: 179–90

Nadin-Davis, P. 1982. *Sentencing in Canada*. Ottawa: Carswell

Nagel, W.G. 1977. 'On Behalf of a Moratorium on Prison Construction,' *Crime and Delinquency* 23/2: 154–72

National Institute of Justice. 1980. *American Prisons and Jails: Population Trends and Projections*, Vol 2. Washington, DC: National Institute of Justice

– 1986. *The Enforcement of Fines as Criminal Sanctions: The English Experience and Its Relevance to American Practice*, by S.G. Casale and S.T. Hillsman. Vera Institute of Justice (grant recipient). Washington, DC: National Institute of Justice

National Task Force on the Administration of Justice. 1979. *Justice Services in Canada 1977–78*. Victoria, BC: The Task Force

Neilsen, E. [Chairman]. 1986. *The Justice System: A Study Team Report to the Task Force on Program Review*. Ottawa: The Task Force

Nelken, D. 1989. 'Discipline and Punish: Some Notes on the Margin,' *The Howard Journal* 28: 245–54

Nettler, G. 1974. *Explaining Crime*. New York: McGraw-Hill

Newton, A. 1981. 'Alternatives to Imprisonment: An International Perspective,' *Criminal Justice Abstracts* 13/1: 134–48

Nicolaus, M. 1973. 'The Professional Organization of Sociology: A View from Below.' In R. Blackburn, ed., *Ideology in Social Science: Readings in Critical Social Theory*. New York: Pantheon

Offe, C. 1984. 'Some Contradictions of the Modern Welfare State,' *Critical Social Policy* 2/2: 7–16

Ohlin, L.E. 1956. *Sociology and the Field of Corrections* [prepared for the American Sociological Society]. New York: Russell Sage Foundation

Oki, G., N. Giesbrecht, P.J. Giffen, and S. Lambert. 1976. *Decriminalization of Public Drunkenness: A Statistical Profile of Patterns and Trends* [ARF substudy no. 740]. Toronto: Addiction Research Foundation

Oki, G., and R. Sirman. 1970. *A Social History of Skid Row in Toronto 1793–1950*. Toronto: Addiction Research Foundation

Olaussen, L.P., and R.K. Sørensen. 1977. *Norwegian Criminology and*

Changes in the Political and Ideological Structure in Norway. Oslo: Institute of Criminology, University of Oslo

Oliver, P. 1985. *Unlikely Tory: The Life and Politics of Allan Grossman.* Toronto: Lester and Orpen Dennys

Oliver, P., and M. D. Whittingham. 1987. 'Elitism, Localism, and the Emergence of Adult Probation Services in Ontario, 1893–1972,' *Canadian Historical Review* 68/2: 225–57

O'Malley, P. 1987. 'Marxist Theory and Marxist Criminology,' *Crime and Social Justice* 29: 70–87

O'Neill, J. 1986. 'The Disciplinary Society: From Weber to Foucault,' *British Journal of Sociology* 37: 42–60

Ontario, Ministry of the Attorney General. 1976. 'Background Paper: The Challenge of the Minor Offence,' *Annual Report*, 44–7. Toronto

– 1978. *Provincial Offences Procedure: An Analysis and Explanation of Legislative Proposals.* (The Provincial Offences Act, 1978, and The Provincial Courts Amendment Act, 1978). Toronto

– 1987a. *Parking Tickets: Why You Can No Longer Get Away without Paying.* A Guide to the Provincial Offences Act: Part II. Toronto

– 1987b. *Procedural Guide to the Provincial Offences Act.* Toronto

Ontario, Ministry of Correctional Services. 1982. *Community Resource Centres: Information Book.* Toronto: Ontario Ministry of Correctional Services

– n.d. (*c.* 1973). 'Historical Development,' manuscript detailing the development of corrections in Ontario from 1792 until 1972. Toronto: Ontario Ministry of Correctional Services

Ontario, Ministry of Treasury, Economics and Intergovernmental Affairs. 1972. *Ontario Budget.* Toronto

– 1975. *Ontario Budget.* Toronto

Ontario Committee on Corrections. 1969. See Ouimet

OPSEU (Ontario Public Service Employees Union). 1983. *A Crisis behind Bars: Ontario's Correctional System.* Toronto: Report by Ontario Public Service Employees Union

Oswald, R.G. 1972. *Attica – My Story.* New York: Doubleday

Ouimet, R. [Chairman]. 1969. *Towards Unity: Criminal Justice and Corrections.* Canadian Committee on Corrections Report. Ottawa: Queen's Printer

Outerbridge, W.R. 1970. 'Re-Thinking the Role of Treatment in Probation,' *Chitty's Law Journal* 18/6: 189–200

– 1973. *Report of the Task Force on Community-Based Residential Centres.* Ottawa: Information Canada

– 1979. Unpublished interview by the Ontario Ministry of Correctional Services' Oral History Project

Packer, H., 1968. *The Limits of the Criminal Sanction.* London: Oxford University Press

Pease, K., 1981. *Community Service Orders: A First Decade of Promise.* Report of Howard League for Penal Reform. London: Howard League
– 1985. 'Community Service Orders.' In M. Tonry and N. Morris, eds., *Crime and Justice: An Annual Review of Research*, vol. 6. Chicago: University of Chicago Press
Pease, K., S. Billingham, and I. Earnshaw. 1977. *Community Service Assessed in 1976: A Home Office Research Unit Report.* London: HMSO
Pease, K., and W. McWilliams. 1980. *Community Service by Order.* Edinburgh: Scottish Academic Press
Penrose, L.S. 1939. 'Mental Disease and Crime: Outline of a Comparative Study of European Statistics,' *British Journal of Medical Psychology* 18: 1–15
Pepinsky, H. 1975. 'Police Decision-Making.' In D. Gottfredson, ed., *Decision-Making in the Criminal Justice System: Reviews and Essays.* Rockville, MD: NIMH
– 1988. 'Violence as Unresponsiveness: Toward a New Conception of Crime,' *Justice Quarterly* 5/4: 539–63
Peters, A.A.G. 1986. 'Main Currents in Criminal Law Theory.' In J. van Dijk, C. Haffmans, F. Ruter, J. Schutte, and S. Stolwijk, eds., *Criminal Law in Action.* Antwerp: Kluwer
Platt, T. 1988. '"If We Know, Then We Must Fight": The Origins of Radical Criminology in the U.S.,' *Critical Sociology* 15: 127–38
Platt, T., and P. Tagaki. 1982. 'Meeting the Challenge of the 1980s,' *Crime and Social Justice* 17: 1–3
Poulantzas, N. 1973. *Political Power and Social Classes.* London: New Left Books
Pratt, J. 1987. 'Dilemmas of the Alternatives to Custody Concept: Implications for New Zealand in Light of International Evidence and Experience,' *Australian and New Zealand Journal of Criminology* 20: 148–62
PREAP [Prison Research Education Action Project]. 1976. *Instead of Prisons: A Handbook for Abolitionists.* Syracuse, NY
Punch, M. 1979. *Policing the Inner City.* London: Macmillan
Radzinowicz, L. 1961. *In Search of Criminology.* London: Heinemann
– 1964. *The Role of Criminology and A Proposal for an Institute of Criminology.* Report presented to the Special Committee on the Administration of Justice, Association of the Bar of the City of New York.
– 1988. *The Cambridge Institute of Criminology: Its Background and Scope.* London: HMSO
Ratner, R.S. 1987. 'Mandatory Supervision and the Penal Economy.' In J. Lowman et al, eds., *Transcarceration: Essays in the Sociology of Social Control.* Aldershot: Gower
Ratner, R.S., and J.L. McMullan, eds. 1987. *State Control: Criminal Justice Politics in Canada.* Vancouver: University of British Columbia Press

Ratner, R.S., J.L. McMullan, and B. Burtch. 1987. 'The Problem of Relative Autonomy and Criminal Justice System in the Canadian State.' In R.S. Ratner and J.L. McMullan, eds., *State Control: Criminal Justice Politics in Canada*. Vancouver: University of British Columbia Press

Rauma, D. 1981. 'Crime and Punishment Reconsidered: Some Comments on Blumstein's Stability of Punishment Hypothesis,' *Journal of Criminal Law and Criminology* 72: 1772–98

Reichman, N. 1987. 'The Widening Webs of Surveillance: Private Police Unraveling Deceptive Claims.' In C.D. Shearing and P.C. Stenning, eds., *Private Policing*. Beverly Hills: Sage

Reid, S., and M. Reitsma-Street. 1984. 'Assumptions and Implications of New Canadian Legislation for Young Offenders,' *Canadian Criminology Forum* 7/2: 1–19

Reiss, A. 1971. *The Police and the Public*. New Haven: Yale University Press

– 1984. 'The Control of Organizational Life.' In A.N. Doob and E.L. Greenspan, eds., *Perspectives in Criminal Law*. Aurora, ON: Canada Law Book

Renner, J. 1978. *The Adult Probationer in Ontario*. Toronto: Ministry of Correctional Services

Rock, P., ed. 1988. *A History of British Criminology*. Oxford: Oxford University Press

Rodger, J.J. 1988. 'Social Work as Social Control Re-examined: Beyond the Dispersal of Discipline Thesis,' *Sociology* 22: 563–81

Roe, J. 1980. 'Involving the Private Sector in Administering the Ontario Community Service Order Program.' Paper presented at the Fourth National Symposium on Restitution and Community Service Sentencing in Minneapolis, Minnesota

– 1981. 'Private Sector Contracts,' *Correctional Options* 1/1: 54–61

Rolston, B., and M. Tomlinson. 1986. 'Long-Term Imprisonment in Northern Ireland: Psychological or Political Survival?' In B. Rolston and M. Tomlinson, eds., *The Expansion of European Prison Systems*, Working Papers in European Criminology no. 7. Belfast: European Group for the Study of Deviance and Social Control

– eds. 1986. *The Expansion of European Prison Systems*, Working Papers in European Criminology no. 7. Belfast: European Group for the Study of Deviance and Social Control

Rosenhan, D.L. 1973. 'On Being Sane in Insane Places,' *Science* 179: 250–8

Rothman, D.J. 1971. *The Discovery of the Asylum*. Boston: Little, Brown

– 1973. 'Decarcerating Prisoners and Patients,' *Civil Liberties Review* 1: 8–30

– 1980. *Conscience and Convenience: The Asylum and Its Alternatives in Progressive America*. Boston: Little, Brown

Ruby, C. 1987. *Sentencing*, 3d ed. Toronto: Butterworths

Rumgay, J. 1989. 'Talking Tough: Empty Threats in Probation Practice,' *The Howard Journal* 28: 177–86

Rusche, G., and O. Kirkcheimer. 1939. *Punishment and Social Structure*. New York: Columbia University Press

Rutherford, A. 1984. *Prisons and the Process of Justice*. London: Heinemann

– 1986. *Growing Out of Crime*. Harmondsworth, Middlesex: Penguin

– 1988. 'The English Penal Crisis: Paradox and Possibilities.' In R. Rideout and J. Jowell, eds., *Current Legal Problems* 41: 93–113

Ryan, M., and T. Ward. 1989. *Privatization and the Penal System: The American Experience and the Debate in Britain*. Milton Keynes: Open University Press

– 1990. 'The Penal Lobby in Britain, 1950–1990: From Positivism to Post-structuralism – An Autocritique.' Presentation to the 18th Annual Conference of the European Group for the Study of Deviance and Social Control, Haarlem, The Netherlands

– 1991. 'Restructuring, Resistance and Privatisation in the Non-Custodial Sector,' *Critical Social Policy* 10: 54–67

Sanders, W. 1977. *Detective Work*. New York: Free Press

Santos, B. 1985. 'On Modes of Production of Law and Social Power,' *International Journal of the Sociology of Law* 13: 299–336

Sapers, H. 1985. 'Contracting in Context: The Selling of Criminal Justice Services.' Paper presented to the American Society of Criminology, San Diego, November

– 1988. 'Critique of "Punishing for Profit,"' *Canadian Journal of Criminology* 30/3: 313–18

Scheerer, S. 1986. 'Towards Abolitionism,' *Contemporary Crises* 10: 5–20

Scheff, T. 1966. *Being Mentally Ill: A Sociological Theory*. Chicago: Aldine

Schneider, H.J., ed. 1982. *The Victim in International Perspective*. New York: de Gruyter

Schön, D.A. 1979. 'Generative Metaphor: A Perspective on Problem-Setting in Social Policy.' In M. Ortony, *Metaphor and Thought*. Cambridge: Cambridge University Press

Schur, E. 1971. *Labeling Deviant Behavior*. New York: Harper and Row

– 1973. *Radical Non-Intervention*. Englewood Cliffs, NJ: Prentice-Hall

Schwartz, M.D., and W.S. DeKeseredy. 1991. 'Left Realist Criminology: Strengths, Weaknesses and Feminist Critique,' *Crime, Law and Social Change* (formerly *Contemporary Crises*) 15: 51–72

Scott, D.K. 1990. 'The Politics of Voluntary Sector Involvement in Community Corrections: Privatization in Ontario.' MA thesis, Centre of Criminology, University of Toronto

Scraton, P., ed. 1987. *Law, Order and the Authoritarian State: Readings in Critical Criminology*. Milton Keynes: Open University Press

Scraton, P., and C. Chadwick. 1987. 'Speaking Ill of the Dead: Institutionalized Responses to Deaths in Custody.' In P. Scraton, eds,. *Law, Order and the Authoritarian State*. Milton Keynes: Open University Press

Scraton, P., J. Sim, and P. Skidmore. 1988. 'Through the Barricades: Prison Protest and Penal Policy in Scotland,' *Journal of Law and Society* 15/3: 247–63

Scull, A.T. 1977. *Decarceration: Community Treatment and the Deviant – A Radical View*. Englewood Cliffs, NJ: Prentice-Hall

– 1979. *Museums of Madness: The Social Organization of Insanity in Nineteenth-Century England*. New York: St Martin's Press

– 1981. 'Progressive Dreams, Progressive Nightmares: Social Control in Twentieth Century America,' *Stanford Law Review* 33: 575–90

– 1983. 'Community Corrections: Panacea, Progress or Pretence?' In D. Garland and P. Young, eds., *The Power to Punish*. London: Heinemann

– 1984. *Decarceration: Community Treatment and the Deviant – A Radical View*, 2d ed. Cambridge: Polity Press

– 1987. 'Decarceration Reconsidered.' In J. Lowman, R.J. Menzies, and T.S. Palys, eds., *Transcarceration: Essays in the Sociology of Social Control*. Aldershot: Gower

– 1991. 'A Critical Analysis of the Decarceration Movement.' In L. Samuelson and B. Schissel, eds., *Criminal Justice: Sentencing Issues and Reforms*. Toronto: Garamond

Shearing, C.D., and P.C. Stenning. 1981. 'Modern Private Security: Its Growth and Implications.' In M. Tonry and N. Morris, eds., *Crime and Justice: An Annual Review of Research*, vol. 3. Chicago: University of Chicago Press

– 1983a. *Private Security and Private Justice: The Challenge of the 80s*. Montreal: Institute for Research on Public Policy

– 1983b. 'Private Security: Implications for Social Control,' *Social Problems* 30: 493–506

– 1984. 'From the Panopticon to Disney World: The Development of Discipline.' In A.N. Doob and E.L. Greenspan, eds., *Perspectives in Criminal Law*. Aurora, ON: Canada Law Book

– 1987. *Private Policing*. Newbury Park: Sage

Sheldon, W.H. 1936. *Psychology and the Promethean Will*. New York: Harper

– 1940. *The Varieties of Human Physique*. New York: Harper

– 1942. *The Varieties of Temperament*. New York: Harper and Row

– 1949. *Varieties of Delinquent Youth*. New York: Harper

– 1954. *Atlas of Men*. New York: Harper

Sheridan, A. 1979. 'Translator's Note.' In M. Foucault, *Discipline and Punish*. New York: Vintage

Sim, J. 1986. 'Working for the Clampdown: Prisons and Politics in England and Wales.' In B. Rolston and M. Tomlinson, eds., *The Expansion of European Prison Systems*, Working Papers in European Criminology no. 7. Belfast: European Group for the Study of Deviance and Social Control

Sim, J., P. Scraton, and P. Gordon. 1987. 'Introduction: Crime, the State and Critical Analysis.' In P. Scraton, ed., *Law, Order and the Authoritarian State*. Milton Keynes: Open University Press

Skolnick, J. H. 1966. *Justice without Trial: Law Enforcement in Democratic Society*. New York: Wiley

Smandych, R. 1986. 'Toward an Understanding of the Phenomena of Controls.' Unpublished manuscript, Centre of Criminology, University of Toronto

Smith, D. 1974. 'The Ideological Practice of Sociology,' *Catalyst* 2: 39–54

– 1983. 'No One Commits Suicide: Textual Analyses of Ideological Practices,' *Human Studies* 6: 309–59

– 1984. 'Textually-Mediated Social Organization,' *International Social Science Journal* 36/1:59–75

Smith, R. 1976. 'Preface.' In I. Sone, *Community Resource Centre Study*. Toronto: Ministry of Correctional Services

Snider, D.L. 1985. 'Legal Aid, Reform, and the Welfare State,' *Crime and Social Justice* 24: 210–42

Snider, L. 1991a. 'Critical Criminology in Canada: Past, Present and Future.' In R.A. Silverman, J.J. Teevan, and V.J. Sacco, eds., *Crime in Canadian Society*, 4th ed. Toronto: Butterworths

– 1991b. 'Rethinking Feminism and Law.' Presentation to the International Conference on Women, Law and Social Control, Mont-Gabriel, Quebec, 18–21 July

Solicitor General of Canada. 1983. *Canadian Urban Victimization Survey Bulletin*. Vol. 1: *Victims of Crime*. Ottawa: Programs Branch

– 1984a. *Canadian Urban Victimization Bulletin*. Vol. 2: *Reported and Unreported Crimes*. Ottawa: Programs Branch

– 1984b. *Selected Trends in Canadian Criminal Justice*. Ottawa: Research and Statistics Group, Programs Branch; Minister of Supply and Services

– 1984c. *Canadian Urban Victimization Survey Bulletin*. Vol. 3. *Crime Prevention: Awareness and Practice*. Ottawa: Programs Branch

– 1985. 'Prisons for Profit,' in *Liaison: The Monthly Journal of the Criminal Justice System*, 10–19. Ottawa: Ministry of the Solicitor General of Canada, March

– 1986. *Edmonton Victimization Survey (1985): Finding and Preliminary Comparisons of 1982 and 1985 Data*, vol. 1. Ottawa: Programs Branch

Sone, I. 1976. *Community Resource Centre Study*. Toronto: Ministry of Correctional Services

Sparks, R. 1971. 'The Use of Suspended Sentences,' *Criminal Law Review* July: 384–401

Special Program Review Committee. 1975. *Report of the Special Program Review Committee*. Toronto

Spitzer, S. 1982. 'Marxist Perspectives in the Sociology of Law,' *Annual Review of Sociology* 9: 103–24

Stanley, P.A. 1977. *Prisoners Remanded in Custody*. Toronto: Ministry of
    Correctional Services
Steadman, H.J., and J. P. Morrissey. 1987. 'The Impact of Deinstitutionaliza-
    tion on the Criminal Justice System: Implications for Understanding
    Changing Modes of Social Control.' In J. Lowman et al, eds., *Transcarcer-
    ation: Essays in the Sociology of Social Control*. Aldershot: Gower
Steinert, H. 1985. 'The Amazing New Left Law and Order Campaign,'
    Contemporary Crises 9: 327–33
– 1986. 'Beyond Crime and Punishment,' *Contemporary Crises* 10: 21–39
Stewart, W.J. 1954. *Report of the Select Committee to Study and Report Upon
    Problems of Delinquent Individuals and Custodial Questions, and the Place of
    Reform Institutions Therein*. Toronto: Ontario Legislative Assembly
Stoops, J.H. 1983. 'Community Service Orders and Social Control: The Views
    of Clients and Agents.' MA thesis, Centre of Criminology, University of
    Toronto
Stratton, J. 1973. 'Cops and Drunks: Police Attitudes and Action in Dealing
    with Indian Drunks,' *International Journal of the Addictions* 8/4: 613–21
Strauss, M. 1985. 'Justice Officials Stymied by Lack of Data,' *Globe and Mail*,
    10 August, 15, 17
Sudnow, D. 1965. 'Normal Crimes: Sociological Features of the Penal Code
    in a Public Defender Office,' *Social Problems* 12: 225–76
Sumner, C. 1979. *Reading Ideologies*. London: Academic Press
Sutherland, E.H. 1934. 'The Decreasing Prison Population of England,'
    Journal of Criminal Law and Criminology 24: 880–900
Swaaningen, R. van. 1990. 'Pressure groups for Penal Reform in the Nether-
    lands – A National Report.' Presentation to the 18th Annual Conference of
    the European Group for the Study of Deviance and Social Control,
    Haarlem, The Netherlands
Swaaningen, R. van, G. de Jonge, and M.W. McMahon. 1989. 'The Labori-
    ous Conspiracy against the Penal System: Comments on the Third Aboli-
    tionist Conference, Montreal, 1987,' *Canadian Criminology Forum* 10: 67–75
Swackhamer, J. 1972. *Report of the Commission of Inquiry into Certain
    Disturbances at the Kingston Penitentiary during April 1971*. Ottawa:
    Solicitor General of Canada
Sykes, G. 1958. *The Society of Captives*. Princeton, NJ: Princeton University
    Press
Szasz, T.S. 1961. *The Myth of Mental Illness*. New York: Harper and Row
– 1965. *Psychiatric Justice*. New York: Macmillan
Taft, D.R. 1942. *Criminology*. New York: Macmillan
Task Force on the Creation of an Integrated Canadian Corrections Service.
    1977. *The Role of Federal Corrections in Canada*. Ottawa: Ministry of
    Supply and Services
Task Force on the Role of the Private Sector in Criminal Justice. 1977.

Community Involvement in Criminal Justice, vol. 1. Ottawa: Ministry of Supply and Services

Taylor, D. 1981. 'Probation: Changes and Challenges,' *Correctional Options* 1/1: 21–30

Taylor, I., P. Walton, and J. Young. 1973. *The New Criminology*. London: Routledge and Kegan Paul

Taylor, I., P. Walton, and J. Young, eds. 1975. *Critical Criminology*. London: Routledge and Kegan Paul

Third International Congress of Criminology. 1955. *General Reports*. Third International Congress of Criminology, London, 12–18 September

Thomas, J., and A. O'Maolchatha. 1989. 'Reassessing the Critical Metaphor: An Optimistic Revisionist View,' *Justice Quarterly* 6: 143–72

Tomlinson, M., and B. Rolston, eds. 1986. *The Expansion of European Prison Systems*. Working Papers of the European Group for the Study of Deviance and Social Control. Belfast: European Group for the Study of Deviance and Social Control

Torrie, J. 1987. 'Cops and Indians: The Making of the Chronic Public Drunkenness Offender, Kenora, Ontario 1944–1984.' Unpublished report to the Kenora Legal Clinic

Tournier, P. 1986. *Quelques données statistiques sur les populations carcerales des Etats-Unis, du Canada, et du Japon*. Paris: Centre de Recherches Sociologiques sur le Droit et les Institutions Pénales

Vass, A.A., and A. Weston. 1990. 'Probation Day Centres as an Alternative to Custody: A "Trojan Horse" Examined,' *British Journal of Criminology* 30: 189–206

Vold, G.B. 1958. *Theoretical Criminology*. New York: Oxford University Press
– 1979. *Theoretical Criminology*, 2d ed, prepared by T.J. Bernard. New York: Oxford University Press

Waegel, W. 1982a. 'Case Routinization in Investigative Police Work.' *Social Problems* 28: 263–75
– 1982b. 'Patterns of Police Investigation of Urban Crimes.' *Journal of Police Science and Administration* 10: 452–65

Wagner-Pacifici, R.E. 1986. *The Moro Morality Play: Terrorism as Social Drama*. Chicago: University of Chicago Press

Walker, J., P. Collier, and R. Tarling. 1990. 'Why Are Prison Rates in England and Wales Higher than in Australia?' *British Journal of Criminology* 30: 24–35

Wallace, D. 1981. 'The Political Economy of Incarceration: Trends in Late U.S. Capitalism: 1971–77,' *The Insurgent Sociologist* 10: 59–66

Waller, J.I. and N. Okihiro. 1978. *Burglary: The Victim and the Public*. Toronto: University of Toronto Press

Ward, T. 1989. 'Resistance and Commodification in the Non-Custodial Sector.' Presentation to the 17th Conference of the European Group for the Study of Deviance and Social Control, Ormskirk, England

Warren, C.B. 1981. 'New Forms of Social Control: The Myth of Deinstitu-
tionalization,' *American Behavioral Scientist* 24: 724–40
Webster, J. 1970. 'Police Task and Time Study, *Journal of Criminal Law,
Criminology and Police Science* 61: 94–100
Weiss, R. 1987. 'The Reappearance of the "Ideal Factory": The Entrepreneur
and Social Control in the Contemporary Prison.' In. J. Lowman et al, eds.,
Transcarceration: Essays in the Sociology of Social Control. Aldershot:
Gower
West, G. 1987. 'Vigilancia Revolucionaire: A Nicaraguan Resolution to
Public and Private Policing.' In C.D. Shearing and P.C. Stenning, eds.,
Private Policing. Newbury Park: Sage
Whitney, K. 1970. 'Skid Row.' In W.E. Mann ed., *The Underside of Toronto*.
Toronto: McClelland and Stewart
Whittingham, M.D. 1984. The Adult Probationer in Ontario: A Thirty Year
Profile (1950 to 1980).' Preliminary Overview for the Ontario Corrections
History Project, Ministry of Correctional Services. Unpublished
Wicker, T. 1978. *A Time to Die*. Harmondsworth: Penguin
Wilkins, L.T. 1964. *Social Deviance: Social Policy, Action and Research*.
London: Tavistock
– 1969. *Evaluation of Penal Measures*. New York: Random House
Willet, T. 1964. *Criminal on the Road*. London: Tavistock
Willis, P. 1977. *Learning to Labour*. Farnborough: Saxon House
Wilson, J. 1968. *Varieties of Police Behavior*. Cambridge, MA: Harvard
University Press
Woods, G. 1984. 'Costs of Municipal Police Services,' *Impact* 2: 13–22
Wright, E. 1973. *The Politics of Punishment*. New York: Harper
Yeager, M.G. 1979. 'Unemployment and Imprisonment,' *Journal of Criminal
Law and Criminology* 70: 586–8
Young, J. 1986. 'The Failure of Criminology: The Need for a Radical Realism.'
In R. Matthews and J. Young, eds., *Confronting Crime*. London: Sage
Young, P. 1983. 'Sociology, the State and Penal Relations.' In D.Garland and
P. Young, eds., *The Power to Punish*. London: Heinemann
– 1986. 'Review of S. Cohen, *Visions of Social Control*,' *Sociological Review*
34: 222–4
– 1989. 'Punishment, Money and a Sense of Justice.' In P. Carlen and D.
Cook, eds., *Paying for Crime*. Milton Keynes: Open University Press
– forthcoming. *Punishment, Money and Legal Order*.
Young, W. 1979. *Community Service Orders: The Development and Use of a
New Penal Measure*. London: Heinemann
– 1986. 'Influences Upon the Use of Imprisonment: A Review of the Literature,' *The Howard Journal* 25/2: 125–36
Zubrycki, R.M. 1984. 'Long-Term Incarceration in Canada,' *Canadian
Journal of Criminology* 26/4: 397–402

Index